Teaching
the
Culturally Disadvantaged Pupil

Teaching
the
Culturally Disadvantaged Pupil

Compiled and Edited By

JOHN M. BECK, Ph.D.
Professor of Education
Chicago Teachers College South
Chicago, Illinois

RICHARD W. SAXE, Ph.D.
Associate Professor of Education
Chicago Teachers College South
Chicago, Illinois

With an Introduction by
Robert J. Havighurst

9946

CHARLES C THOMAS · PUBLISHER
Springfield · Illinois · U.S.A.

Published and Distributed Throughout the World by

CHARLES C THOMAS • PUBLISHER

BANNERSTONE HOUSE

301-327 East Lawrence Avenue, Springfield, Illinois, U.S.A.

NATCHEZ PLANTATION HOUSE

735 North Atlantic Boulevard, Fort Lauderdale, Florida, U.S.A.

With THOMAS BOOKS careful attention is given to all details of manufacturing and design. It is the Publisher's desire to present books that are satisfactory as to their physical qualities and artistic possibilities and appropriate for their particular use. THOMAS BOOKS will be true to those laws of quality that assure a good name and good will.

CONTRIBUTORS

MARVIN A. BROTTMAN, *Assistant Professor of Education, Chicago Teachers College South.*

RAYMOND M. COOK, *Dean, Chicago Teachers College South.*

MARTIN DEUTSCH, *Director of the Institute for Developmental Studies and Professor, Department of Psychiatry, New York Medical College.*

LILLIAN DIMITROFF, *Professor of Education, Chicago Teachers College South.*

WALTER J. FOLEY, *Coordinator, Pupil Personnel Services, Iowa Educational Information Center, University of Iowa.*

WILLIAM E. GORMAN, *Chairman, Department of Guidance and Counseling, Associate Professor of Education, De Paul University.*

KATHRYN A. GRAHAM, *Principal, William Bishop Owen Elementary School, Chicago.*

ROBERT J. HAVIGHURST, *Professor of Education, University of Chicago.*

JAY G. HIRSCH, M.D., *Research Child Psychiatrist, Institute for Juvenile Research, Chicago.*

JOHN J. HOBGOOD, *Human Relations Officer, Chicago Commission on Human Relations, and Mayor's Committee on New Residents.*

WILLIAM ITKIN, *Professor of Psychology, Chairman, Special Education Program, Chicago Teachers College North.*

BRUCE R. JOYCE, *Assistant Professor of Education, Director, Elementary Teacher Education, University of Chicago.*

LLOYD J. MENDELSON, *Principal, John Farren Elementary School, Chicago.*

JANE NEALE, *Chairman, Art Department, and Assistant Professor, Chicago Teachers College South.*

DOLORES NICOSIA, *Supervisor of Music, Chicago Public Schools.*

ILLA PODENDORF, *Chairman, Science Department, Laboratory Schools, and Lecturer in Education, University of Chicago.*

MILDRED LETTON WITTICK, *Professor of English, Patterson State College, Wayne, New Jersey.*

INTRODUCTION

THE ELEMENTARY SCHOOL AND THE DISADVANTAGED PUPIL

ROBERT J. HAVIGHURST

THE WAR ON POVERTY is concentrating, where it should, on preventing a generation from growing up to become members of a permanent *welfare class*. We know that a large subgroup of children are growing up in our city slums and our pockets of rural poverty without the kind of educational experience that will enable them to become self-supporting adults.

We also know that the kind of behavior that leads to poverty is learned, and that, while learning this behavior, these children are failing to learn the things that would make them succeed in school and in urban life.

The President of the United States has told us in clear and simple terms that we can and should do something about this condition. We cannot afford to have the social pathology—the juvenile delinquency, adult crime, family disorganization, physical and mental disease—that goes with unemployment, illiteracy, and slum living. Neither can we afford in terms of our social pride to be part of an affluent society which has such a seamy side to it.

We can afford the financial cost of the War on Poverty, no doubt about it. But it is not so clear that we can win this war. This requires knowledge of the causes of the conditions that breed poverty in a wealthy urban society. It requires knowledge of how the human mind develops or fails to develop in low income families. It requires ingenious and creative teaching. It requires the administrative genius to organize a system of teaching children and youth the necessary things for competent urban living that their families and home neighborhoods do not now teach them.

Who Are the Disadvantaged?

Disadvantaged pupils should be distinguished from mentally handicapped and physically handicapped pupils. Socially disadvantaged pupils are ones who have been denied some social experiences that "normal" children have had.

The social experiences which socially disadvantaged children have not had are certain experiences in the family. Compared with other children whose parents give them average or better advantages for getting started in modern life, the socially disadvantaged child lacks several of the following:

1. A family environment which sets an example of reading; provides a variety of toys and play materials with colors, sizes, and objects that challenge his ingenuity with his hands and his mind.

2. A family conversational experience which answers his questions and encourages him to ask questions; extends his vocabulary with new words and with adjectives and adverbs; gives him a right and a need to stand up for and to explain his point of view on the world.

Systematic study of the language behavior of families by Bernstein and others indicates that there are major differences in the complexity and the content of language between the middle class and the working class, when relatively large samples of families are studied. (At the same time, some working-class families are like typical middle-class families and vice versa.) Generally, the working-class families use a "restricted" form of language, while the middle-class families use a more "elaborated" form.

A child who has learned a *restricted* language at home is likely to have difficulty in school, where an *elaborated* language is used and taught by the teacher; and the difficulty of the child is likely to increase as he goes further in school, unless he learns the elaborated language that is expected in the school. On the other hand, the child who has had experience with an elaborated language from his earliest years has a relatively easy time in school, because he must simply go on developing the kind of language and related thinking which he has already started.

Some family environments with a restricted language also handicap the child by failing to answer his questions, failing to bring him into family conversation (if there is any) and failing to stimulate him with playthings and other experiences on which the developing mind must feed. Martin Deutsch has studied such children with techniques of the experimental psychologists, and he finds them to have inferior auditory discrimination, inferior visual discrimination, inferior judgment concerning time, number and other basic concepts. He finds that this inferiority is not due to physical defects of eyes and ears and brain, but is due to inferior *habits* of hearing and seeing and thinking. Presumably, the family environment of these children did not teach them to pay attention to what was being said around them, or to the visual scene. Then, when they came to school, their school performance suffered because they had not learned to listen to the teacher and other important people or to see the things they are shown in the school.

It is important to avoid the error of saying that all children of working-class families are socially disadvantaged. Approximately 65 per cent of the children of this country are living in working-class homes. That is, their fathers or mothers do manual work for a living. The great majority of these families give their children a fairly good start for life in an urban industrial democratic society. Their children are adequately fed and clothed. They are loved and protected by their parents. They learn to respect teachers and to like school. They do fairly well or better than that in school.

While working-class children as a group are somewhat different from the children of white-collar workers, it would not be reasonable to say that the working-class children are socially disadvantaged or culturally deprived. Working-class children as a group score slightly below children of white-collar families in intelligence tests; they fall slightly below on tests of school achievement; they attain somewhat less formal education. But the differences are relatively small, and become even smaller when the socially disadvantaged children are removed and the majority of working-class youth who remain are compared with white-collar children.

Who, then, are the socially disadvantaged when we attempt to describe them in terms of observable social groups? They are groups with the following characteristics:

1. They are at the bottom of the American society in terms of income.
2. They have a rural background.

3. They suffer from social and economic discrimination at the hands of the majority of the society.
4. They are widely distributed in the United States. While they are most visible in the big cities, they are present in all except the very high income communities. There are many of them in rural areas, especially in the southern and southwestern states.

In racial and ethnic terms, these groups are about evenly divided between whites and nonwhites. They consist mainly of the following:

Negroes from the rural South, many of whom have migrated recently to the northern industrial cities.

Whites from the rural South and the southern mountains, many of whom have migrated recently to the northern industrial cities.

Puerto Ricans who have migrated to a few northern industrial cities.

Mexicans with a rural background who have migrated into the West and Middle West. Also rural Spanish-Americans in the southwestern states.

European immigrants with a rural background, from eastern and southern Europe.

Altogether, these groups make up about 15 per cent of the United States population. Since they tend to have large families, their children make up as much as 20 per cent of the child population. Not all socially disadvantaged children come from these groups, but the great majority do. Not all children in these groups are socially disadvantaged, but the great majority are.

Since these children and their families tend to concentrate in the large cities, while upper-income people tend to move out from the cities to the suburbs, the socially disadvantaged children are in big cities in larger proportions than 15 per cent. Probably *30 per cent of the children* in such cities as New York, Chicago, Philadelphia, Washington, Detroit, Cleveland, and Baltimore fall into the socially disadvantaged category.

What We Can Do About It

We have enough research on socially disadvantaged children to show us where the emphasis should be placed in our attempts to solve the problem. The emphasis should be in the elementary school, and in the pre-school years. The Elementary and Secondary Education Act of 1965 provides substantial amounts of federal government support for work with these children at these ages. No doubt school people will do the following things:

Set up a large number of pre-school classes for disadvantaged children.

Work in experimental ways with the parents of such children. Revise and expand a program of "readiness building" at the kindergarten level to take account of the difficulties that socially disadvantaged children have in getting ready to learn to read.

Revise our methods of teaching reading to use methods during the primary grades which fit disadvantaged children better.

Reorganize our teaching in the intermediate grades so as to use teaching materials which will work better with these children. Develop elementary school libraries that stimulate and facilitate children's reading. Adapt the new mathematics and science materials to the learning styles of these children. Supplement the classroom teacher with visiting teachers or social workers who can bring the parents into better ways of helping their children through school.

The next five years will see an all-out effort to:

1. Raise the average IQ of children from low-income families by ten points.
2. Eradicate that large segment of mental retardation which is due to environmental deprivation.
3. Clear out 50 to 75 per cent of the severe retardation in reading and arithmetic which now exists in elementary schools.

These will not be easy to accomplish. A good deal of well-meaning but fruitless labor will be expended by people who have an abundant supply of good will but not much understanding of the problem and not much experience with it.

However, there are some promising practices which have been worked out by creative people and have been evaluated. Teachers in service can use the methods and materials that have been found to work at least fairly well. Prospective teachers can be trained to use these procedures.

It is a challenge and an opportunity for the teachers of our big-city school systems.

EDITORS' PREFACE

T HIS BOOK IS about ways of improving the education of the culturally disadvantaged children in the elementary school. For this purpose we have emphasized classroom practices which readily may be utilized by capable teachers. However, rather than prescriptions, these suggested methods and materials are intended as concrete models for teaching. To provide a comprehensive understanding of this basic teaching problem, we have carefully synthesized the latest research and reports in the field as they relate to the many dimensions of education for the culturally disadvantaged.

In Part I of the book, we have described the scope of the problem and the important advances made in the education of the culturally disadvantaged children. The four chapters in this part stress the principal theoretical and empirical aspects of the problem. We have drawn upon the research and experiences of educational specialists and community groups in probing for the direction and aim of the new education which our urbanized society demands. A variety of alternative solutions are explored and analyzed. While much of the recent experimentation is not yet complete, there is ample evidence to support the view that imaginative and creative programs can be devised which will improve the opportunities and achievements of the culturally disadvantaged pupil.

The eight chapters in Part II concern the curriculum and instruction in the elementary school. Each author has drawn on school experiences, based on sound principles, in suggesting new paths that can be taken in developing more effective methods and materials for the culturally disadvantaged. The effective utilization of the how-to-do-it suggestions presumes, of course, the teacher's understanding of the basic psychosocial principles of learning discussed in the previous section by Martin Deutsch and Jay Hirsch.

Finally, in Part III, three chapters are devoted to school and community responsibilities for the improvement of education for the culturally disadvantaged. Specifically, attention is given to characteristics and preparation of teachers, the dynamic role of the principal, and the urgent need for mobilization of community resources. The focus in the chapter on the community is on the overriding need for close cooperation between the school and community.

It is our hope that this book will be read not only by prospective teachers and teachers in service but by all those interested in this growing problem in education.

The editors wish to thank the contributing authors for their many acts of cooperation, often at considerable personal sacrifice, in the preparation of this volume.

Special recognition is given to the assistance rendered by Dr. Melvin R. Karpas, Crane Branch of Chicago Teachers College South.

John M. Beck
Richard W. Saxe

CONTENTS

Teaching
the
Culturally Disadvantaged Pupil

PART I

BASIC CHARACTERISTICS OF THE DISADVANTAGED PUPIL

THE MAJOR AUDIENCE for this book is the elementary school teacher or the soon-to-be elementary school teacher. These readers will be well versed in theories of learning and alert to the need to provide for the individual differences of their pupils. They may not be so well aware of the special problems presented by culturally disadvantaged pupils. It is our purpose in Part I to acquaint our readers with these problems, their possible and probable causes, and to describe and evaluate attempts to improve the situation.

The professional literature dealing with the culturally disadvantaged pupils has grown from a trickle to a flood. When one considers the many issues which center about the problem of the culturally disadvantaged pupil, it can be said that this is the most crucial of all the crucial issues facing education today. We have been fortunate in securing the cooperation of scholars directly involved in this area whose training, special knowledge, and professional position make it possible for them to bring together an analysis of the problems of disadvantaged pupils and to supplement this analysis with their own findings. Writers in this section have been selective. Each has brought together and organized the most promising and the most recent work in his field. For this reason, both the novice and the veteran educator will profit by a careful study of these reports which provide a synthesis which will serve as the foundation for a later treatment of more particular problems of teaching the culturally disadvantaged pupil.

Part I should be considered as a prerequisite for Part II. It is the basis for the presentations by the subject matter experts on how to teach *something*. In these pages, we learn to whom the *something* is to be taught. This prior knowledge is essential to an interpretation of the more practical discussions of the school curriculum which are to follow.

3

Chapter I

DIMENSIONS OF THE PROBLEM OF THE DISADVANTAGED PUPIL

Marvin A. Brottman[*]

ANY INDIVIDUAL, to fully participate in all aspects of our society, should be well informed, possess skills, both social and occupational which are valued by the society, and be accepted by the groups or institutions to which he aspires. Few, if any, of these conditions are being met by an increasingly large segment of our population.

One may object to the resulting alienation of these groups on grounds that social injustice is being done, economic damage is occurring, or democratic principles are being violated. This writer takes the position that all of these reasons and more, justify the concern for maximum participation of all groups to the maximum of their inclination and ability. Further, that the process and institutions of education, both formal and informal offer the best means available to maximize the involvement and acceptance of all groups in the larger society.[1]

DEFINITION OF TERMS

In this text, the term used to describe the population of concern is the *culturally disadvantaged* pupil. Current writers use several synonymous terms. These include *culturally deprived,*[2] *socially disadvantaged,*[3] *under-privileged,*[4] and *culturally disadvantaged.*[5] All these terms share a common factor in that there is an "identifiable set of attitudes and behavior patterns which prevail among in-migrants who settle in the inner city."[6] These attitudes and behaviors reflect a limited acquaintance with social amenities and cultural attributes usually associated with middle-class society. The adults are frequently hostile to many of these manifestations and, as a result, their children do not have those predisposing experiences which appear to be related to success in school.

*Assistant Professor of Education, Chicago Teachers College South.

From the view of educators, it is of little value to consider behaviors associated with a particular group in society to be either positive or negative or better or worse than those of the middle-class. It would be far more useful to consider the behavioral characteristics exhibited by the group which appear to affect learning within the milieu of the school and to explore aspects of that milieu which may be modified by school personnel within a reasonable time.

Questions raised by inexperienced teachers assigned to difficult schools frequently include concerns of how to handle these children. This type of question implies a lack of recognition by the teacher of how best to teach these children, considering the attendant problems of modification of curriculum, relationships with parents, attendance, acceptable classroom behavior, and evaluation procedures. The focus of this chapter and text is on the educational process to be employed in teaching the disadvantaged.

CHARACTERISTICS OF DISADVANTAGED PUPILS

Several deficiencies of current attempts to determine characteristics of disadvantaged pupils have been: (1) the lack of any consistent rationale based on relationships among various aspects of experience and ability of pupils as related to experiences and demands made by the school, (2) an exploration of the family and community of the learner as an environment affecting learning, and (3) research being too little, broad or restrictive and not attacking the problem in a systematic manner.

In an attempt to draw together many aspects of the larger problem, it is appropriate to focus on the learner within the community, family, peer environments, and educational milieu. These interrelationships may be examined by placing all of these variables within the structure of a model of social behavior in psychosociological terms. Although the model was developed primarily for use in the study of administration, it is general enough in its scope to suggest ways of examining the behavior of any individual within a specified environment. After a consideration of the general model, it will be suggested that it may be applied to observations of disadvantaged pupils, their teachers, parents and the school.[7]

The most common context of interpersonal behavior is a social system. This involves

> ... two major classes of phenomena which are at once conceptu-
> ally independent and phenomenally interactive. There are first
> the institutions with certain roles and expectations that will
> fulfill the goals of the system. And there are second the indivi-
> duals with certain personalities and need-disposition inhabiting
> the system, whose interactions comprise what we generally call
> social behavior. We assert that this social behavior may be un-
> derstood as a function of the following major analytic elements:
> institution, role, and expectation, which together constitute
> the *nomothetic* dimension of activity in a social system; and in-
> dividual, personality, and need-disposition, which together con-
> stitute the *idio*graphic dimension of activity in a social system.[8]

(NOMOTHETIC DIMENSION)

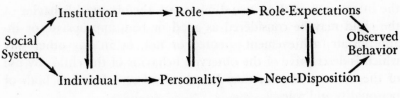

(IDIOGRAPHIC DIMENSION)

Figure 1. A model representing two-way social behavior.

The general model may be represented pictorially as indicated in Figure 1. The nomothetic dimension appears at the top and has institutions deriving from the social system, each institution defined by the roles which comprise it, and each role by the expectations attaching to it. At the lower part of the diagram, the idiographic axis is shown. The individual is part of the social system with personality defining the individual; it, in turn, is defined by need-dispositions. Any given act should be interpreted as deriving simultaneously from both dimensions with the resulting social behavior a function of an individual's attempt "to cope with an environment composed of patterns of expectations for his behavior in ways consistent with his own independent pattern of needs."[9]

For example, the model may serve to describe in general the dynamics of a behavioral act of a pupil in a particular school. The role of *pupil* is defined by the school and by the teacher as possessing characteristics evidenced by regular attendance, participation in class, being polite, and appearing interested. These are among the expectations a teacher may have for every pupil. The child comes to the school with characteristics peculiar to himself, these having been developed over the lifetime of the child through numerous and varied experiences. Some aspects of personality are manifested by need-dispositions which have been described as psychological, physiological, emotional, and social.[10] An individual's needs include food, water, elimination, recognition, and security, which may be demonstrated in various ways. Let us suppose that a child *needs* recognition from adults and behaves in a particular manner to achieve it. The teacher, reflecting views of the school, expects a pupil to behave in *other* ways. As a result of the interaction of these two dimensions, the observed behavior of the child may be considered as good or bad, appropriate or inappropriate, achievement-oriented or not, or in any other way which is descriptive of the observed behavior of the child. By use of the model, behavior may be perceived as a function both of personality and role.

The example presented above considers the general model as it may apply to the behavior of any individual within a social system. However, our emphasis is upon various characteristics of the disadvantaged pupil and methodologies utilized to describe them. I will review some of the current relevant literature and place it within the most appropriate dimension of the model. This will point up areas where additional research is needed and will suggest relationships among existing studies.

CHARACTERISTICS, THE PROFESSIONAL LITERATURE

Little of the burgeoning literature is representative of research in the empirical sense. Most findings are based on deduced concepts dependent upon real or interpreted contact with children. Few of the research studies have proceeded in a systematic manner or have been predicated upon theoretical considerations of child development or theories of learning. Perhaps this is why teachers receive few answers to questions related to specific effective teaching techniques, approaches to modification of curricula, treatment of discipline problems, or relations between home and school.

Rather than separating research from nonresearch literature, it may be useful to indicate the general areas considered by recent writers. There is a literature concerned with personality characteristics,[11] with related topics on components of intelligence,[12] attitudes toward learning, toward authority,[13] measurements of intelligence,[14] and school achievement.[15] Articles dealing with the structure of the family, the community,[16] and economics with consideration of social class structure,[17] are represented by materials dating back to 1949. There is no lack of articles; questions may be raised as to the accuracy of much of the information and the implications for action derived from them.

An example of a writer who presents an overview of the problem in general terms and one of the earliest and most widely read authors in this field is Riessman.[18] He presents the disadvantaged child and parents as poorly informed, reading ineffectively, aggressive, not concerned with status, illiberal on civil liberties and foreign policy, informal, pragmatic, and anti-intellectual. In terms of our model, Riessman is describing the idiographic dimension without considering the nomothetic.

More useful than the knowledge that these pupils are anti-intellectual and aggressive is the concept that the teacher expects the child to want to learn; the child wants to learn, but not what the teacher is teaching. As a result, the student appears anti-intellectual — to the material presented in class. This same student might learn well enough when presented with sex education or playing drums in band when his interests and "needs" lie in these areas.[19]

The problem of describing the disadvantaged is apt to become more solvable when presented within the dimensions of the model than if presented as traits subject to little modification by the individual or his environment. The model directs attention to the dynamics of interactions by the institution and attempts at modi-

fying needs of the individual which may result in pupil achievement-oriented behavior.

THE PROBLEM IN THE INSTITUTIONAL DIMENSION

We now examine characteristics of the nomothetic dimension
through studies related to it. This will be followed by a summary
of studies which explore the idiographic dimension. Suggestions
for future studies to correlate both dimensions as an approach
yielding data more reality-oriented than many current studies will
conclude this aspect of the problem.

Because of lack of space, one example must suffice to illustrate
each segment of the institutional dimension. The discussion will
follow the model and begin with a definition of the school.

Other than the physical plant, a school consists of teachers,
administrators, and curricula which combine to define a school in
terms of its educational functions. As the school has an historical
tradition which influences its current practices, it also is subject
to forces which continue to exert pressures for change or maintenance of the *status quo*. Both unions and the National Association of Manufacturers have programs and staffs concerned with
school programs. Teacher organizations, both local and national,
have varying degrees of success in shaping school policy in hiring
practices. Accrediting agencies and state legislation influence curricula more than do parent teacher organizations. Finally, as school
boards are either elected or appointed, they reflect values of the
groups supporting or electing them. What emerges is the realization that a multitude of factors interact to define the school as
an institution.[20]

The role of a student is defined in terms of the expectations
attached to it. These are derived from the traditions and values
held by the particular school as well as the expectations of teachers within it. The role has attached to it certain rights and obligations. A student is expected to maintain regular attendance,
attend to his studies, work or compete with other students, and
participate in various activities. He may be expected to be polite,
to use proper language, to conform to rules, and, in general, to
exhibit behaviors appropriate to his role.[21] Those experiences the
child brings to the school (his role of son at home, or that of

friend with peers) may be such that his expectations either reinforce or contradict those of the school. To the extent that the various roles are complementary, there will tend to be less conflict for the child and he will be more likely to perceive his role as student paralleling that of the school.

Few empirical studies which explore role-expectations for pupils have been performed. Most expectations are described or implied in somewhat idealistic terms in general education texts or are listed negatively by boards of education as "reasons for suspension or exclusion."[22] An exception to this paucity of studies is one by Kitano[23] in which he reported that in a nursery school, thirty-two children were classified by teacher as exhibiting normal behavior and fourteen as being problem children. With teacher descriptions as a basis, a seven-point problem rating scale was developed. Two graduate students observed and rated all children. When the scores of both problem and normal children were compared, no significant difference existed between both groups. Kitano concludes that a problem child was defined by the expectations set by the teacher; pupil behavior *per se* did not constitute problem behavior. Although the author did not indicate specific characteristics of any group studied, it would appear that the results have applicability to any school situation.

All aspects of the nomothetic dimension are directed toward specific goals. In our society, educational goals may be expressed as ideals and include such statements as "education for all according to their abilities" and "development of skills appropriate to membership in a free society." Such idealized goals are vague and do not lend themselves to meaningful examination by comparison to goals of individuals along the idiographic dimension. Short-term goals expressed in more precise terms are useful here. A school may indicate that it expects its pupils to develop the ability to communicate with others or to acquire computational skills necessary for living in an urban society. These goals imply that certain behavioral characteristics will be required. Indeed, to have students achieve these goals is the only purpose for which a school exists. Modify the goals in a way unacceptable to the supporting society and the school may cease to exist.

THE PROBLEM IN THE INDIVIDUAL DIMENSION

Explorations of the idiographic dimension will constantly involve that of the nomothetic. Every individual is a composite of his biological and social self. From birth, the individual interacts with various environments, beginning with physical and immediately involving the social environment of the family. The family is part of the nomothetic dimension and is the primary factor influencing personality development. As personality affects need-disposition, it is similarly affected by the role of the individual with its expectations. The interdependence is so pervasive that even though it may not be constantly referred to, the reader should be aware of it.

The influence of the family in the development of personality is of prime importance. It is through contact with the family that an organism becomes socialized as an individual and develops certain needs which will be manifested as behavior patterns in the school. Obviously, the child interacts simultaneously with grandparents, aunts, uncles, peers, siblings, and the larger community.

Let us consider a ten-year-old child of a disadvantaged family and describe some factors which may influence his behavior. The parents, aunts, uncles, peers, siblings, and the larger community. and their experiences with school have not been happy. When he can find employment, the father is a skilled laborer. Housing for the family consists of four rooms which are inadequate for two parents, a grandmother, and six children. The children are frequently ill because of crowded living conditions and a minimally adequate diet. The child in our example comes to school in fair physical condition, not highly motivated toward achievement in school, but with a need for recognition that is unsatisfied in the home. His world outside of the classroom produces recognition by his being part of a gang and defying certain types of authority.

This child has learned that methods for gaining recognition in school differ considerably from those outside. Because of the role definition of pupil, and teacher expectations attached to it, he may find that he cannot get the recognition he needs within the classroom and so he works for and receives most recognition outside of the school.

As oversimplified as this example is, it points to the reality resulting from the interaction between aspects of the idiographic and nomothetic dimensions. It would appear that learning would be aided when pupils are able to have some of their needs satisfied within the classroom.[24]

Studies on this dimension center about four problem areas which are not mutually exclusive. These are in family and child rearing practices, sex differences, cognition and language development including auditory discrimination, and the last, which includes parts of those preceding, factors of social class status.

Child Rearing

Child rearing practices have been studied extensively. It appears that lower-class parents exercise control over their children by harsh, corporal punishment. The father particularly has as a large part of his role the administration of punishment. If a father is not in the home, then the mother may assume this role, but more often is casual about applying constraints.[25] The child is familiar with corporal sanctions; indeed, he may anticipate these as his proper due. The role of each parent in child rearing appears to vary with the particular racial or ethnic group. In the lower-class Negro family, mother, grandmother, or aunt may exercise pervasive influence on the children. When the father is present, he frequently takes little part in child rearing.[26] Opposite to the matriarchal lower-class Negro family is the patriarchal family organization among Mexican-American, Puerto Rican, and Appalachian whites. Within families of these groups, the father is usually present and controls not only the behavior of his children, but also that of his wife.[27]

Sex and Personality Differences

Closely allied with child rearing are studies regarding sex and personality. Within the Negro family, girls are more highly accepted than boys and have access to models in the availability of their mothers. Girls have greater verbal fluency than boys and are more conforming to adult authority. These factors appear to relate to greater achievement in school.[28] Among Mexican-American, Puerto Rican, or Appalachian whites, parents favor boys over girls, or neither is shown unusual preference.[29]

Language Development

The role of cognition in language development has been the subject of many studies in recent years. Piaget's[30] studies strongly suggest that the development of cognitive functions in children is causally related to earlier experiences in the cognitive domain. The relationship may be so strong that lack of relevant experiences may restrict the development of subsequent cognitive abilities. A sequence of development is suggested: sensory-motor, concrete, and formal operations. The sequence does not change among children experiencing an impoverished environment; what may change is the rate with which a child masters one phase then moves to the next.

Bruner[31] agrees with Piaget and points out that once language is acquired, an individual may use it ". . . for the translation of experience . . ." to hasten the succeeding steps in the further acquisition of understanding and knowledge. Bruner places greater emphasis on experience, while Piaget is concerned with capacity in influencing the course of cognitive development. Disadvantaged children are handicapped in their exposure to situations which provide experience with cognitive skills. This position is supported in an increasing body of research.[32]

A corollary to the concept that environment is perhaps the most important consideration in language development is that lower-class retarded readers show a decided lack of ability in auditory discrimination when compared to retarded readers of the middle class.[33] One might speculate that crowded living conditions of the disadvantaged predispose a selective "tuning-out" of sounds in the home with a carryover to school learning situations.

The relationship of language and cognition to social class has been theorized by Bernstein.[34] He suggests that in British society, the use of language not only serves to identify social class membership, but reflects abilities of individuals to understand concepts and communicate them to others. Bernstein postulates that a *public* language is used by the working class and that this language is restrictive in the sense that the individual does not create a language use but utilizes existing idiomatic and traditional phrases to express himself. Members of the middle class use a *formal* language which is elaborative in that the user can communicate nuances of feeling and complex concepts. One may question whether the British lower-class is analogous to our population of disadvantaged. There appears to be some empirical support that these groups are comparable. John and Goldstein[35] found that a crucial difference between lower class and middle class first grade children was that lower-class children demonstrated a consistent lack of language utility as compared to a similar sample from the middle class.

Social Class

Social class is the result of generalizing from characteristics of individuals to those comprising a group. Our model represents the generalizations of interactions between the idiographic and nomothetic dimensions applied to a social group. As our primary concern here is with persons, not institutions, a discussion of a gross representation of social class is presented.

The now classical study establishing criteria for describing social class structure was performed by Warner.[36] He developed a scale whereby an individual could be categorized as a member of a particular class by assigning numerical values to characteristics such as occupations, income, and housing. This classification scheme is useful in that it provides a basis for research into the behavior modalities existent for individuals assigned to a particular class. On this basis, disadvantaged persons may be considered to be members of the lower class. Havighurst and Davis used the concept of class to document behavioral characteristics which may be generalized for any social class and related to success in school.[37]

Studies relating social class status to school performance occur in several areas. These generally include intelligence, achievement, and motivation. A majority of studies focus on the lower-class Negro but many of the results can be generalized to all disadvantaged.

An excellent summary of research on intelligence test scores of Negroes is presented by Pettigrew.[38] He concludes that Negroes consistently score lower on IQ tests than do their white counterparts primarily because of social class and caste factors. Research is cited demonstrating that where Negroes have been integrated into all-white schools or where special instruction has been provided, IQ scores increased significantly, approaching but not reaching those of white students.

Success in school is frequently related to understanding and utilizing abstract concepts. Bernstein[39] postulated that lower-class children used language expressing concrete rather than abstract ideas. This hypothesis is supported in part by Miller and Swanson[40] in their discussion of expressive styles. When the child-rearing practices (most associated with middle-class practices) approved of maternal self control, symbolic reward, and psychological discipline, the child tended to develop a conceptual or abstract style. When, as in lower-class families, maternal self-control was limited, rewards were tangible, and discipline was physical, the child more often developed a motoric or concrete style. Significant social class differences in pupil selection of concrete as opposed to abstract explanations of solutions to problems has been found by Siller.[41] Since achievement and IQ test scores may be related to the ability of the child to understand and work with abstracts, the role of social class in predisposing the family and peers to provide the necessary experiences is critical.

Motivation towards academic achievement may be considered from the point of view of the role played in its development by the family and school. The middle class is education oriented to the extent that parents support the school and its agents, encourage children to succeed, and aid the child in performing school tasks. In the school, teachers are either from the middle class or have accepted its values which tend to regard as successful, children who subscribe to similar value systems. Lower-class parents may not support the school and may even be hostile to it. They may want their children to succeed without knowing how to go about doing it. In the school, teachers of these children may not understand their value systems or if they do, may reject them. When the educational role of the family and school are complementary, there is a predisposition for success; the converse is also true.[42]

In summary, extensive research findings are available on the idiographic (individual) dimension of the model in areas involving social class in which are subsumed studies in family, child rearing practices, sex differences, and aspects of language development. There are few studies relating complementary points on both dimensions. Areas needing exploration include: (1) relating classroom to family structure in terms of the roles played by the teacher-mother versus pupil-child; (2) what role expectations are held for the pupil-in-school, versus the child-at-home, and how are they fulfilled in each situation, and (3) what kinds of experiences may be provided for all individuals involved to increase convergence of both dimensions with a subsequent increase in academic achievement? The preceeding are a few of the *many* areas needing exploration.

In the sections to follow, emphasis is shifted from specifics of the disadvantaged to a setting of the problem within the context of the society. The problem will be examined historically as well as related to the school as a social institution.

WHO ARE THE DISADVANTAGED PUPILS?

There are several ways in which those constituting the disadvantaged are identified. The most direct approach is in terms of people who have been affected by changes in technology to the extent that they now have modified prerequisites for a constructive life. These technological changes have influenced rural populations so that some cannot adapt themselves to the change. Others migrate to cities where their inadaptability becomes even more conspicuous. Of the groups fitting the preceeding discriptions, the largest populations are among Negroes, Appalachian whites, Puerto Ricans, Mexican-American farm workers, and the reservation Indians.[43]

A second identification may be made by inference from examination of community programs for aiding the immigrant in adjusting to urban living. When migration was at its peak following the end of World War II, many cities established commissions for human relations or welfare councils to aid in isolating and attacking these problems. Most of these organizations identify the same groups as constituting the disadvantaged.[44]

Programs throughout the country vary in their emphasis on

one group or another depending on which groups predominate in a community.[45] Thus we find New York, Detroit, and Chicago concerned with Negroes and Appalachian whites; New York and Milwaukee exploring programs for Puerto Ricans; and Los Angeles and San Francisco working with Mexican-Americans.[46]

Of all the groups mentioned, Negroes, by weight of numbers alone, constitute the most important. According to the 1960 U.S. Census, of the almost twenty-one million nonwhite inthis country, nineteen million were Negro. Of the Negroes, almost eleven million lived in urban centers in 1960 as contrasted to 9.5 million in 1950. Much of the increase can be accounted for by migration from rural areas, as well as a high birth rate.[47]

The civil rights movement, as well as the rise of militant Negro groups such as the Congress of Racial Equality and the Muslims, has focused attention on various problems of the Negro including that of education.[48] Writers, such as James Baldwin, have dramatized the intensity of feeling being manifested.[49]

Let us turn our attention briefly to the factors contributing to the development of the problem.

HISTORY OF THE PROBLEM

Although recognition of the problem of disadvantaged pupils may appear to the reader to have occurred within the last half-dozen years, this impression is due to increased publicity at the national level rather than to sudden recognition of the existence of a problem. Before 1950, criticism of educational practices resulting in changing programs occurred primarily at the local level. Then, as critics of educational practices such as Bestor, Lynd, and Rickover gained a national audience, attention shifted from problems of local concern to a generalization of these problems at the national level.[50] At that time, controversy centered about "fads and frills" in education and a lack of *excellence* of standards. The debate reached its peak in 1957 when the launching of the Russian Sputnik triggered federal support of selected programs in science, mathematics, and foreign languages through the passage of the National Defense Education Act of 1958. The uproar did result in much soul searching and reevaluation of goals within the educational enterprise directed towards locating and training talented young people. It was a byproduct of this evaluation that resulted in new concerns with the *other end* of the academic spectrum.

The main factors affecting the development of disadvantaged groups originated as far back as 1860 when the urban-rural population ratio changed. Urban population increased seventeen times while the rural population (rural-farm and rural-nonfarm) increased less than two and one-half times.[51] Edwards and Richey concur that:

> The growth of urban population and the increasing differentials in urban-rural growth have been among the most important factors in social and education problems.[52]

Along with increased urban growth came the shift from an agrarian to an industrial economy. New skills were needed, new professions developed, and as the home and church declined in importance in education, that of educational agencies such as the school increased. This increase in importance was demonstrated more in urban than in rural areas by more money spent per pupil for superior physical plants and teachers salaries. Reflecting an increased birth rate, between 1890 and 1930 public school enrollments more than doubled and nonpublic school enrollment substantially increased. By 1930, more than 95 per cent of children between the ages of seven and thirteen years were enrolled in school. Enrollment declined in 1940 and 1950, but this decrease was a reflection of a reduced school age population. Between 1950 and 1960 enrollment was up 25 per cent and it was anticipated to increase another 25 per cent by 1965.[53]

Although urban centers spent more money on education than did rural areas and more facilities were available, all parts of the population did not make equal use of the facilities. The predominant factors affecting use then as now appear to be family occupation and income. In Maryland in 1938, two out of three children of unskilled parents did not complete eighth grade compared to one out of thirteen of the professional group.[54] In Detroit in 1961, Sexton found parallel relationships between different levels of occupation and school achievement, but not to the extent occurring in 1938.[55]

The problem of motivation toward occupational status should be noted. A cycle has been established in which discrimination because of caste or competence over a period of time resulted in a lowered motivation in persons who recognized that their preparation would have been wasted. Recently, as jobs have become available, there were few qualified persons available. Continuing the cycle, individuals who now are motivated to prepare for newly available jobs may find their jobs automated out of existence before they are in the job market. Relationships among occupations, preparation, and motivation need to be viewed against the general background of automation. This added complexity is not unique to the disadvantaged, but it adds another burden to the difficulties of finding adequate occupations.

The historical and social development of this country demonstrates the relationships among the factors of population growth and movement, industrialization of the economy, social-class status, and educational achievement. It underscores the duration and magnitude of the problem at the national level and perhaps hints at directions for attempted resolutions.

ECONOMICS OF THE DISADVANTAGED

As our society increases in complexity and occupations become more specialized than ever before, those individuals who are unable to function effectively within this framework are immediately at an economic disadvantage. Recognition of this lack of competence has occurred at many levels within the community and has recently been accompanied by training and retraining programs. The most elaborate effort is at the national level through the "Economic Opportunity Act of 1964."[56] Embodied within this Act are provisions for youth and urban and rural community action programs, whose emphases are towards disadvantaged individuals.

It has been suggested earlier that a predisposition toward educational achievement is associated with many factors in the home and school. The disadvantaged do not generally achieve in school and this lack of education is directly related to occupational status and income. The U.S. Department of Labor has published some data on this relationship.[57] Table 1 shows that in 1960 three fourths of professional and technical workers have had some college while only about one fourth of any other large group has had that much education. Conversely, four fifths of all occupations listed and classed as "blue-collar" is composed of people having less than high school graduation. The second category of proprietors and managers is a composite of business executives and owners of small businesses. Executives may need a college education while proprietors do not. A study showed that 57 per cent of business executives were college graduates in 1952 as compared to 32 per cent in 1928.[58]

TABLE 1

OCCUPATION AND EDUCATION

Occupation (in broad categories)	Education (in per cent)		
	Less than High School Graduation	*High School Graduation*	*Some College Education*
Professional and Technical Workers	6	19	75
Proprietors and Managers	38	33	29
Sales or Clerical	25	53	22
Skilled Workers	59	33	8
Semi-skilled Workers	70	26	4
Service Workers	69	25	6
Unskilled Workers	80	17	3
Farmers and Farm Workers	76	19	5

Source:
   Manpower: Challenge of the 1960's (U.S. Dept. of Labor, 1960) p. 17.

The points to be noted are the contributions made by this group to society by occupations and by expenditure of income. The amount of income varies with education. In 1958, the average annual income of men age forty-five to fifty-four ranged from $3,000 with some elementary training to $12,000 for those completing college.[59] The differences in lifetime income are almost as great. In 1958, income from age eighteen to death was estimated at $182,000 for those who have completed only elementary school, ranging to $435,000 for those with four or more years of college. The differences dramatize the importance of education.

THE SCHOOL AND THE DISADVANTAGED

A unique feature of American public schools in comparison to those of other countries is that each school district is legally responsible for the development and financial support of all aspects of its schools. This means that financing, selection of personnel, maintenance of physical plants, and development of curricula may vary considerably from one part of the country to another and among districts within the same state. The variations may reflect differences of available funds as well as the prevailing philosophy of how much should be spent for what.

These wide differences do not encourage generalizations about schools and the disadvantaged, but certain statements may be made about relationships of the staff, organization of the school, and curricula to the disadvantaged. When considering the effectiveness of a total educational program, there can be no real division among these three. However, for purposes of examination they will be individually considered.

Sources of Teachers

The reasons why a person selects teaching as an occupation may be intimately related to his performance as a teacher. Undoubtedly, there is an interaction of factors affecting this choice. These may include psychological, social, and economic factors at the personal level to economic and social conditions at the national level. Increased unemployment may result in a desire for personal security and an increased national birth rate provides a basis for broad encouragement of young people to enter teaching.

As well as entering teaching for a variety of reasons, teachers possess a variety of backgrounds. Perhaps most important for our purposes are those identifying social class. Before 1920, teachers predominantly came from the middle classes, both upper and lower. Because of the stigma attached to women working, moreover, teaching provided one of the few respectable occupations available. Beginning in the late 1920's a change occurred in the social composition of the profession from that of middle to upper-lower class. Today, all but the extremes of the social spectrum are represented. The importance is not so much the social origin of teachers but rather the attitudes and values they bring to the classroom in disadvantaged areas.[60]

One might reasonably expect that most teachers who *moved up* from the lower to middle class ranks would be sensitive to the needs of disadvantaged students and subsequently demonstrate outstanding teaching techniques. The somewhat limited observations of this writer do not support this contention. Instead, it appears that there is a distribution of effective and less effective teachers similar to that found in advantaged schools where teachers may be from middle-class backgrounds. It may be that when an individual has become a teacher with its attendant high status, he might not care to be reminded of his social class origin. His origin might be denied by insisting on perfection in class or by being more middle class in expectations of students than a teacher from a middle-class environment. A conclusion to be derived from these observations is that social class origin does not in itself predispose teachers to be effective in the classroom. Knowledge of individual personality characteristics, attitudes, and training apart from broad social characteristics would be a more accurate predictor of effective teaching.

School Organization

Schools are organized in a variety of ways. For many years, an eight-year elementary and four-year high school arrangement was standard in many districts. Then, there was a change to a six-year elementary, two-year junior high and four-year senior high school plan. Modifications, including the addition of junior college, were added with further variations at all levels. However, no matter what the organizational pattern, traditional requirements for promotion from one grade or year to the next were observed. Today, the same criteria for promotion are used that were in use twenty years ago: teacher evaluation of achievement based on certain standards; achievement test scores, IQ, age, social maturity, and other criteria both subjective and objective. A student who fails a semester or a subject must repeat or make it up in some way.

Schools are beginning to recognize that traditional organizational and promotion policies are not helping the disadvantaged to achieve. The drop-out rate continues to rise, "problem" schools have increased teacher turnover, and in general the disadvantaged continue to under-achieve.

Recognition of organizational problems has been widespread. Under the Great Cities Program, fifteen school systems have been exploring various practices of teaching the disadvantaged. Some experiments include modifications in organization.[61] Chicago schools are adopting an organizational plan for the primary grades in which the student achieving success in reading and mathematics moves through eight levels in grades kindergarten through third. There are no failures; a child moves from one level to the next when he is ready, not necessarily at the end of a school year.[62]

If there is a trend towards reorganization, it is in the direction of modification of grade levels no longer regulated by the calendar and a change in subject matter sequence and duration. Further recognition of the special learning problems of disadvantaged may suggest even more imaginative innovations in organization and promotion.

Curriculum

As considered from the broad view, a curriculum includes subject matter to be taught, teaching methods, materials to be utilized, approaches to evaluation, and, as previously indicated under organization, the sequence to be followed. Most school districts follow some form of a curriculum whether formally printed as a course of study or informally derived by teachers. Some guides specify objectives to be achieved, methodologies to be employed for those objectives, teaching aids and techniques, and evaluative devices. Student texts may imply these; teacher's editions make them explicit.

Objectives of the curriculum are crucial in that they set forth what the entire learning experience is to accomplish. If objectives are poorly conceived, then the total curriculum may be mediocre at best and inappropriate at worst. Bloom suggests that all objectives which can be stated as descriptions of student behavior may be placed into three groupings: cognitive, affective, and psychomotor. Cognitive has to do with "recall or recognition of knowledge and the development of intellectual ability and skill;" affective with "changes in interests, attitudes, and values, and the development of manipulative skills."[63] Tyler emphasizes that the process of developing objectives is intricate and must be based in part, on the needs, interests, and abilities of the learner.[64]

Here is the center of the curriculum problem. Under the best of conditions with students of rich experiential backgrounds, where needs, interests, and abilities are known, only cognitive objectives can be clearly delineated and classified. Affective objectives can be placed into some systematic order and psychomotor objectives have not been classified.[65]

So little is known about the *real* needs, interests, and abilities of the disadvantaged that the formulation and even classification of objectives for a unique curriculum is in a primordial stage of development. This lack of knowledge and understanding has been reflected in an almost complete lack of curricula developed with this population in mind. It is no accident that although many school systems recognize this problem area, little is being done about it.

Curriculum guides used by the Chicago schools have suggested activities for the "slow learner." They do not have modified objectives, suitable approaches for the teacher, or special ways of evaluating achievement; nor do they have a modified scope or sequence of various parts of a curriculum.[66] They have a standard subject matter curriculum including suggestions for slow and gifted students. There may be an assumption that slow learners are disadvantaged and simplification is all that's needed. The fallacies of such an assumption are explicit throughout the several chapters of this book.

An attempt to develop a curriculum uniquely suited to the disadvantaged is underway at Queens College. A project called BRIDGE is coded for the following phrase: Building Resources of Instruction for Disadvantaged Groups in Education. One of the lines of inquiry involves attempts at modifying and experimenting with a prescribed three-year junior high school syllabus. No results are yet available but some practices show promise.[67]

Beilin and Gotkin make other suggestions in developing mathematics curricula for the disadvantaged. They cite theoretical and empirical studies which indicate some direction for curriculum builders but also conclude as was previously indicated, not enough is known of the learners to warrant large scale efforts in curriculum construction.[68]

SCHOOL-HOME RELATIONS

The final section of this introductory chapter concerns the interrelationship between home and school, more specifically, relationships between the parents and school personnel. Through this entire chapter references were made to the interactions occurring between the child and his family, peers, teacher, school administrations, and curriculum. It was suggested that attitudes held by the child toward school were largely the result of attitudes of parents toward education in general and school in particular. The importance of the relationship between parents and school must be stressed.

Fusco[69] has surveyed twenty schools in five large cities to determine how the school perceived the existing behavior of parents relating to the demands made by the school on their children. Some parents appeared to be distrustful of school personnel by refusing to visit the school unless sent for. In other cases, parents wouldn't come but sent an older brother or sister in their place. Where no father was in the home or available for visitations, mothers expressed frustration with having a large number of children to supervise alone.

A somewhat unusual response was reported from parents in highrise housing. They expressed a sense of isolation because of their impersonal surroundings and appeared to respond to them with indifference to the school.

Of prime concern here is the inability of parents to provide an intellectually stimulating environment for their children, coupled with lack of information on what they might do to support school and classroom activities. This implies a problem within the school of lack of information about parents, coupled with poor communications between school and home.

The writer has been unable to locate any studies ascertaining how disadvantaged parents perceive the school, teachers, curriculum, or their own role in relation to the educational tasks required of their children. The importance of this area suggests a need for research with a high priority.

SUMMARY

This chapter sketched various dimensions of the problem of disadvantaged pupils. No attempt has been made to suggest remedial measures; these will be discussed in the remaining sections of this book.

1. Characteristics of disadvantaged pupils were described as a function of the interaction between social institutions, such as the school, and the individual child. To place this interaction within a context which can be used to summarize relevant research and suggest areas where research is needed, a psycho-social model was employed. The model used contained only two dimensions, both derived from the social system: a nomothetic or institutional and idiographic or individual dimension. The nomothetic consists of the institution, roles derived from it, and role-expectations. The idiographic dimension is defined by the individual, personality, and need-disposition, each position on the continuum defines the one preceding. Both dimensions interact constantly at all points, resulting in the observable behavior of an individual or group.

2. Placed in historical perspective, the problem has evolved as has the American social order. Social, political, and economic events have affected the lives of segments of the Negro, Puerto Rican, Mexican-American, Appalachian white, and American Indian subcultures to the extent that these people cannot participate to the maximum of their potential in the larger society. It was emphasized that the extended duration of the problem mitigates against rapid solutions.

3. In considering economic effects disadvantaged groups have on society, as well as the effects on income of being disadvantaged, it was pointed out that there is a direct relationship between income and education. Those individuals with least education have occupations that are menial and have the lowest annual as well as lifetime income. They contribute the least of any groups in society in terms of productivity and expenditure of income.

4. Exploration of the role of the school in defining the problem focused on three aspects: staff, organization, and curricula.

Staffing of schools has changed in sex, sources, status, and income. Today more males, from upper-lower class, with higher status and higher income than ever before in this century comprise elementary school teacher populations.

Both organization and curricula are evolving from a rather rigid to a flexible structure which considers some of the unique needs of these learners. Even with the change, much research is needed to document the specifics of changes needed for more effective schools.

5. Apparent throughout this chapter is the contention that the home is the key to modification of behavior patterns antithetical to academic, occupational, and economic achievement. Programs to evaluate and improve home-school relations are needed. When the parents know *how* and are *able* to aid their children in maximal participation in society, the problem of the disadvantaged will be in the process of resolution.

REFERENCES

1. Benjamin Bloom, Allison Davis, and Robert Hess, *Compensatory Education for Cultural Deprivation,* Research Conference on Educational and Cultural Deprivation (Dept. of Educ.: University of Chicago, 1964) (Mimeographed.)
2. Frank Riessman, *The Culturally Deprived Child* (New York: Harper & Row, 1962) .
3. Educational Policies Commission, *Education and the Disadvantaged American,* (Washington: NEA, 1962) .
4. Warren Cutts, "Reading Unreadiness in the Under Privileged" *NEA Journal,* 52 (April 1, 1963) , 23-4.
5. Bernard Kaplan, "Issues in Educating the Disadvantaged" *Phi Delta Kappan,* 45 (November, 1963) , 70-76.
6. Gene Fusco, *School-Home Partnership in Depressed Urban Neighborhoods* (Washington: U. S. Government Printing Office, 1964) p. 4.
7. Jacob Getzels and Egon Guba, *Social Behavior & the Administrative Process,* Paper read at the annual meeting of the American Sociological Society, September, 1965. (Mimeographed.)
8. Getzels and Guba, *op. cit.,* p. 3.
9. *Ibid.*
10. Glenn Blair, R. Stewart Jones, and Ray Simpson, *Educational Psychology* (2nd ed.; New York: Macmillan Co., 1962) .
11. *Journal of Social Issues,* Vol. XX, No. 2, 1965.
12. Jerome S. Bruner, "The Course of Cognitive Growth," *American Psychologist,* Vol. 19, No. 1 (January, 1964) , pp. 1-15.

Martin Deutsch, "The Role of Social Class in Language Development and Cognition," *Journal of Orthopsychiatry,* (in press).

Harry Beiling and Lassar G. Gotkin, *Psychological Issues in the Development of Mathematics Curricula for Socially Disadvantaged Children,* Presented at the Invitational Conference on Mathematics Education for Below Average Achievers, School Mathematics Study Group, April, 1964, (Mimeographed.).

13. Frank Riessman, *The Culturally Deprived Child, op. cit.,* pp. 26-30.

A. Harry Passow (Ed.), *Education in Depressed Areas* (New York: Teachers College, Columbia University, 1963), pp. 101-180.

Welfare Council of Metropolitan Chicago, *Institute on Cultural Patterns of Newcomers,* (Chicago, 1958).

14. Irwin Katz, "Review of Evidence Relating to Effects of Desegregation on the Intellectual Performance of Negroes," *American Psychologist,* Vol. 19, No. 6 (June, 1964), 381-399.

Chicago Board of Education, *Data Concerning the Community and The Public School Pupils of Chicago* (Chicago: July 8, 1964). (Mimeographed.)

15. *Ibid.*

16. A. Harry Passow, *op. cit.,* pp. 1-100.

17. Allison Davis, *Social Class Influences Upon Learning* (Cambridge: Harvard Press, 1948).

A. Harry Passow, *op. cit.,* pp. 181-236.

Robert Havighurst and Bernice Neugarten, *Society and Education* (Boston: Allyn and Bacon, 1957).

Patricia C. Sexton, *Education and Income: Inequalities of Opportunity In Our Schools* (New York: Viking, 1961).

18. Frank Riessman, *op. cit.*

19. Allison Davis, *Teaching the Culturally Disadvantaged Pupil,* (Dept. of Education, University of Chicago, n. d.), pp. 12-14. (Mimeographed.)

20. *Social Forces Influencing American Education,* The Sixteenth Yearbook of National Society for the Study of Education, Part II (Chicago: University of Chicago Press, 1961).

21. Frederick Elkin, *The Child and Society* (New York: Random House, 1960), pp. 56-57.

Chicago Board of Education, *Pupil Conduct and Discipline,* November, 1961. (Brochure.)

22. Chicago Board of Education, *Rules of the Board of Education,* Sec. 6-8, 6-9.

23. Harry H. L. Kitano, "Adjustment of Problem and Nonproblem Children to Specific Situation: A Study in Role Theory," *Child Development,* 33, 1962, 229-233.

24. H. Maas, "Some Social Class Differences in the Family Systems and Group Relations of Pre-and Early Adolescents," *Child Development,* 22, 1951, 145-152.

Eleanor Maccoby, P. K. Gibbs *et al.*, "Methods of Child Rearing in Two Social Classes," in W. E. Martin and C. B. Stendler (Eds.), *Readings in Child Development* (New York: Harcourt-Brace, 1954), pp. 380-396.

25. David Jenkins, "Interdependence in the Classroom," *Journal of Educational Research,* XLV (October, 1951), 137-144.

26. B. Dai, "Some Problems of Personality Development in Negro Children," in Clyde Kluckhohn and H. A. Murray (Eds.), *Personality in Nature, Society, and Culture* (New York: Korph, 1944), pp. 437-458.

27. Welfare Council of Metropolitan Chicago, *Institute on Cultural Patterns of Newcomers. op. cit.*

28. David Ausubel *et al.*, "Perceived Parent Attitudes as Determinants of Children's Ego Structure," Child Development, 1954, 173-183.

29. *Institute on Cultural Patterns of Newcomers, op. cit.*

30. J. H. Flavell, *The Developmental Psychology of Jean Piaget* (New Work: Van Nostrand, 1963).

31. Jerome Bruner, "The Course of Cognitive Growth," *American Psychologist,* 19 (January, 1964), 1-15.

32. Martin Deutsch, "The Role of Social Class in Language Development and Cognition," *Journal of Orthopsychiatry,* (In press.)
William Fowler, "Cognitive Learning in Infancy and Early Childhood," *Psychological Bulletin,* 59, 1962, (2), 116-152.

33. Cynthia Deutsch, "Auditory Discrimination and Learning: Social Factors," *The Merrill-Palmer Quarterly.* Vol. 10, No. 3 (July, 1964), 227-296.

34. Basil Bernstein, "Social Class and Linguistic Development" in A. H. Halsey, J. Floud, and C. A. Anderson (eds.), *Education, Economy and Society* (New York: Free Press, 1961), pp. 288-314.

35. Vera P. John and Leo S. Goldstein, "The Social Context of Language Acquisition," *The Merrill-Palmer Quarterly,* Vol. 10, No. 3 (July, 1964), 265-275.

36. W. Lloyd Warner, Marchia Meeker and Kenneth Eells, *Social Class In America* (Chicago: Science Research Assoc., 1949).

37. Havighurst and Neugarten, *Society and Education, op. cit.*, pp. 1-55. Allison Davis, *Social Class Influence on Learning, op. cit.*

38. Thomas F. Pettigrew, *A Profile of the Negro American* (Princeton: Von Nostrand Co., 1964), pp. 100-135.

39. Basil Bernstein, *op. cit.*

40. Davil R. Miller and Guy E. Swanson *Inner Conflict and Defense* (New York: Henry Holt, 1960.)

41. Jerome Siller, "Socio-Economic Status and Conceptual Thinking," *Journal of Abnormal and Social Psychology,* 55, 3 (November, 1957).

42. Robert J. Havighurst and Bernice T. Neugarten, *Society and Education, op. cit.*, pp. 79-105: 181-198.

43. Educational Policies Commission, *Education and the Disadvantaged American op. cit.,* pp. 3-10.
44. These include: Welfare Council of Metropolitan Chicago; The Mayor's Friendly Relations Committee, Cincinnati, Ohio; Maryland Department of Economic Development; The Harlem Youth Organization, New York.
45. U. S. Department of Health, Education, and Welfare, *Programs for the Educationally Disadvantaged* (Washington, D. C.: U. S. Govt. Printing Office, 1963).
46. Research Council of the Great Cities Program for School Improvement, *Promising Practices for the Culturally Deprived* (Chicago, 1964).
47. United States Bureau of the Census, *U. S. Census of Population. General Social and Economic Characteristics, U. S. Summary.* Federal Report PC (1) -1c (Washington, D. C.: U. S. Govt. Printing Office, 1962).
48. Charles E. Silberman, *Crisis in Black and White* (New York: Random House, 1964).
49. James Baldwin, *Another Country* (New York: Dell Publishing Co., 1960).
50. Arthur E. Bestor, *Educational Wastelands* (Urbana: University of Illinois Press, 1953); Albert Lynd, "Quackery in the Public Schools," *Atlantic Monthly,* (March 1950), 33-38; Hyman G. Rickover, *Education and Freedom* (New York: E. P. Dutton, 1960).
51. United States Bureau of the Census, *Historical Statistics of the United States, 1789-1945* (Washington, D. C.: U. S. Govt. Printing Office, 1949), p. 29.
52. Newton Edwards and Herman Richey, *The School in the American Social Order* (2nd ed. rev., Boston: Houghton Mifflin, 1963), p. 485.
53. *Ibid.,* pp. 497-511.
54. Bernard Karpinos and Herbert Sommers, "Educational Attainment of Youth in Various Income Classes," *Elementary School Journal,* XLII (May, 1942), 677-687.
55. Patricia C. Sexton, *op. cit.*
56. U. S. Congress, *Economic Opportunity Act of 1964,* Public Law 88-452, 99th Cong., Aug. 20, 1964.
57. U. S. Dept. Labor, *Manpower: Challenge of the 1960's* (U. S. Department of Labor, 1960), p. 17.
58. W. Lloyd Warner and James C. Abeglen, *Occupational Mobility in American Business and Industry, 1928-1952* (Minneapolis: University of Minnesota Press, 1955), p. 108.
59. Herman P. Muller, "Annual Lifetime Income in Relation to Education: 1939-1959, "*The American Economic Review,* 50, 5 (December, 1960), 962-986.
60. Havighurst and Neugarten, *Society and Education, op. cit.,* pp. 355-375.
61. The Research Council of the Great Cities Program for School Improvement, *Promising Practices from the Projects for the Culturally Deprived, op. cit.*

62. *Guidelines for the Primary Program of Continuous Development,* (Chicago: Chicago Board of Education, 1963).

63. Benjamin S. Bloom (Ed.) *Taxonomy of Educational Objectives, Handbook I: Cognitive Domain* (New York: Longmans, Green & Co., 1956), p. 7.

64. Ralph W. Tyler, *Basic Principles of Curriculum and Construction* (Chicago: University of Chicago Press, 1950).

65. Benjamin S. Bloom (Ed.), *Taxonomy of Educational Objectives, Handbook II: Affective Domain* (New York: David McKay Co., 1964).

66. *Compensatory Education,* Study Report No. 4 (Chicago: Chicago Board of Education, 1964), p. 48.

67. Leonard Kornberg, "Meaningful Teachers for Alienated Children," in *Education in Depressed Areas,* A. Harry Passow (ed.), *op. cit.,* pp. 262-277.

68. Harry Beilin and Lassar G. Gotkin, *op. cit.*

69. Gene C. Fusco, *School-Home Partnership, op. cit.,* pp. 8-10.

Chapter II

PROGRAMS FOR THE CULTURALLY DISADVANTAGED

WILLIAM E. GORMAN*

ELEMENTARY SCHOOL systems across the nation have moved in a variety of directions in attempting to meet the challenge of educating culturally disadvantaged pupils. "Culturally disadvantaged youth, and by this we usually mean poverty stricken youth, are the subject of growing interest among the nation's educators."[1]

In those words, Kaplan emphasized the fact that there has been increased concern for the culturally deprived child as he finds his way into the middle class oriented structure of the typical metropolitan school system. The mores and folkways of the culturally deprived child differ radically from those of the culture represented in the new educational surroundings in which he finds himself.

In a recent, comprehensive report, Havighurst and his staff have evaluated the education of the socially disadvantaged in the schools under the supervision of the Board of Education of the City of Chicago.

The report indicates that the term *socially disadvantaged* is a "convenient abbreviation to cover a multitude of factors affecting many of the children in our city schools."[2] The report further indicates that "these factors include low educational level of the parents, low family income, and little or no experience of the wider community outside the rural or city slum environment in which the child has lived."[3]

Further characteristics typical of the socially disadvantaged child include poor housing, poor health conditions, and broken or incomplete families. The report further states: "Such socially disadvantaged children may be white or Negro, but if they are Negro, they are also affected by the whole complex of problems and attitudes relating to race."[4]

---

*Chairman, Department of Guidance and Counseling and Associate Professor of Education, De Paul University.

Thus, there has arisen a need to explore possible new approaches to the education of these children. Many programs and projects have been reported to date. For the moment, there does not appear to be any distinct nationwide pattern developing regarding methods, systems or administrative procedures for coping with the massive problem of the education of the disadvantaged elementary school child. While a national *modus operandi* does not exist, there is, nevertheless, a good deal of effort being put forth in elementary schools to effect a major breakthrough in the field of education for the disadvantaged child. Some of this effort may be reported as successful while some of the effort may be considered less successful than hoped for. Some of the effort may be, for the moment, in the experimental stage, where hopes of success are high, but where results are not yet reportable. Indeed, it may be that most such efforts are really in the last of these three categories. As with education for other children, the total results of the educational efforts that are expended on the disadvantaged child may not be fully known for many more years in the life of each child recipient of the educational effort. This is to say, that, as in other examples of educational opportunity which we might employ, we dare not lose sight of the fact that we are dealing with individual differences that most surely exist within the broad confines of any cultural strata.

In selected geographical areas across the United States, there is an ongoing shift of families with children of elementary school age. Included are migrant workers and their families following the crops. One of the most bitter educational facts of life in modern American society is echoed in the following statement: "Tens of thousands of American migrant children, it is estimated, today do not have an opportunity for education equal to that of other children in our society."[5]

Included also in the geographic shift of culturally disadvantaged persons are some recently arrived families who have come to the mainland from Puerto Rico. This shifting population flow of culturally different elementary school children and their families also includes the Appalachian mountaineers and Southern Negroes who have sought new hope in the becoming atmospheres of the great cities of our land.

No matter what their original geographic derivation, it would be presumptuous to assume that all of these persons are equally culturally disadvantaged. Environment includes many internal and external factors which affect the individual, we are told.

Throughout this section we have used the term *culturally disadvantaged* quite frequently. However, for the reason suggested by Pikunas and Albrecht, we must approach the use of this term with a degree of caution. Two children coming from the same cultural background will neither necessarily both experience identical advantages nor disadvantages. Such factors as personal motivation and the attitudes of parents toward the child and toward the school are constantly at work in individual instances. For these reasons, it is necessary to indicate that a child may be culturally *different* without necessarily being culturally *disadvantaged per se.*[6] Havighurst suggested the following concerning the matter of the aspirations of culturally disadvantaged persons.

"Contrary to popular notions, people who are culturally deprived do place a high value on education, but they lack confidence and know-how in how to go about getting one. In the case of working class Negro families, the generally wary, lower-class attitudes toward school authorities may be further reinforced by resentment and frustration arising from racial problems."[7]

There are recognized differences in the complexity and scope of the varieties of problems attendant to the education of the culturally disadvantaged child. Hence, one would not expect all American communities to exhibit the same identical educational circumstances to the same and exact degree. Nevertheless, there are basic or common denominators which exist according to the recent survey by Havighurst. "The Chicago School Survey is important primarily because it attempts to diagnose and advise concerning the problems of education in the big city—the central and major practical problem of education in the United States. What was found to be true of Chicago and what is proposed for Chicago in the survey apply equally to all big cities."[8]

A recent report lists the project activities of large city school systems which have been involved in "The Great Cities Program for School Improvement."[9] A review of the Great Cities Report suggests that much of what is currently being done for culturally disadvantaged elementary school children may be described under the following general headings:

1. Special classes
2. Summer school
3. Guidance
4. In-service education of teachers
5. Early admissions
6. Special training for teachers
7. Home visitors .
8. Other compensatory education.

It is not the intention of this chapter to suggest that the above list is all inclusive, either in terms of what is being done or in terms of what should be done. Neither do we intend to suggest that the examples used herein even approach all inclusiveness. In most cases, we have attempted, for example, to use one or more Great City Programs as illustrative of an area of particularized educational action on behalf of the socially deprived elementary school child. With these limitations in mind, let us approach an overview of programs for the culturally disadvantaged.

Special Classes

The urgent need for the provision of meaningful curricular offerings in educating youth for democracy has been well expressed by Gross and Zeleny:

"... The curriculum and youth must be so correlated that the needs of society and of youth become satisfied in one living process. The two, that is, the curriculum (reflecting society) and youth, cannot be considered as two separate things. The individual and his school environment are one."[10]

The Milwaukee Public Schools Orientation for In-migrant and Transient Children is an example of what can be accomplished for the culturally disadvantaged by way of special classes. In the Milwaukee Project of Orientation for In-migrant and Transient Children, there has been an assignment of a full-time social worker and a school psychologist who devotes 80 per cent of his time to the project. This system allows, among other factors, for "continuous assistance in mutually interpreting the contributing social, emotional, and educational factors influencing each child's progress"[11] through the weekly consultations between the teachers and these specialists.

Milwaukee also reported as a promising practice, the special placement of deprived children in small classes taught by selected teachers. These classes utilize small group and individual special help techniques as well as intensive assistance from instructional supervisors.

Summer School

Another procedure used in the education of the culturally deprived is attendance during summer school classes. Variations exist, of course, but there is a definite emphasis on improvement in reading and arithmetic in a large number of summer school programs. The Detroit Public Schools Great Cities Program for School Improvement is a case in point. Among other practices, the Detroit Summer School Program is a good example of affording special educational opportunity to the culturally disadvantaged child. "Summer school enrichment, particularly in reading and arithmetic, tends to affect the academic recession which generally occurs during the typical inner city summer."[12]

Affording the culturally disadvantaged with additional weeks in school during the summer months is one way of implementing a suggestion of Conant: "In the slum school, the development of reading skill is obviously of first importance. The earlier the slow readers are spotted and remedial measures instituted, the better."[13]

The public schools of the District of Columbia Great Cities Gray Areas Project report beneficial academic results stemming from summer school remedial reading programs which have been offered to children with IQ's of 85 and above in grades three through six.[14]

The advantage of summer school educational opportunities to the disadvantaged child and the necessity for the continuance of such programs are inferred in the following excerpt from a report published by the Chicago schools.

"As has been noted, many environmental factors interfere with the educational progress of the culturally disadvantaged child. These have produced a pupil who is often overage and retarded in his grade placement. Unless this pupil is afforded the opportunity to catch up, he freqeuntly becomes an early school leaver. The summer school provides a special compensatory opportunity for the child with a disadvantaged background."[15]

Guidance

Still another exciting avenue through which the disadvantaged elementary school child is being provided with services is in the area of guidance. Again, there have been a number of approaches to the guidance effort that have been identified. For example, the St. Louis Public Schools report that they have a primary level guidance project in which a guidance counselor and a school social worker are assigned to work with children, teachers, and parents in the primary levels of two project schools. The objective is early identification of problem behavior patterns with the provision of early remedial help.

St. Louis Public Schools have also provided on an experimental basis, counselors to seventh and eighth grade students in selected project schools. The program has resulted in superior transition of these pupils to departmentalized secondary school programs.[16]

A broad based approach to guidance has been suggested by Peters: "The guidance function provides strategically-placed stimuli for assisting, altering, accelerating or adjusting the life motion and direction for the individual. The guidance function stresses realistic self-appraisal, rational planning, preparation for alternatives (flexibility), problem-solving of self concerns, and analysis of one's social interactive processes. Above all, the guidance function mandates a consideration of the fullest use of one's qualities based on a foundation of intellectual development."[17]

The City of New York reports a demonstration guidance project which includes individual counseling of junior high school students with support of services including social workers, psychologists, and consultative psychiatry services. This comprehensive project also includes opportunities for group guidance and has been reported as costing about $100 additionally per junior high school pupil per year (or about 25 per cent above regular cost).[18]

The demonstration guidance project provides opportunities

for cultural enrichment through such activities as trips to theatres, special movies, assembly programs, etc. In addition, classes totaling ten to fifteen youngsters are provided with math and foreign language instruction.

Another feature of the demonstration guidance project is its use of small and large group meetings with parents for purposes of attempting to raise the aspiration level of parents for their children. An additional program of junior guidance classes has been started in New York City. As stated, the goals are:

1. To develop effective procedures which will identify emotionally and socially disturbed children in the earliest grades.
2. To provide a resource for disruptive children who are damaging the normal functioning of regular classes.
3. To prevent the development of serious maladjustment by helping disturbed children before their problems become deep rooted.
4. To build a coordinated program that will include teacher selection, teacher training, and a carefully planned curriculum and other built in protections for a rehabilitative program."[19]

Additionally, there are two types of junior guidance classes reported in New York City. The first are closed register junior guidance classes which "serve poorly functioning children with a wide range of personality and behavior symptoms. These classes are single grades divided between boys and girls and are balanced to include both withdrawn and aggressive children of at least average intelligence."[20] Each class contains fifteen children and attempts are made to minimize the mobility of these children.

Children are retained in the program whenever possible, for at least one year. There are three teachers for thirty children with the third auxiliary teacher providing extra services to the children.

Open registration junior guidance classes are set up "primarily to provide an emergency therapeutic resource for the very disruptive who cannot be contained in regular classes and who require placement during the school year. The maximum number of children in this class is ten."[21]

The necessary interrelationship of education and guidance has been accentuated by Glanz: "Guidance, as the profession charged with helping the person to use his opportunity and to learn to be free and responsible, is a part of education. Guidance could not exist without education, and education as we now know it is not complete without guidance. The interrelationship of education, teaching and guidance, can now be better understood as the historical roots of guidance are understood and as guidance faces its future."[22]

An approach to elementary school guidance for the disadvantaged is found in the Chicago Public Schools, which provide an improved program for boys and girls who are fourteen years of age and older and who have not graduated from grade school. Educational and Vocational Guidance Centers have now been established in seven locations in various parts of the City of Chicago. The pupils, in each of the centers are grouped in nongraded classes of about twenty, on the basis of achievement in arithmetic and reading, the results of group tests, teacher estimates, and chronological age.

> "This individualization of the instruction program, and the personalized but firm relationship between pupil and teachers which are made possible by the reduced class size, the intensive counseling and guidance services available in the center, and the knowledge that he may move ahead as rapidly as he develops the necessary skills, have proven to be important factors in changing the attitude of the pupils, improving his motivation, accelerating his entrance to high school and increasing the probability of his graduation."[23]

In-service Education of Teachers

The necessity for special efforts at teaching excellence on the part of teachers of the disadvantaged has been mentioned by Harris: "Teachers whose schools are located in such neighborhoods can succeed when they make the learning situation in the classroom vital enough to arouse interest and effort. Unfavorable socio-economic conditions do not make it impossible to teach well, but they do make extra effort necessary."[24]

The Philadelphia Public Schools have been cognizant of the

importance of in-service education of teachers: "In-service education of teachers is recognized universally as one of the most important supports to a vital, functional educational program."[25] In the Philadelphia Public Schools Great Cities School Improvement Program there is a continuing effort to improve on teacher's competencies through in-service education. The program includes released time in-service education where, on one morning each week, the teachers of classes in project schools have an opportunity to attend grade group in-service sessions in their own school. These sessions are held on a regularly scheduled basis. The grade groups meet with special consultants for a period of time ranging up to forty-five minutes in duration. This time is spent in developing theory and practice which is designed to improve the instruction of the culturally disadvantaged child. While the teachers are so engaged, their classes are attending a highly constructed literature program in an auditorium-type situation which is conducted through the use of the best literature films and filmstrips available.

The in-service program is further augmented by the use of workshop sessions and extended faculty meetings.

Early Admission

Still another approach to the education of the culturally disadvantaged child is found in the matter of early admission to school. In many instances, the purpose of an early admission policy would be to bring culturally disadvantaged children into a school, during the summer before their first year in school. In Baltimore, early admission is utilized in an attempt to enrich the experiences of children.

The Baltimore City Public Schools Early School Admissions Project is an experiment which involves early admission to school. This $330,000, three-year program, has been co-financed by the Baltimore City Public Schools and the Ford Foundation. This project is in the process of "attempting to determine whether early admission to school can overcome any of the barriers to learning which environmental factors seem to impose."[26]

The apparent value of the program may be viewed through the following gains reported to Baltimore authorities by interested adults:[27]

Teachers have identified gains on the part of children in a number of areas, including understanding and using language, developing skills in auditory discrimination, developing skills in visual discrimination, developing skills in using materials such as paint and scissors, working with others, pursuing individual interests with less support from adults, caring for personal needs with less assistance from adults, following directions, and participating in new activities.

At least 70 per cent of the parents indicated that their children had shown marked progress in their ability to get along better with other children, to talk to adults, to use more words to express ideas, and to use materials.

Kindergarten teachers who received the children of the early school admissions project noted the following:

1. There were no first-week-of-school adjustment problems.
2. A minimum of time was consumed in establishing routine procedures.
3. Children expressed themselves more readily and at a more advanced level than typical kindergarten entrants in the given community.
4. Children were eager to participate in activities that were new to them.

Special Training for Teachers of the Disadvantaged

The Cleveland Public Schools Great Cities Program includes an internship opportunity for prospective teachers. In cooperation with a local college, education majors working in their junior year spend one morning per week, for twelve weeks, working with each of three different teachers at an inner city Junior High School. Cleveland also reports: "Fourteen juniors participated in this program this year. All of them selected inner-city schools for practice teaching in their senior year."[28]

Home Visitors

Educators must be aware of the home conditions from which disadvantaged children come to school. The differences between the intellectual atmosphere of many such homes, as compared with typical middle-class home is suggested by Harris:

"Unfortunately, many children come from homes in which the parents are either indifferent to the school or actually antagonistic. Parents whose own educational experiences were unsatisfying and whose work demands little or no education tend to place little importance on education in general, or reading in particular. Often they live in a neighborhood in which general attitudes are anti-intellectual. This is especially true when child society is organized along gang lines, as it is in many underprivileged areas. In such a neighborhood, conformity to an anti-educational pattern may be necessary for social acceptance."[29]

Small wonder that children springing from such circumstances would be anti-intellectual and, in the long run, antischool. Endeavors exist in many cities to help bridge the gap between the structures of the school and the disadvantaged home by way of home visitations. For example, in Cleveland, home visitors have been assigned to each of six elementary schools in which they work with parents, students and teachers. The role of the home visitor is to serve as a liaison between the home and the school and to help keep the parent appraised of the child's adjustment in school. These home visitors also evaluate the home situation "so as to provide the teachers with insights and understandings of the problems facing the children of the community."[30]

The Houston Independent School District Talent Presentation Project included some interesting techniques. This city conducted a very successful back-to-school drive. "Twenty classroom teachers were employed at regular salaries to screen records of incoming seventh grade students to prepare for the organization of new classes."[31]

They also visited the homes of project students. Statistically, 94 per cent of the project students returned to school. Some 200 dropouts returned to school, some after an absence of two years.

Other Compensatory Education

A recent report from the Chicago Board of Education describes Compensatory Education in the following manner:

"Compensatory Education refers to educational programs, practices, techniques and projects designed to overcome the deficiencies of children from culturally disadvantaged homes to enable them to fulfill the fundamental purposes of education."[32]

In San Francisco, the Superintendent's Compensatory Program operates on funds which are budgeted exclusively for the improvement of the instruction of culturally disadvantaged children. In this program, a typical procedure is for an experienced teacher, who has been shifted from a regular classroom to a new reading and language laboratory, to serve about ten different pupils each period of the day. The Superintendent's Compensatory Program has had, as a primary objective, the "improvement of the pupils communications skills—listening, speaking, reading and writing."[33] In the school year 1963-64, the Superintendent's Compensatory Program provided $230,000. This money allowed thirty-eight teachers to provide special instruction in reading and in the language arts in nineteen elementary schools, thirteen junior high schools, and six senior high schools.

A final statement provided by San Francisco authorities is well worth our attention. "The typical teacher takes for granted the practice of individualizing instruction. When a student needs a bit of extra help, he lends a hand. However, when he is faced with a large number of culturally handicapped pupils, the situation is beyond his good intentions. Extra services as have been described here, are justified and accepted in San Francisco as a worthy budget item."[34]

The Buffalo Public Schools have attempted the development of a program adopted to the needs of the culturally different. Buffalo has reported on a program for the culturally deprived in its Public Schools which lately involved about 3,100 pupils in five elementary schools "located in the heart of an area of the city characterized by high population density, substandard housing, high youth crime and delinquency rate, high in-migration from out of state and the lowest percentage of recreational space of any area in the city."[35]

One of the primary objectives of the project has been to raise the academic achievements of culturally deprived pupils particularly in the area of reading.

In order to put the original pilot program into operation, the following teaching positions were added to the regular staff of the original pilot project school: a reading specialist with a chief function of the improvement of the teaching of reading; a remedial reading teacher to teach selected low achievers in reading; a speech teacher; an additional art teacher to act as both teacher and as a consultant to teachers; an additional music teacher to act as both teacher and as a consultant to teachers; a part time "coaching" teacher to aid children in arithmetic; a school social worker; and a school nurse.[36]

Now that we have taken a look at some programs for the disadvantaged elementary school child in our nation, let us attempt to evaluate what we have seen. Many spirited efforts on behalf of the educational advancement of the culturally disadvantaged child are under way in many parts of the United States. These programs represent a good start and appear, by and large, to be headed in proper directions. We must recognize, however, that our programs to date are merely the beginnings of the educational efforts we must make on behalf of the disadvantaged child. Such efforts must be expanded and even greater heed must be paid by other schools to the solution of the myriad problems attendant to the education of the disadvantaged elementary school child in our society. Detjen and Detjen have written:

"It is said that 40 per cent of the pupils who enter the fifth grade drop out before high school graduation. Many of these are capable of doing the academic work. Some of the reasons for their withdrawal are economic pressures, conflicting values, emotional problems, community forces, and influence of family and peer groups. But the greatest cause of school dropouts is lack of interest and incentive."[37]

It is with the twin matters of interest and incentive in the learner that all programs and projects aimed at the disadvantaged must be concerned. At least part of the problems faced by school people in turning their attention to the matters of the interests and incentives of disadvantaged children is described in the following:

"The schools in disadvantaged areas find it exceedingly difficult to accomplish the goals established for them by tradition because children come to school lacking the background ordinarily furnished by their first teachers, their parents. As a result, it is necessary that schools provide those experiences that are taken for granted as part of a middle class child's everyday life. The differences have significance for education, and it requires reflection for adults to understand the extent, the depth and the seriousness of the problem involved."[38]

With the preceding commentary in view, the question arises as to the role the school must play in the life of the disadvantaged child. Just what should the cultural role of the school become? Townsend and Burke help answer this question in the following manner:

"The cultural role of the school is midway between the primary groups, such as the family and playmates, and the secondary groups, such as social and industrial organizations. The school aids the acculturation process by providing training and knowledge appropriate to the society. It offers a wealth of material with which the child can identify, and supplies him with persons who support rather than protect and dominate him."[39]

In short, then, we must say that education for the disadvantaged must be education for full involvement with freedom. Through education, we must help our disadvantaged children to move in the direction of the full challenge of democracy, with its rights and privileges and attendant responsibilities. Which of today's programs hold the greatest hope for helping the disadvantaged child to be prepared to accept that challenge? All of the programs cited earlier in this section offer some such hope. Each program has its own special advantages, and offers its own special type of hope in the field of the education of the diasadvantaged. Certainly, programs for the disadvantaged elementary school child must be kept in constant review. The education of the disadvantaged elementary school child must remain a burning educational item until the problem has been overcome through massive effort, and successful action.

Federal attention has recently been given to the culturally disadvantaged child in the modern American school. These children will be benefited by a 1964 revision of the National Defense Education Act which Congress has broadened to include, among other subjects, the teaching of disadvantaged youth. This has caused Cutts to comment: "Improvement of reading instruction and help for disadvantaged youth will be implemented in three ways:

1. Improvement of the quantity and quality of instructional equipment and materials. Such improvement may also include minor remodeling in order to make best use of new equipment and materials (Title III).
2. Provision of supervisory and consultative services from the state, half the cost of which would be paid from NDEA funds (Title III).
3. Training through state sponsored workshops (Title III)) and help through college sponsored NDEA institutes (Title XI)."[40]

The same National Defense Act expansion provides under Title V for the extension of guidance services to children in grade school, kindergarten through eighth grade (as well as to persons in grades nine through thirteen).[41] Chandler has suggested the need for such a program:

"The importance of guidance services for those in school has already been emphasized through provisions of the National Defense Education Act that helps school systems strengthen guidance services. The impact of these trends on schools in urban areas is clear: they must give greater attention to students individual differences through programs of guidance, curricular provisions and teaching procedures."[42]

There is a driving national need to continue with compensatory services in our schools. This has been well stated by authorities of the San Francisco schools: "In a city such as San Francisco, to equalize class size, teacher competence, buildings, supplies, equipment, and extra services throughout all the schools, as has been done in the past, is not enough. The predominance of culturally handicapped children in some neighborhoods, in contrast to others, places upon the administration and the Board of Education, the responsibility of compensating by means of extra services and programs for those cultural shortages evidenced in groups of children."[43]

Responsible educators will continue to react to the presence of large numbers of culturally disadvantaged children in American schools. They will continue to use and to improve upon present compensatory programs and services. They will also continue to attempt new and promising procedures in their ceaseless efforts to bring the very best of compensatory education to the disadvantaged elementary school child.

REFERENCES

1. Bernard A. Kaplan, "Issues in Educating the Culturally Disadvantaged," *Phi Delta Kappan,* Vol. XLV, No. 2 (November, 1963) , 70.
2. Robert J. Havighurst, *The Public Schools of Chicago,* A Survey for the Board of Education of the City of Chicago (Chicago: Board of Education of the City of Chicago, 1964) , p. 57.
3. *Ibid.*
4. *Ibid.*
5. *The Education of Migrant Children,* U. S. Department of Health, Education, and Welfare (Office of Education 200 38; Washington, D. C.: Supt. of Documents, U. S. Printing Office, 1962) , p. 1.
6. Justin Pikunas and Eugene Albrecht, *Psychology of Human Development* (New York: McGraw Hill Book Co., Inc., 1961) , p. 21.
7. Havighurst, *op. cit.,* p. 59.
8. Robert J. Havighurst, "The Chicago School Survey," *Phi Delta Kappan,* Vol. XLVI, No. 4 (December, 1964) , 70.
9. The Research Council of the Great Cities Program for School Improvement, *Promising Practices from the Projects for the Culturally Deprived,* (228 North LaSalle Street, Chicago, April, 1964) .
10. R. E. Gross and L. D. Zeleny, *Educating Citizens for Democracy* (New York: Oxford University Press, 1958) , p. 12.
11. The Research Council of the Great Cities Program for School Improvement, *op. cit.,* p. 45.
12. *Ibid.,* p. 30.
13. James Bryant Conant, *Slums and Suburbs* (New York: McGraw Hill Book Co., 1961) , p. 23.
14. The Research Council of the Great Cities Program for School Improvement, *op. cit.,* p. 81.
15. Chicago Public Schools, *Compensatory Education in the Chicago Public Schools,* Study Report No. 4 (Chicago: Chicago Public Schools, August, 1964) , p. 111.
16. The Research Council of the Great Cities Program for School Improvement, *op. cit.,* p. 75.
17. Herman Peters, "Fostering the Developmental Approach in Guidance," *The Educational Forum,* November, 1963, p. 39-90.
18. The Research Council of the Great Cities Program for School Improvement, *op. cit.,* p. 47.
19. *Ibid.,* p. 50.
20. *Ibid.*
21. *Ibid.*

22. Edward C. Glanz, *Foundations and Principles of Guidance* (Boston: Allyn and Bacon, Inc., 1964) , p. 37.

23. The Research Council of the Great Cities Program for School Improvement, *op. cit.,* p. 13.

24. Albert J. Harris, *Effective Teaching of Reading* (New York: David McKay Company, Inc., 1962) , p. 7.

25. The Research Council of the Great Cities Program for School Improvement, *op. cit.,* p. 53.

26. *Ibid.,* p. 3.

27. *Ibid.,* pp. 4-5.

28. *Ibid.,* p. 15.

29. Harris, *loc. cit.*

30. The Research Council of the Great Cities Program for School Improvement, *op. cit.,* p. 15.

31. *Ibid.,* p. 34.

32. Chicago Public Schools, *op. cit.,* p. 1.

33. The Research Council of the Great Cities Program for School Improvement. *op. cit.,* p. 78.

34. *Ibid.,* p. 80.

35. *Ibid.,* p. 9.

36. *Ibid.*

37. Ervin W. Detjen and Mary F. Detjen, *Elementary School Guidance* (New York: McGraw Hill Book Co., Inc., 1963) , p. 201.

38. Chicago Public Schools, *op. cit.,* p. 25.

39. Edward A. Townsend and Paul J. Burke, *Learning for Teachers* (New York: The MacMillan Co., 1962) , p. 7.

40. Warren G. Cutts, "How the Extension of NDEA Will Benefit Reading Teachers," *The Reading Teacher,* Vol. 18, No. 3 (December, 1964), 223.

41. United States, *National Defense Education Act* (Amendments, 1964) Title V, Sec. 502, Para. 2.

42. B. J. Chandler, Lindley J. Stiles, and John I. Kitsuse, *Education In Urban Society* (New York: Dodd, Mead and Co., 1962) , p. 3.

43. The Research Council of the Great Cities Program for School Improvement, *op. cit.,* p. 77.

Chapter III

SOME PSYCHOSOCIAL ASPECTS OF LEARNING IN THE DISADVANTAGED

Martin Deutsch*

It has long been known that some general relationship exists between the conditions of social, cultural, and economic deprivation and cognitive deficit. The environment having the highest rate of disease, crime, and social disorganization also has the highest rate of school retardation. Deficiencies in linguistic skills and reading are particularly striking. School dropout and failure, apart from what they represent in lost potential to the individual and his community, mean that as adults, those who have failed or dropped out will be confined to the least skilled and least desirable jobs and will have almost no opportunity for upward social mobility.

A large body of empirical literature supports the assumption that certain environmental conditions may retard psychological processes, including intellectual development. This conclusion is borne out in both animals and human beings (e.g., Hebb, 1949; Hunt, 1961). One of the most comprehensive reviews of the effects of environmental impoverishment on intellectual development, by Clarke and Clarke (1959), presents data collected on adolescents and young adults who have experienced severe deprivation as a result of cruelty, neglect, or parental separation. Bruner (1960, pp. 203-204) writes that ". . . exposure to normally enriched environments makes the development of such (cognitive) strategies possible by providing intervening opportunities for trial and error . . . that there is impairment under a deprived regimen seems . . . to be fairly evident." Although he does not refer specifically to the environment of the lower-class child, Bruner's remarks seem especially relevant there. The obvious implication is

---

*Director, Institute for Developmental Studies and Professor, Department of Psychiatry, New York Medical College.

that disadvantaged children, who have a meager environmental basis for developing cognitive skills, are often unprepared to cope with the formal intellectual and learning demands of school.

Nevertheless, a fostering environment for such children can facilitate intellectual development. Bruner (1964), for example, suggests that certain environmental conditions increase the likelihood of learning cognitive strategies. Clarke and Clarke (1959) report striking increases in IQ in a deprived group during a six-year program aimed at reversing deprivation effects. That improved environmental conditions may have a positive impact on the intellectual development of children is also supported by the studies of the Iowa group (e.g., Skeels, Updegraff, Wellman, and Williams, 1938; Wellman, 1940; and Skodak and Skeels, 1949). Informal observation shows that, even in the most economically depressed areas, where school retardation rates are highest, some children manifest considerable school success and academic proficiency. If we assume a causal relationship between environmental conditions and cognitive development, then variation in cognitive development could partially reflect variations within the environment. We can assume that no so-called underprivileged area is homogeneous: there are, indeed, considerable variations in the home environments of children from such areas—variations ranging from large fatherless families supported by public assistance to small intact families with inadequate but regular income.

Moreover, learning contexts are as heterogeneous as environmental backgrounds. Although the two contexts are not actually disparate, early socialization, mediated through home and neighborhood environments and mass media, requires responses different from those necessary for school learning and subject mastery. The formal learning processes carry well-defined criteria of failure and success not mediated through such behavioral indices as group leadership, influence, and the like, whereas the informal learning environment has no explicitly stated criteria or marking systems. In the latter, success may be more highly related to leadership, and failure to rejection or subordination by the group.

Even as his learning context changes when the child enters school, so does his psychological context for achievement. At this point, the amount of continuity between the home environment and that of school can strongly influence the child's responses to the learning and achievement context of school. The discontinuity between the lower-class child's background and the school impairs his successful responses in the new situation.

The middle-class child is more likely to have been continuously prodded intellectually by his parents and rewarded for correct answers, whereas, in the main, the lower-class child's parents have seldom subjected him to the pressure of a formal adult-child learning situation. The middle-class child is likely to have experienced, in the behavior of adults in his environment, the essential ingredients implicit in the role of teacher. For the lower-class child, relating to the teacher and school officials requires a new kind of behavior, for which he has not necessarily been prepared.

School curricula and learning techniques usually imply an assumption that the child has had prior experience in the complex learning area, where there are logical assumptions as to appropriate behavior and where success is rewarded and failure is disapproved. The teacher, trained in our not-so-modern teacher-education institutions, assumes—probably consciously as well as unconsciously—that the school child is a quasi-passive recipient of knowledge, and that he clearly understands the teacher's educative and remedial functions. In this, the teacher is as likely to be confused about the child's expectations as the child is confused about the school's expectations.

Lacking sufficient sociological sophistication, school authorities understandably tend to expect from children a level of comprehension and motivation that can only be built through positive experiences in the learning situation. Children who are used to a great deal of motor activity and who have certain environmentally determined deficiencies in learning to learn, often respond with an inappropriate academic orientation. Teachers meet this situation in several ways, most of which cause serious problems for the socially marginal child. Some teachers establish low expectations, anticipate failure, and, true to the Mertonian self-fulfilling prophecy, find an increasing rate of failure.

Another reaction seems to be, "They can't learn; they don't care; their parents are not concerned." This projective device serves to relieve the professional of responsibility, since it does contain a grain of truth: often older siblings and neighbors of the lower-class child have experienced so much failure and so much class and cultural arrogance as to generate a great apathy out of which none of them expects positive consequences from the school experience. This very apathy is sometimes reflected in the attitudes of the educational apparatus toward the lower-class community.

Still other teachers say, "It is all the environment—impoverishment, economic insecurity, segregation, second-class citizenship, historical chains. Of course, none of these things is the child's fault, but neither are they the school's fault." This approach has greater validity, invoking as it does social circumstances obviously crucial to the developing organism. Yet such a view often leads to negation not only of the essential responsibility of the school but also of the actual and potential strengths of the children. Most important, it induces an elaborate rationale for the further alienation of teachers from their primary function, teaching. The essential element, which is both professionally and psychologically threatening, is simply that, for the child inadequately equipped to handle what the school has to offer, it is up to the school to develop compensatory strategies through a program of stimulation appropriate to his capabilities. Essentially, the disadvantaged child is still further disadvantaged when the school, as the primary socializing and teaching agent, refuses to accept its own failure whenever any such child fails.

For the school to assume its full responsibility requires constant self-criticism and self-evaluation; these have not been characteristic of educational systems, despite noteworthy exceptions. To put it more bluntly, when teacher-training institutions and educational systems foster an atmosphere of critical evaluation of their procedures and establish high criteria for professional training and development, teachers will maintain a psychological connection with their children that today is often severed, especially when the teacher, with neither a theoretical nor a working model, must bridge social-class discontinuities. Were more of today's children succeeding in learning to read at grade level, we would be forced to reconstruct our theory considerably. They are not, and the total atmosphere in the majority of our urban schools having large groups of disadvantaged youngsters becomes less and less conducive not merely to the learning process but also to the positive child-teacher relationship that establishes motivation and gives rise to high standards of achievement.

Responsibility for this unfavorable learning situation is not the school's alone. It lies in a combination of social circumstances, historical apathy, economic exploitation, and a society that does not put its money where its explicit values are. Even so, the school most directly reflects society's failure: it is the one institution that has the opportunity to directly affect the situation.

In this total atmosphere, what are some of the additional handicaps that the disadvantaged child brings into school? If we expect the school to organize so as to meet the child on his own developmental level, then we must know a good deal about the specific intellectual sequelae likely to be associated more with economic impoverishment than with affluence. Further, we need simple and adequate ways of measuring the actual development of each child's abilities, because they are the foundation for the skills the school is to teach him. Such specific information will enable the teacher to teach him more adequately and to present him with the most appropriate stimuli. Moreover, the child's probable success will increase when the material presented is truly consistent with his developmental level, since engendering a sense of competence, in White's (1959) terms, can sustain motivation, thereby facilitating learning.

The self-image is vital to learning. School experiences can either reinforce invidious self-concepts acquired from the environment, or help to develop—or even induce—a negative self-concept. Conversely, they can effect positive self-feelings by providing for concrete achievements and opportunities to function with competence, although initially these experiences must be in the most limited and restricted areas. The evidence leads us to the inescapable conclusion that, by the time they enter school, many disadvantaged children have developed negative self-images, which the school does little to mitigate.

Another significant element, usually ignored, probably helps shape the perception of himself that the child develops in school, namely, the use of time. Generally, time is inefficiently used, there is minimal individualized attention, and the child often spends much time in unproductive rote activities, while the teacher focuses her attention on remedial subgroups or the omnipresent paper work. Given the high pupil-teacher ratio, the critical need is for autoinstructional devices or preprogramed curriculum elements to which the child can turn. This is part of a situation where responsibility cannot be placed on the teacher, and the frequent use of this downtrodden professional as a scapegoat reflects chiefly only his position as the psychologically operative instrument in the education of the child. In a sense, after passing through the whole of society's educational echelons, the buck stops with him (but not in his pocket). Nevertheless, this understanding does not improve the situation. Too often, the child is seriously understimulated, even with the best of teachers, and there is little overall curriculum planning for the needs of disadvantaged children. Most important, society has furnished neither funds nor the educational leadership and training necessary for the new supplementary technologies that would enormously increase the effective use of time. These would, in turn, help the child develop a sense of purpose and belonging in the school context.

Autoinstructional and programed devices and methods might also give the child a sense of greater mastery over the unfamiliar school environment: they could reduce his passivity by giving him greater control over the timing of stimuli, thus minimizing cultural differences in time orientation. Further, in the self-corrective feedback of programed materials, the teacher's role of giving reward and disapproval would be shared; for a child unaccustomed to these as means of motivation for intellectual performance, it might help decrease his alienation from the school. If these hypotheses are valid, then the new educational techniques could socially facilitate the learning process.

The extent of the disadvantaged child's alienation as a crucial factor in handicapping his school performance and achievement has been emphasized. Much of this is structural, and much of the psychosocial problem lies in the interaction between the child and the school. However, cognitive variables which have been socially influenced or determined also contribute to the whole process of increasing the mutual alienation of the school and the child. Among these one of the major difficulties is the often nonfunctional language system he brings to school. My colleagues and I have discussed this at length elsewhere (Deutsch, Maliver, Brown, and Cherry, 1964; Deutsch, 1964a; 1964b; 1965; John 1963).

I would like to point out here that social-class determination of linguistic styles and habits is an effective deterrent to communication and understanding between child and teacher. To illustrate, the child is unaccustomed to both attending to, and being the object of, what are for him long, orderly, focused verbal sequences. Yet this is the primary scholastic teaching and discipline method. Further, because the disadvantaged child is less familiar with the syntactical regularities and normative frequencies of the language, he has difficulty in ordering its sequences and in both deriving meaning from, and putting it into, context. This is all the more disadvantageous for the lower-class child because he has a short attention span for the verbal material to which he is exposed in school. Consequently, he is likely to miss a great deal, even when he is trying to listen. For such a child it is extremely important to feel some mastery in handling at least receptive language. This is made more difficult by what Bernstein (1960; 1961; 1962a; 1962b), the English sociologist, has described as the different dialects spoken by lower- and middle-class people.

This discussion keeps returning to the need for helping the educator to develop a comprehensive consciousness of the psychological, as well as the learning, difficulties of the disadvantaged child; the real potential for change; the specifics involved in training children, for example, to ask questions, or to become aware of syntactical regularities, or to use autoinstructional materials; and the imperative need to maintain as high as possible the level of stimulation and relevancy in the classroom. Here the research and insights of the behavioral sciences should be able to contribute significantly, provided the educational albatross takes a few "risks" to accommodate social change.

REFERENCES

1. B. Bernstein, "Language and Social Class," *Brit. J. Sociol.,* 11, (1960), pp. 271-276.

2. B. Bernstein, "Social Structure, Language and Learning," *Educ. Res.,* Vol. III, (June 1961).
3. B. Bernstein, "Linguistic Codes, Hesitation Phenomena and Intelligence," *Lang. and Speech,* 5, 1962, p. 1.
4. B. Bernstein, "Social Class, Linguistic Codes and Grammatical Elements," *Lang. and Speech,* 5, 1962, p. 4.
5. J. S. Bruner, *The Process of Education* (Cambridge, Harvard University Press, 1960).
6. J. S. Bruner, "The Course of Cognitive Growth," *Amer. Psychologist,* 19, 1964, pp. 1-15.
7. A. D. B. Clarke, and A. M. Clarke, "Recovery from the Effects of Deprivation." *Acta Psychol.,* 16, 1969, pp. 137-144.
8. M. Deutsch, Facilitating Development in the Pre-school Child: Social and Psychological Perspectives," *Merrill-Palmer Quart.,* 10, 1964, pp. 249-263.
9. M. Deutsch, Training Programs as Preparation for Social Change. Paper read at American Orthopsychiatric Assn., Chicago, March, 1964.
10. M. Deutsch, "The Role of Social Class in Language Development and Cognition," *American J. Orthopsychiatry,* 1, 1965, pp. 78-88.
11. M. Deutsch, Alma Maliver, B. Brown, and Estelle Cherry, *Communication of Information in the Elementary School Classroom.* Washington D. C.: Cooperative Research Project No. 908 of the Office of Education, U. S. Department of Health, Education and Welfare, 1964.
12. D. O. Hebb, *The Organization of Behavior* (New York: Wiley, 1949).
13. J. McV. Hunt, *Intelligence and Experience* (New York: Ronald Press, 1961).
14. J. McV. Hunt, "The Psychological Basis for Using Pre-school Enrichment as an Antidote for Cultural Deprivation," *Merrill-Palmer Quart.,* 10, 1964, p. 3, pp. 209-243.
15. Vera P. John, "The Intellectual Development of Slum Children: Some Preliminary Findings," *American Journal Orthophychiatry,* 5, 1963, pp. 813-822.
16. H. M. Skeels, Ruth Updegraff, Beth L. Wellman, and A. M. Williams, "A Study of Environmental Stimulation: an Orphanage Pre-school Project," *Univer. Iowa Stud. Child Welf.,* 1938, 15, No. 4.
17. Marie Skodak, and H. M. Skeels, "A Final Follow-up Study of One Hundred Adopted Children," *J. Genetic Psychology,* 75, 1949, pp. 85-125.
18. Beth L. Wellman, "Iowa Studies on the Effects of Schooling," *Yearbook National Soc. Study Education,* 39, 1940, pp. 377-399.
19. R. W. White, "Motivation Reconsidered: the Concept of Competence," *Psychol. Rev.,* 66, 1959, pp. 279-333.

Chapter IV

INDIVIDUAL CHARACTERISTICS AND ACADEMIC ACHIEVEMENT

JAY G. HIRSCH, M.D.*

T HE INDIVIDUAL CHARACTERISTICS of the disadvantaged pupil in the United States are determined by three major circumstances with which each child must cope:

1. *He is a child.* This means that he is a not-yet-fully-grown, not-yet-completely-matured, not-yet-totally-developed human organism, who is in a constant state of dynamic change.
2. *He is an individual.* Biologically, psychologically, and socially he is like all other children in many important ways. As a unique individual, however, he differs from all other children in some important ways.
3. *He is living in a particular environment.* Through the two major institutions which affect young people, the home and the school, as well as the influence of many factors in the wider society, his environment affords him life experiences upon which his academic learning will be based.

The disadvantaged pupil shares the above three circumstances with all children everywhere. He is, as we have said, simply an individual child who lives in a particular environment. What, then, distinguishes him from his age-mates who are not labelled "disadvantaged"?

Behavioral scientists (and philosophers, as well) have perennially chosen to separate the bases of human behavior into the two broad general categories of heredity and environment. From this division has sprung the age-old "nature-nurture controversy." This has led to a setting forth of the evidence for the relative importance of biological endowment and experience on the develop-

*Research Child Psychiatrist, Institute for Juvenile Research.

ment of individual characteristics. The truth appears to be that both are essential, and that neither can be adequately assessed or measured.

Hereditary factors are particularly resistant to study.[1] Despite numerous attempts to prove that differences between groups on dimensions relevant for academic achievement can be accounted for on a purely genetic basis,[2,3] there is still insufficient evidence to allow for such a conclusion.[4,5]

Environmental influences on individual characteristics have not been especially well studied either. There is, however, a growing body of data which points to experience as a major determiner of observed differences in certain important categories of personal functioning, including learning.

This chapter will focus on certain environmental factors and their influence upon the development of individual characteristics important for academic achievement. We will see that the experiences of some lower status children differ markedly from those of many youngsters from higher status groups. Insofar as such differences relate in the expected direction to their respective academic achievement levels, the nature and extent of the difference in experiences of the lower status child and his upper status counterpart constitute a measure of the former's relative "disadvantage."

Figure 1 is a schematic representation of some of the more important dimensions of academic achievement, and the relationship of environmental factors to their development.

On the left of the diagram are seen the three major loci of environmental influence upon the child: the home, the school, and the wider society.

The influence of the wider society is greatest upon the development of the first three factors in achievement. These are called factors external to the child, and are listed as:

    I. Social factors
   II. Administrative factors
  III. Teaching factors

These external factors are defined as conditions which influence a child's academic achievement level by indirect means,

Figure 1. SOME FACTORS IN ACADEMIC ACHIEVEMENT

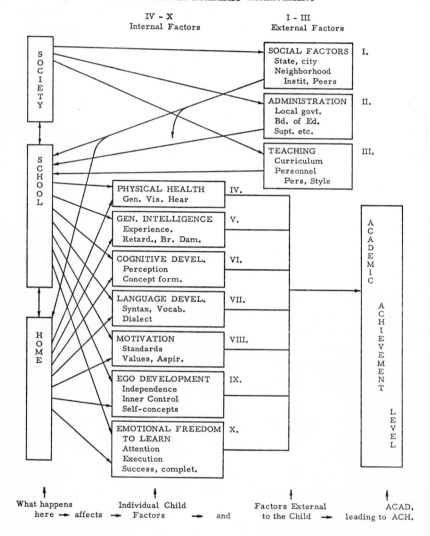

IV - X	I - III
Internal Factors	External Factors

What happens here → affects → Individual Child Factors → and → Factors External to the Child → ACAD. leading to ACH.

either through their affect upon the school or the home, or upon the development of some of the individual child factors to be defined below. The means by which society makes its impact felt upon these factors may be exemplified by the contention that performance in the academic achievement situation is influenced by society's values, standards, and expectations regarding the achievement of particular groups, and by the economic and social opportunities (or lack of same) which society offers in return for attainment. A chief exponent of this point of view has been Clark,[6] who invokes the principle of the *self-fulfilling prophecy*[7] as a major cause of academic failure among the disadvantaged. The thesis is merely that the wider society does not expect the lower status minority group youngster to succeed. This very expectation significantly effects administrative policy regarding his education, the way in which he is taught, and the methods by which he is approached. These, in turn, contribute to the child's ultimate failure, and the prophecy becomes reality. As Clark puts it, "children who are treated as if they are ineducable almost invariably become ineducable."[8]

The social factors, which include laws and customs of the particular city and state, as well as the circumstances in the local community and immediate neighborhood in which the child lives, have a direct affect upon the development of the individual child, as well as an influence upon the experiences he will have through his home and school. These issues are considered in some of the succeeding chapters.

Administrative factors, such as the enrollment policies and the nature of the relationship between and among the public, the board of education, and the superintendent of schools, and teaching factors, such as curriculum arrangement, teacher personality, and teaching style, all have their effect upon the child at the local school level. These categories are covered at length in the chapters to follow, and hence will not be mentioned in detail here.

We are left, then, to consider the individual child factors (internal factors) in academic achievement. Referring to the diagram in Figure 1, we see that the home and the school converge to influence all seven of the major categories under this heading. These are:

IV. Physical health
V. General intelligence
VI. Cognitive development
VII. Language development
VIII. Motivation for academic achievement
IX. Ego development
X. Emotional freedom to learn

These internal factors are defined as characteristics of the individual pupil which have direct bearing upon his school achievement. The main function of this classification is to aid us in conceptualizing the complex area we wish to cover; it will provide us with convenient landmarks around which to proceed.

The various factors as outlined are not intended to necessarily constitute discrete and separate categories. They overlap in their scope, and most certainly have a great influence upon one another. Each has a contribution to make toward academic success, and yet the relative importance of each category is likely to vary considerably between individuals.

Referring to each of these factors in its turn, we will review the theoretical notions that have been evinced to show its relationship to achievement, as well as the evidence adduced to back up these notions, if such is available. We will wish to discover in what ways each of the internal factors contributes to academic achievement, and also learn how certain aspects of the child's total experience lead to his relative standing on each of the internal factors.

INTERNAL FACTORS IN ACADEMIC ACHIEVEMENT

Physical Health

A child must be healthy in order to meet the physical and mental demands made of him in the classroom and at school. Poor health diminishes the capacity for involvement in school work, and serves to depress the child emotionally. Serious problems of general health, such as cardiac, respiratory, neurological or extensive orthopedic difficulties, necessitate special school programs. Even minor illnesses, which are more frequent and do not require special handling, lead to absence from school and the threat of falling behind in learning. In addition, specific health problems relating to vision and hearing have special and obvious relevance for academic performance.

Many statistical studies have shown that lower income groups have higher rates of morbidity and mortality than do upper income groups. Pettigrew[9] has reviewed the evidence for Negro-white differences in the incidence and prevalence of communicable disease. Negro incidence and death rates are significantly higher for pulmonary tuberculosis, venereal disease, and the infectious diseases of childhood. The death rates from the childhood diseases early in life are reported to be at least twice that of the rates among whites. In addition to this mortality due to infectious disease, Negroes are reported to have a much higher incidence of prematurity and other complications of pregnancy than are whites, even when an attempt is made to control socioeconomic status. Knobloch and Passamanick[10] cite figures from Baltimore to show that lower economic status white women have one and one-half times the incidence of prematurity and twice the incidence of bleeding and toxemia of pregnancy than do upper economic status white women. Lower status Negro women have twice the incidence of prematurity and three times the incidence of bleeding and toxemia when compared to the same upper status white group. There is a corresponding elevation in the incidence of brain damage in infants with a low birth weight and maternal complications of pregnancy. However, even with such elevated rates for these conditions in association with socioeconomic status and race, the total incidence of such neurological abnormality could account for perhaps no more than 5 to 10 per cent of the learning problems seen among the disadvantaged.

There is general agreement that certain noxious influences found in association with poverty, such as poor nutrition, overcrowding, inadequate heating and plumbing facilities, and little or no medical attention play a significant role in the higher morbidity and mortality among this group.

For other conditions, although the rates of incidence are not very different between groups, the approach to therapeutic intervention may differ radically. School personnel observe how often that previously—undiscovered and—untreated vision and hearing problems are found in disadvantaged neighborhoods. This appears to be directly related to an initial relative lack of sophistication on the part of parents, and the absence of a feeling of immediacy about the necessity of obtaining medical help for a given deficit or ailment once it is discovered. The lack of economic resources would appear to play a major role here also, since even when free clinics are available, a trip to the doctor may mean that the mother must stay home from work to accompany the child, which results in the loss of sorely-needed income.

General Intelligence

It is widely acknowledged that measured IQ, especially certain verbal measures, is a rather good predictor of academic achievement.[11] Some psychologists contend that such high correlations exist because the IQ test is merely another test of achievement. Most psychologists agree that there has not yet been devised an adequate measure of innate intellectual potential, and that there is not yet a suitable culture-free instrument for intelligence testing. Although innate potential certainly has something to do with IQ, there is a growing rejection of the concept of fixed intelligence, in favor of an information-processing model for intelligence, with emphasis on the crucial role of experience.[12]

On those tests that are in use, measured intelligence scores vary directly with socioeconomic status.[13,14] Shuey,[15] in a review of seventy-two different studies involving over 36,000 subjects, found that the average IQ on group verbal tests for Negro children is 85. This is in agreement with Klineberg's finding of a median IQ for Negro children of 86. Klineberg also found that children of Italian, Mexican, and Portuguese parents had median IQ scores at the same level, and that the scores of American Indian children were below the scores of these other disadvantaged groups.[16] Whereas the average scores of disadvantaged groups are depressed relative to the average scores of upper socioeconomic groups, individual scores reveal that many "disadvantaged" youngsters score very high, and many "advantaged" youngsters score very low. The degree of overlap of scores and the significance of this have been discussed by Pettigrew[17] and Klineberg.[18]

Deutsch and Brown[19] studied the IQ in first and fifth graders (Lorge-Thorndike, nonverbal) in a New York City sample, and broke down their data by race, socioeconomic status, presence of father in the home, and presence or absence of nursery school or kindergarten experience. They found no statistical difference between the first and fifth grade scores for the whole group, but did find, like the investigations mentioned above, highly statistically significant Negro-white differences and socioeconomic status differences. Negroes at each socioeconomic level scored lower than whites at the same level. However, Negro children in the upper middle class group scored significantly higher than white children in the lowest socioeconomic group. An interesting finding is that as the socioeconomic level increases the Negro-white difference in IQ also increases. Six points on the mean IQ score separate the two races in the lower status group (97 to 91) whereas the racial groups are separated by twelve points in the highest status group (115 to 103). These investigators also found significant differences in IQ at all socioeconomic levels between children who live in homes with a father and those living without fathers, the results favoring the intact family group. They also found that those children who attended preschool nursery or kindergarten programs score higher in IQ than do those who did not attend such programs, although the results were statistically significant at the .05 level of significance only for the fifth grade group.

Knobloch and Pasamanick offer some data which supports the contention that racial groups start out with essentially the same developmental levels.[20,21] In a follow-up study of a large group of full term infants of both races, they found no significant differences between the Negro and the white infants on the Gesell Developmental Examination at forty weeks of age.

Hunt's volume[22] has reviewed a great deal of the evidence that has accumulated to support the notion that to a large extent differences in measured intelligence are reflective of the differences in experience between subjects. He emphasizes the importance of preverbal experience in the development of the intellect. He supports this contention by quoting animal studies by Hebb[23] which show that early enriched perceptual experience was associated with superior performance on problem-solving tasks, and also points to the observations of Piaget[24,25] in which he described in detail the intellectual development of young children. Fowler[26] has also emphasized the role of early experience in the development of intelligence.

In the absence of demonstrable innate differences in intellectual potential between groups, we must consider the effects of differential experience in explaining differences in measured IQ between groups. What, then, are the crucial elements of the lower class child's experience which determine his poor standing on this important corollary of academic achievement?

The answer to this question must at this point be tentative and incomplete. This is mainly because we have difficulty translating the gross correlates of low IQ, such as race, socioeconomic status, father absence, and absence of nursery or kindergarten experience, into smaller, more specific, and more easily definable elements.

Deutsch and Brown[27] state the following in regard to this point: "We are now attempting to measure the ingredients of deprivation with the aim of developing a typology of deprivation which organizes experience in developmentally relevant groupings that can be related to sources of socially determined group variation in IQ performance. It would seem probable that when behavioral scientists have been able to classify and measure the elements and variables in social deprivation, the observed differential in intelligence test scores between Negro and white samples will be accounted for."

Cognitive Development

When we leave the area of general intelligence and move on to other categories of intellective capacity such as cognitive development and language development, we find an even greater paucity of controlled research. This is true for youngsters of all types including those in the disadvantaged group.

The word *cognitive* is derived from the Latin *cognitio* meaning "to get a knowledge of." Cognitive development may be defined as the growth of those capacities which contribute to the process of knowing. Some important capacities here are perception, concept formation, and problem solving. This is an area which has only recently become a major focus of research in the field of psychology, following upon the work of the Swiss psychologist, Piaget, who has thrown light upon many of the phenomena involved in cognitive development.[28] There seems little doubt that the human organism develops an increasing capacity for problem solving as he grows and matures. Our concern is to understand the process by which the child learns problem solving techniques from an early age, and to understand the influence of environmental factors upon the development of these skills.

Fowler's review[29] on the subject of cognitive learning in infancy and childhood suggests that appropriate stimulation in the early years, if presented in a flexible, play-oriented context that can be grasped by the young child, could be extremely important in promoting the development of intellectual functions. It may be, according to Fowler, that conceptual learning sets, habit patterns, and interest areas can be more favorably established during early stages of the developmental cycle, rather than later.

Although they are not stated in the same terminology as we utilize today, the writings of Maria Montessori[30] espouse a doctrine of early education which is similar in many ways to that suggested by Fowler. Rambusch[31] has interpreted Montessori in more modern language. One of the major approaches within the Montessori system is the use of perceptual stimuli of gradually increasing complexity, which are specifically designed to lead to concept formation and ultimately to problem solving.

One study in which perceptual skills have been shown to be important for intellectual achievement among disadvantaged youngsters is the work of C. Deutsch, in which she studied auditory discrimination among good and poor readers from within a lower socioeconomic Negro population. Good readers were found to be superior to poor readers in auditory discrimination. Poor readers were also found to have greater difficulty in shifting from one perceptual modality to another, and are less efficient in a serial learning task when the stimuli are auditory. The differences in auditory discrimination between the good and poor readers tended to diminish with chronological age, suggesting that this function, and perhaps other perceptual and cognitive skills as well, have their most important influence during the early school years.

To explain her findings on auditory discrimination, Deutsch turns to the lower class home. A high "noise" to "signal" ratio is postulated as having importance in the poor development of auditory discrimination skills. The child is not given training or experience in attending to listening, nor is he rewarded for doing so. As Deutsch states, "one could expect that a child raised in a very noisy environment with little directed and sustained speech stimulation might well be deficient in his discrimination and recognition of speech sounds. He could also be expected to be relatively inattentive to auditory stimuli and further to have difficulty with any other skill which is primarily or importantly dependent on good auditory discrimination. The slum child does indeed live in a very noisy environment and he gets little connected and concentrated speech directed to him."[32] Deutsch's explanation may have considerable merit, although we cannot say yet that it has been proven.

Before we are able to draw final conclusions in regard to the matter of cognitive development and its association with certain environmental conditions, it is important that more studies be carried out on different aspects of cognitive development, and that reliable observations be made in the homes of disadvantaged youngsters in order to delineate the experiential correlates of their cognitive abilities and deficiencies.

Language Development

The importance of language development for intellectual learning and academic achievement is obvious. Language is the mode of communication between people and it is the mediator in concept formation and problem solving. Hence, without the development of language skills, we are greatly limited in our ability to determine the level of a child's cognitive capabilities, and in the absence of language, cognitive growth is greatly retarded.

John[33] and Deutsch[34] have reported some findings in regard to a study of language development in a group of lower class minority group children in Harlem. These findings indicate that in the early years language deficiencies are largely a function of lower class status and are not significantly related to racial grouping. As children get older, however, both socioeconomic status and race appear to play important parts in the development of language deficits. This deficiency appears to be on language measures which reflect abstract and categorical use of language as opposed to denotative and labeling usage of language, which is largely intact.

The hypothesis put forth to explain these differences in language development between groups is that certain language deficiences and patterns in the utilization of language within the lower class home have an adverse effect upon the development of language skills in the children of these families. For example, John suggests that the middle-class child has an advantage over the lower-class child in the amount of help available to him in his home. Without such help in the development of language he has little opportunity to acquire abstract skills and precision in the use of language.

Bernstein[35,36] has postulated the presence of two kinds of language codes, an elaborated code and a restricted code. The restricted code is one which is in use in day-to-day contact with friends, relatives and people with whom we are closely associated. This does not require a complicated syntax, nor a sophisticated vocabulary or grammar. It is the kind of language that is utilized in conversation with people who know the way we think and the ideas we have, but to whom we wish to communicate certain feelings. This can be done largely nonverbally through gesture and expression and does not require a complicated language code. All people have this restricted language capability.

The elaborated language code is that which has a more complicated syntax and a more accurate grammatical order, with logical modifiers and frequent use of impersonal pronouns and prepositions. This is the kind of language which is required in academic learning, in order to communicate ideas to someone with whom the student is unfamiliar. It is the kind of language code which is increasingly important for learning as the child goes further in school.

Bernstein suggests that the lack of development of such an elaborated code in the lower-class situation determines the very nature of the social relationships which are possible for the children in question. This notion has gained acceptance through the popularization of Shaw's *Pygmalion* on the stage and in the movies in the form of the play *My Fair Lady*. The essence of the idea is that social relationships are determined by the kind of language which a person develops and that without the appropriate language skills one cannot participate fully within society.

It certainly appears true that in the United States the presence of language differences between disadvantaged groups and other segments of the population function as barriers to social intercourse. The presence of language deficiencies appears to contribute heavily to the problems of learning that certain children possess. This would appear to be particularly true as children progress further in school.

As Deutsch has pointed out,[37] it would appear as if cognitive developmental factors are in ascendence in the early years of schooling, and differences in this area tend to diminish as children get older. Cognitive development is replaced in its position of importance by language deficiencies, which appear to be less important early in the child's school life but which become much more prominent as he progresses further in school.

Motivation for Academic Achievement

Motivation for academic achievement may be defined as the desire and incentive to achieve at a high standard of excellence in academic learning. It is to this that we refer when we ask the question: "How hard was Johnny trying?" This factor is a potent contributor to achievement level. It is a category of behavior which, according to McClelland, involves not only competition with a standard of excellence, but also affect, or emotional feeling, in connection with the evaluation of one's performance.[38] The pupil must *want* to achieve.

The attainment of a high standard of accomplishment leads

to pleasure for oneself and/or praise and approval from others. White has written about the "feeling of efficacy" which is the internal pleasure derived from a task well done, and the "sense of competence" which is the expectation of success and confidence in oneself that comes from repeated experiences of efficacy.[39,40] This is similar in psychological terms to what Hunt has called *intrinsic motivation* from the theoretical framework of a neurophysiological model.[41]

Approval in the form of praise or reward from others is also an important motivating factor in achievement, and could be termed *extrinsic motivation,* i.e., satisfaction in attainment which has its source outside the individual.

Motivation for achievement has been studied largely in adult subjects. McClelland *et al.,*[42] McClelland,[43] and Atkinson *et al.*[44] report many studies of motivation for achievement among adults. These investigators have worked out a means of measurement of motivation for achievement (hereafter referred to as n Ach, i.e., need for achievement) through the use of TAT projective material. This was adapted by Winterbottom for use with children.[45] Rosen[46] and Merbaum[47] have done the only inter-racial studies of n Ach in children. Winterbottom found that boys who are high in n Ach are more independent in problem solving and evidenced greater pleasure when successful than boys low in n Ach. Merbaum found that n Ach increases with chronological age for both Negro and white southern subjects, although the group of white boys scored higher on n Ach than did their Negro counterparts. Rosen, in comparing six different ethnic groups of boys, found that n Ach was more significantly related to social class membership than to ethnicity per se.

Crandall[48] reviewed the work that had been done on motivation for achievement among children, and noted the sparseness of data in this important area. He takes exception to the approach of McClelland and Atkinson when they lump all forms of achievement motivation together. Crandall refers to different subtypes of achievement motivation, covering such areas as intellectual achievement, physical skills, artistic-creative achievement, mechanical skills, and social skills achievement.

Crandall and his associates studied motivation for academic achievement among middle class elementary school children, and found that neither n Ach nor anxiety level predicted achievement behavior.[49] They found that for girls, the desire for intellectual competence (intellectual achievement value) correlated with achievement effort. For boys, intellectual achievement value did not predict achievement, but other variables such as high standards, and expectation of success did. Also, boys who were high on self-responsibility, (the degree to which the children feel they *cause* the reinforcement that accrues from achievement efforts) were high in achievement. Crandall concludes that motivation for academic achievement appears to be very different for boys and girls. After further study, he goes on to say that elementary school girls seem to demonstrate the need for external approval and affection, whereas boys' achievement appears to be more autonomously determined by their own internal achievement standards and by their need for self-approval. Sears also found that need for affection predicted achievement for elementary school girls, whereas n Ach scores predicted achievement for boys only.[50] Mischel also found that n Ach was correlated with children's ability to delay gratification.[51] Crandall states that "research to date tends to suggest that academic achievers tend to conform with and incorporate adult values and prescriptions," while at the same time "they appear to be self-reliant, assertive, competitive and even aggressive in their academic experience."[52]

What, then, is the nature of children's experience at home which motivates some to academic success, while others are not so moved?

There is available some data comparing high and low achievement motivation with certain child-rearing practices. Virtually all of this work has been done with boys from middle class families. These studies suggest that high standards of achievement communicated to the child, accompanied by high evaluation of the boys' competence, and emphasis on autonomy and self-reliance, and approval for achievement and disapproval for failure are all related to the development of high achievement motivation in boys.[53,54] Realistic goals and standards appropriate to the child's level of development, and a reasonable margin of failure also are the type of home experiences related to high achievement motivation.[55]

Scheinfeld,[56] pointing to the work of Abegglen,[57] Strodtbeck,[58] Rosen and D'Andrade[59] and Bradburn,[60] suggests that there may be a necessary and important division of labor on the part of the mother and father in socializing achievement in their sons. The optimal situation would be a father who pushes autonomy and self reliance, and a mother who encourages high achievement standards with the use of rewards and punishments, but who is frequently very nurturant and not so encouraging of self-reliance. If the father is present but relatively weak, or if the father is absent from the home, the mother must push high goals and standards but be less nurturant than in the previous case. If the father is absent, a strong outside male figure is helpful in encouraging achievement.

Although there have been studies which compare child rearing across ethnic and class lines, for example; Davis and Havighurst[61] there are not yet data available which compare the child-rearing practices relating to motivation in families of high and low achievers within the disadvantaged group.

Ego Development

The ego is that aspect of the individual personality which serves executive functions, mediating between the demands of inner experience and outer reality. Ordinarily, we speak of these ego functions as personality characteristics. The development of at least some of the following characteristics would appear to be important for academic success: (1) independence, which can be further subdivided into self-reliance and autonomy; (2) inner control, consisting of the ability to delay gratification and to control impulse, and (3) good self-concepts, including high self-esteem, appropriate sex-role identity, and identification with achieving models.

The relationship of these factors to academic achievement bears some further discussion. One could hypothesize that in order to function adequately within a classroom setting, the child must be able to express a measure of independence, but he must not be so "independent" that his behavior is not under control. In order to achieve, he must subordinate some of his own desires to the needs of the classroom. This requires an ability and a willingness to respond to authority and to function both cooperatively and competitively with his peers.

One could also hypothesize that in order to achieve successfully, the child must have a high opinion of himself, or at least of his intellectual capacities. He must also see his present and future sex role as being consistent with academic achievement. If he has achieving adult models with whom he can identify, he is perhaps more likely to be an achiever himself. One cannot tell whether a high score on a variable such as self-esteem represents the cause or the effect of high achievement. Probably both are true. This is expressed well in the old adage: "Nothing succeeds like success."

Ausubel and Ausubel[62] have extensively reviewed the evidence for social class and racial differences on many of the above-mentioned ego functions. They further relate these findings to experiential differences between the groups arising largely in the home, but also in the school and wider society. They point out that many of the differences between groups are largely social-class related. This is especially true in the areas of independence and inner control. In these instances, lower class status and the experiences associated therewith appear to play determining roles.

For example, the Ausubels state that because of less succorant care and more casual supervision of activities, lower-class children are pushed to precocious independence, and that this combines with the more prominent position of the peer group as a socializing influence to produce certain of the personality characteristics commonly associated with the disadvantaged child. These authors also point out that when compared to the Negro family, Puerto Ricans and Mexicans have a closer family life, and that for the Mexican group the role of the peer group is small, relative to its importance for these other groups.

Low self-esteem has been shown by a number of studies to be a characteristic of Negro children.[63,64] Kardiner and Ovesey also cite low self-esteem as one of their "marks of oppression," along with poor sex-role identity for males, and pent-up aggression which must be defended against rather than overtly expressed.[65]

The factor of sex-role seems particularly important in the life of the lower-class male generally, and especially for the disadvantaged Negro youngster. Coming from a situation in which the percentage of broken homes is very high[66,67] and living in a society in which Negro men are least viable in the job market, frequently the Negro child has no stable male identification figure at all, much less one who has been successful academically. The great emphasis upon aggression as a proof of masculinity in the adolescent peer culture leaves little room for pursuits in the area of school achievement to enhance one's group status. Girls would appear to be in a situation of relative strength because they enjoy a higher status in the family, and because it is still true that there are more opportunities available to minority women in jobs requiring academic achievement. Even if they are not academically successful, girls can derive a legitimate social role through being a mother and homemaker.[68] There are perhaps many other reasons why women of this group enjoy a relatively privileged status. Smuts points out that Negro girls predominate over Negro boys at every level of education.[69]

There is a great need for further clarification of the motivation and ego development of disadvantaged youngsters. One fruitful approach would be to take achievers and under-achievers from the same disadvantaged social and economic circumstances, and attempt to delineate some significant differences in personality characteristics within the disadvantaged group itself. Then a further attempt to explain such differences could be made by making corresponding observations on the familial child-rearing practices and socialization experiences of these children. Such a program of research is under way by the author and his co-workers, D. Scheinfeld and D. Solomon, at the Institute for Juvenile Research.[70]

Emotional Freedom to Learn

Emotional freedom to learn may be defined as the capacity to freely invest one's psychic energies in the task of academic learning.[71]

It has been pointed out by Pearson and Rabinovitch, in their reviews of the child psychiatric literature on learning problems, that virtually any form of childhood psychopathology can be accompanied by problems of academic achievement.[72,73] Such problems, therefore, must be viewed as symptoms rather than as definitive diagnostic categories. Both Rabinovitch and Pearson, however, emphasize the necessity to evaluate factors other than purely emotional ones in order to detect the true causation of each individual case of learning difficulty. Each one of the previously described internal factors contributes to academic achievement along with this present category.

Emotional freedom to learn, and its converse, emotional blocks to learning,[74] refer to a broad clustering of phenomena which are traditionally placed in the bailiwick of the child psychiatrist. There is an imperfect relationship between the amount of emotional disturbance and the degree of involvement of the learning process. Some children with serious emotional problems have little or no impairment of their academic achievement, whereas other children with relatively mild psychiatric disturbance have serious difficulties in learning.

Emotional freedom to learn implies the absence of psychic defense mechanisms that operate to diminish the capacity for attention to the task, execution of the task, and/or successful completion of the task. Psychiatric syndromes which could potentially interfere with functioning in this way include anxiety states, depression, obsessional neuroses and phobias, preoccupation with problems outside of school, fear of failure, the reluctance to go to school (school phobia), fear of success, learning problems as counter-aggression, and pre-psychotic or psychotic phenomena of childhood.

Some studies have shown that disadvantaged adult populations have a higher percentage of serious psychiatric impairment.[75,76] Certain forms of social maladjustment, such as delinquency, illegitimacy, crime, alcoholism and drug addiction also occur more frequently in disadvantaged populations. To an unknown extent, we might infer that this is somewhat indicative of a higher incidence of personality disturbance among the group, although it can be argued that at least some of these phenomena arise partly out of adverse social circumstances and are not purely reflective of psychopathology.

The prevalence rates for children of emotional disturbance requiring psychiatric care are influenced largely by selection factors in the respective out-patient clinics or in-patient units, and do not necessarily reflect true prevalence of these conditions in the population at large.[77]

We are therefore not able at this time to make accurate intergroup comparisons in either the incidence or prevalence of emotional disturbance among children of different groups. The experience of the author in both the clinic and public school settings leads him to the conclusion that disadvantaged youngsters are certainly no less susceptible to childhood emotional problems, and are indeed probably more susceptible. It is also true that in all likelihood different psychiatric syndromes occur with different frequencies among groups with differing experiences in socialization. One might expect that upper status youngsters would show a predominance of neurotic manifestations, and lower status youngsters would cluster more toward the character disorders, although this has not yet been accurately statistically demonstrated on a group of young subjects.

The relationship between the emotional disturbances that exist among disadvantaged youngsters and their academic achievement problems is still unknown. The relative part such disturbances play in school learning problems compared to other internal or external factors, or in addition to these factors, is yet to be determined.

DISCUSSION

As we approach the academic achievement problems of the disadvantaged child, we are struck by the number of factors that must be taken into account in order to understand this phenomenon. Even the casual reader of this review will have noted, however, that the categories that have been chosen are really applicable to any group of children, whether disadvantaged or not.

These large categories, representing the internal factors, or individual child factors in achievement, overlap with one another, and the subcategories contained within them interact. One cannot speak about concept formation without also considering the development of language, and one cannot mention elements of motivation or emotional freedom to learn without also referring to certain aspects of ego development. It is likely that many of these factors will be found to cluster one with the other. As we begin to learn more about the details of the differences in socialization experiences between disadvantaged children who grow up in different family environments and who are subjected to different school experiences, it is probable that certain patterns of strengths and weaknesses will emerge as typologies of achievement and under-achievement. The intellective functions of general intelligence, cognitive development, and language tend to form a natural cluster; so do the personality variables represented by motivation for academic achievement, ego development, and emotional freedom to learn.

A high standing on the intellective factors is likely to bring about sufficient rewards and recognition from the environment so as to encourage the healthy growth of the personality factors. Conversely, a child who has internalized standards and values, mastered control of his behavior, and has healthy self-concepts, in the absence of emotional blocks to learning, is much more likely to do well on the intellective tasks which are assigned to him.

The optimal condition for academic success occurs in the case of those children who rate high on all of these internal factors. Successful students from within the disadvantaged group are likely to score high in most of these dimensions. In the case of low achievers, there is likely to be a broader spread in the distribution, with some children demonstrating gross deficiencies in all of these factors, whereas others will score high on some of them and low on others.

Finding adequate means of measurement for the internal factors has more than just theoretical importance. If we were in a position to measure the child's relative standing early enough, we might be able to recommend methods of intervention designed to help the child develop the requisite skills. Such has been the philosophy behind the rise of therapeutic nursery schools for emotionally disturbed children, as well as the preschool programs for disadvantaged youngsters recently pioneered by Deutsch and others. The former type of program works toward the promotion of healthy personality growth, while the latter has the intention to provide the appropriate experiences necessary to develop cognitive and language skills and foster motivation for achievement.

One could see how artificial are the boundaries between the personality and the intellective factors if one were given the task of developing methods for the stimulation of one group of factors without altering the child's functioning in the other group of factors. Most often, the experience which promotes growth in one general area of functioning will also encourage development in the other.

A word must also be added here about feed-back mechanisms and the understanding of the material presented in Figure 1. The reader will note that the arrows flow in a uni-directional manner, for example from home and school to the Individual Child Factors. This designation was adopted to indicate the predominant flow of influence in the development of these characteristics, but it would be more complete to think of the arrows as going in both directions. It is of course true that once the child has demonstrated his standing and capabilities in the respective categories, there occurs a dynamic interplay between his performance and the responses of the people around him, and between the expectations and demands of these people and the child's view of his own capabilities. All of these elements will influence his next performance. This thesis may be illustrated by the use of two examples. (1) Children with special talents which are recognized and positively reinforced, are more likely to develop these gifts, because the positive response of the environment, which consists of pride in one's child's (or pupil's) accomplishment results in even further encouragement of their development. (2) Conversely, those youngsters who do not excel and who in turn do not provide corresponding satisfaction for the people around them, are less likely to be positively reinforced in the future development of those skills. Often children are *type-cast* early in life, and it is difficult to rise above negative expectations and definitions that arise from the environment or the self or both.

SUMMARY AND CONCLUSIONS

A conceptual framework has been herein suggested, as a means of approaching problems of academic achievement. This framework is applicable to the situation of all children in the United States, regardless of social or economic background, although specific reference has been made here to the school problems of economically and socially disadvantaged youngsters.

From the multitudinous elements which make up the child and his environment, ten major areas have been chosen for discussion. The first three of these are called external factors in academic achievement, and consist of social, administrative, and teaching factors. These are largely dealt with in other chapters of this book, and are mentioned only briefly here. The remaining seven factors which together constitute the internal factors in academic achievement, and which are the individual characteristics of the pupil that relate to his functioning in school, are the major subject matter of this chapter, and may be listed thusly: physical health, general intelligence, cognitive development, language development, motivation for academic achievement, ego development, and emotional freedom to learn.

Each of these internal factors is discussed first with the intent to establish it as a legitimate and important area for the understanding of school performance generally, then with special reference to the problems of under-achievement among the disadvantaged. Various research is reviewed which bears upon each of these factors. In instances where there is information available, the environmental influences upon the development of these factors is also considered. Issues of normal growth and development, as well as the unique elements of a child's experience, play a part in his standing on all of these individual factors. These in turn each have their role in determining the child's level of academic achievement.

The need for further research into the etiology of school problems among the disadvantaged cannot be over emphasized. It is indeed astounding to realize how little we know about the development of academic proficiency among any segment of our population. It is especially disconcerting to realize how little we yet know about the achievement problems of such a large number of young people, whose future lives depend so much upon academic success. It is imperative that thoughtful research be carried out so that we can derive an understanding of the natural history of such problems, in order to ultimately be able to prescribe appropriate methods of remediation and/or prevention.

REFERENCES

1. D. J. Ingle, "Racial Differences and the Future," *Science,* 146, (Oct. 16, 1964), pp. 375-379.
2. H. E. Garrett, "The Equalitarian Dogma," *Mankind Quarterly,* 1, (1961), pp. 253-257.
3. A Shuey, *The Testing of Negro Intelligence* (Lynchburg, Bell, 1958).
4. T. F. Pettigrew, *A Profile of the Negro American* (Princeton, Van Nostrand, 1964).
5. O. Klineberg, "Negro-White Differences in Intelligence Test Performance: A New Look at an Old Problem," *Amer. Psychologist,* 18, (1963), pp. 198-203.
6. K. B. Clark, *Prejudice and Your Child* (2nd Ed., Boston: Beacon Press, 1963).
7. R. K. Merton, "The Self-Fulfilling Prophecy," *Antioch Review,* 8, (1948), pp. 193-210.
8. K. B. Clark, "Clash of Cultures in the Classroom," *Learning Together,* M. Weinberg (ed.) (Chicago, Integrated Education Associates, 1964), pp. 18-25.
9. T. F. Pettigrew, *op. cit.*
10. H. Knobloch, and B. Pasamanick, "Environmental Factors Affecting Human Development Before and After Birth," *Pediatrics,* 26, (1960), pp. 210-218.
11. L. J. Cronbach, *Essentials of Psychological Testing,* (New York, Harper and Row, 1960).
12. J. McV. Hunt, *Intelligence and Experience* (New York: Ronald Press, 1961).
13. R. J. Havighurst, *The Public Schools of Chicago:* A Survey for The Board of Education of Chicago. Board of Education, City of Chicago, Chicago, 1964.
14. M. Deutsch, and B. Brown, "Social Influences in Negro-White Intelligence Differences," *J. Soc. Issues,* 20, (1964), pp. 24-35.
15. A. Shuey, *op. cit.*

16. O. Klineberg, *Characteristics of the American Negro* (New York: Harper, 1944).

17. T. F. Pettigrew, *op. cit.*

18. O. Klineberg, *op. cit.*, 1963.

19. M. Deutsch, and B. Brown, *op. cit.*

20. H. Knobloch, and B. Pasamanick, Further Observations on the Behavioral Development of Negro Children. *J. Genet. Psychol.* 83, (1953), pp. 137-157.

21. H. Knobloch, and B. Pasamanick, *op. cit.*, 1960.

22. J. McV. Hunt, *op. cit.*

23. D. O. Hebb, *The Organization of Behavior* (New York: Wiley, 1949).

24. J. Piaget, *The Psychology of Intelligence* (M. Piercy and D. E. Berlyne, Trans.) (London: Routledge and Kegan Paul, 1947).

25. J. Piaget, *The Origins of Intelligence in Children* (Margaret Cook, Trans.) (New York: International Universities Press, 1952). (Originally Published in 1936).

26. W. Fowler, "Cognitive Learning in Infancy and Early Childhood," *Psychol. Bull.*, 59, (1962), pp. 116-152.

27. M. Deutsch, and B. Brown, *op. cit.*, p. 34.

28. J. Piaget, *op. cit.*, 1952.

29. W. Fowler, *op. cit.*

30. M. Montessori, *The Montessori Method* (New York, Schocken Books, 1964). (Translated from the Italian, 1912).

31. N. M. Rambusch, *Learning How to Learn: An American Approach To Montessori* (Baltimore: Helicon Press, 1962).

32. C. P. Deutsch, "Auditory Discrimination and Hearing: Social Factors," *Merril-Palmer Quarterly*, 10, (1964), pp. 277-296.

33. V. P. John, "The Intellectual Development of Slum Children: Some Preliminary Findings," *Amer. J. Orthopsychiat.*, 33, (1963), pp. 813-833.

34. M. Deutsch, "The Role of Social Class in Language Development and Cognition," *Amer. J. Orthopsychiat.*, 25, (1965), pp. 78-88.

35. B. Bernstein, "Linguistic Codes, Hesitation Phenomena and Intelligence," *Lang. and Speech*, 5, (1962), pp. 31-46.

36. B. Bernstein, "Social Class, Linguistic Codes and Grammatical Elements," *Lang. and Speech*, 5, (1962), pp. 221-240.

37. M. Deutsch, "The Disadvantaged Child and the Learning Process: Some Social, Psychological and Developmental Considerations," Passow, A. (Ed.), *Education in Depressed Areas*. New York: Teachers College Bureau of Publications, Columbia University, 1963, pp. 163-179.

38. D. McClelland, J. Atkinson, R. Clark, and E. Lowell, *The Achievement Motive* (New York: Appleton-Century-Crofts, 1953).

39. R. W. White, Motivation Reconsidered: "The Concept of Competence," *Psychol. Rev.*, 66, (1959), pp. 297-333.

40. R. W. White, "Ego and Reality in Psychoanalytic Theory, A Proposal

Regarding Independent Ego Energies," *Psychol. Issues,* Vol. III, No. 3, Monograph 11, 1963. Int. Univ. Press., N. Y.

41. J. McV. Hunt, "The Psychological Basis for Using Pre-School Enrichment as an Antidote for Cultural Deprivation," *Merril-Palmer Quarterly,* 10, (1964), 209-248.

42. D. McClelland, J. Atkinson, R. Clark, and E. Lowell, *op. cit.*

43. D. C. McClelland: *The Achieving Society* (Princeton, Van Nostrand, 1961).

44. J. W. Atkinson, (Ed.), *Motives in Fantasy Action and Society* (New York: Van Nostrand, 1958).

45. M. R. Winterbottom, The Relation of Need for Achievement to Learning Experiences in Independence and Mastery. *Motives in Fantasy, Action, and Society,* (New York, Van Nostrand, 1958), pp. 453-476.

46. B. C. Rosen, "Race Ethnicity, and the Achievement Syndrome," *Amer. Sociol. Rev.,* 24, (1959), pp. 47-60.

47. A. D. Merbaum, "Need for Achievement in Negro and White Children," (Ph.D., dissertation 1961 Univ. of North Carolina), Univ. Microfilms Inc., Ann Arbor, Michigan.

48. V. J. Crandall, Achievement, "In H. W. Stevenson (Ed.), *Child Psychology,* Yearb. Natl. Soc. for Study of Educ., Chicago: University of Chicago Press, 1963.

49. V. Crandall, W. Katkovsky, and A. Preston, "Motivational and Ability Determinants of Young Children's Intellectual Achievement Behaviors," *Child Development,* 33, (1962), pp. 643-661.

50. P. Sears, "Correlates of Need Achievement and Need Affiliation and Classroom Management, Staff Concept, Achievement and Creativity" Unpublished manuscript, Laboratory of Human Development, Stanford University, 1962.

51. W. Mischel, "Delay of Gratification, Need for Achievement, and Acquiescence in Another Culture," *J. Abn. Soc. Psychol,* 62, (1961), pp. 504-513.

52. V. J. Crandall, *op. cit.,* Achievement, p. 387.

53. M. R. Winterbottom, *op. cit.*

54. B. C. Rosen, and R. G. D'Andrade, "The Psychosocial Origins of Achievement Motivation," *Sociometry,* 22, (1959), pp. 185-218.

55. D. C. McClelland, *op. cit.*

56. D. R. Scheinfeld, Personal communication. The Author is greatly indebted to Mr. Scheinfeld for the stimulation and fertilization of many of the ideas expressed here and elsewhere in this paper, which, because of our close work together, I can no longer identify as either his or mine.

57. J. C. Abegglen, "Personality Factors in Social Mobility: A Study of Occupationally Mobile Businessmen," *Genet. Psychol. Monog.* 58, (1958), pp. 101-159.

58. F. L. Strodtbeck, "Family Interaction, Values, and Achievement," in *Talent and Society*, D. C. McClelland, A. Baldwin, W. Bronfenbrenner, and F. L. Strodtbeck: (New York, Van Nostrand, 1958), pp. 135-194.
59. B. C. Rosen, and R. G. D'Andrade, *op. cit.*
60. N. M. Bradburn, "Need-Achievement and Father Dominance in Turkey," *J. Abn. Soc. Psych.*, 67, (1963), pp. 464-468.
61. A. Davis, and R. J. Havighurst, "Social Class and Color Differences in Child Rearing," *Amer. Social. Rev.*, 11, (1946), pp. 698-710.
62. D. P. Ausubel, and P. Ausubel, "Ego Development Among Segregated Negro Children," A. H. Passow (Ed.) *Education in Depressed Areas* (New York: Teachers College Bureau of Publications, Columbia University, 1963), pp. 109-141.
63. K. B. Clark, and M. P. Clark, "Racial Identification and Preference in Negro Children." T. M. Newcomb and E. L. Hartley (Eds.), *Readings in Social Psychology* First Edition, (New York: Holt, 1947), pp. 169-178.
64. H. W. Stevenson, and E. C. Stewart, "A Development Study of Racial Awareness in Young Children," *Child Development*, 29, (1958), pp. 399-409.
65. A. Kardiner, and L. Ovesey, *The Mark of Oppression* (New York: Norton, 1951).
66. R. S. Cavan, "Negro Family Disorganization and Juvenile Delinquency," *J. Negro Educ.*, 28, (1959), pp. 230-239.
67. M. Deutsch, and B. Brown, *op. cit.*
68. M. Deutsch, Minority Group and Class Status as Related to Social and Personality Factors in Scholastic Achievement, Society for Applied Anthropology, Monograph No. 2, 1960, Cornell University, Ithaca, New York.
69. R. W. Smuts, "The Negro Community and the Development of Negro Potential," *J. Negro Educ.*, 26, (1957), pp. 456-465.
70. J. Hirsch, D. Scheinfeld, D. Solomon, *Determinants of Achievement and Under-Achievement Among Lower-Class Urban Negro Children.* A proposal for a research grant from Foundations Fund for Research in Psychiatry, April, 1964, (mimeo).
71. R. D. Rabinovitch, "Reading and Learning Disabilities, in "S. Arieti (Ed.) *Amer. Handbook of Psychiatry*, I, (1959), pp. 857-869.
72. G. H. J. Pearson, "A Survey of Learning Difficulties in Children," *Psychoanal. Study of the Child*, 7, (1951), pp. 322-387.
73. R. D. Rabinovitch, *op. cit.*
74. I. D. Harris, *Emotional Blocks to Learning* (New York, Free Press, 1961).
75. A. B. Hollingshead, and F. C. Redlick, *Social Class and Mental Illness: A Community Study* (New York: Wiley, 1958).

76. L. Srole, T. S. Langner, S. T. Michael, M. K. Olper, and T. A. C. Rennie, *Mental Health in the Metropolis: The Midtown Manhattan Study* (New York: McGraw-Hill, 1962).
77. E. E. Raphael, "Community Structure and Acceptance of Psychiatric Aid." *Amer. J. Sociol.*, 49, (1964), pp. 340-358.

PART II

THE DISADVANTAGED PUPIL IN THE ELEMENTARY SCHOOL

T HE CHAPTERS IN Part I have defined the characteristics of disadvantaged pupils and described the concomitant difficulties in school adjustment. Gorman has surveyed attempts of the schools to solve what seem to be inevitable problems. Nevertheless, it is clear that, although working with disadvantaged pupils is certainly not *terra incognita,* it is not yet an area of firm agreement. We have no one grand theory to rally around. In short, much remains to be learned in anything but an intuitive, pragmatic way. Some adjustments have brought encouraging improvement in school achievement of disadvantaged pupils. Unfortunately, most of the gains have been associated with the efforts of enthusiastic, dynamic leadership and special emphasis programs. The classical Hawthorne experiments of the 1930's taught us that efforts of this type may well succeed because of the very interest and enthusiasm associated with their trial. Hence, to the teacher who wishes definitive answers to his questions, we must reply that we do not now have such answers.

If this were all that we could contribute to help teachers working with disadvantaged pupils, there would be no need for this section of the book. It would suffice to delineate the problem in its many ramifications and to discuss the resources available to work toward its amelioration. This, of course, is a worthy undertaking and we turn our attention to it in the final part of the book, but there is something we can say with some authority to teachers of disadvantaged pupils. In order to do this, we must rephrase their query. If the teachers will now ask not: "How do you teach the disadvantaged pupil," but rather: "How do you teach the disadvantaged pupil *something*," we can proceed in good conscience.

The writers in Part II are all experts in their respective curricular areas. They are aware of the causes of the problems presented by and to culturally disadvantaged pupils. Their reports are based on both theory and practice. In order to reduce repetition to the necessary minimum, they have endeavored to concentrate on the practical aspects of teaching their subject to disadvantaged pupils. This restriction must not lead to the notion that the suggestions arise from practice alone, undirected by theoretical considerations. There are, indeed, reasons why certain tactics have been tried rather than others. They have been generated by a theoretical orientation. An orientation which, though not explicit, can be deduced by readers.

We shall discuss procedures that *work*. These procedures have been suggested by a body of knowledge, by a theory. An experimental vindication of the theory and of the practices is not yet available. However, the pupils are most certainly available. This section of the book is addressed to those who must teach these available pupils while we wait for the results of research programs for further guidance. It begins with an effort by psychologist Foley to develop an approach to teaching which will be especially effective with disadvantaged pupils. We then consider most of the subjects taught by the elementary school teacher and conclude with a presentation by psychologist Itkin on the evaluation of teaching with special emphasis on the particular problem of evaluating the disadvantaged pupil.

Chapter V

TEACHING DISADVANTAGED PUPILS

Walter J. Foley*

T HE OTHER CONTRIBUTORS have presented facts and points of view related to the cultural context, familiar patterns, physical attributes and psychological predispositions of culturally disadvantaged children. Here, we are concerned with elementary school guidance as a means of developing a better understanding of the role of the school in the affective or social learning process.

The section is further specialized by being addressed to counselors, potential counselors, teachers, and potential teachers. The discussion is centered on a better understanding of teacher behaviors, pupil behaviors and their consequent interactions. The unique objective is to present possible teacher behaviors that are designed to influence pupil behaviors. While the methods presented apply to every classroom, they are especially relevant for teachers of culturally disadvantaged pupils.

The reasoning behind the decision to depart from the more traditional *guidance program* approach is a commitment to the belief that the real need is not for more exhortation or organizational patterning, but for the examination of teacher-pupil and pupil-pupil interactions. Specifically, this section presents an examination of these interactions as they contribute to the learning of attitudes and valuations.

Therefore, the implications of current research on the acquisition and modification of social learnings are presented along with a method of evaluating social behavior. Social learning, as we understand it in our day-to-day living, consists of the learning of new behaviors and the alteration of past behaviors to reduce friction in living with others.

*Coordinator of Pupil Personnel Services for the Iowa Educational Information Center at the University of Iowa.

A Review of Attempted Solutions

Gorman, in Chapter II, has reviewed attempted solutions to the educational problems presented by the disadvantaged student. His discussion showed the wide variation in the scope and diversity of the various programs. In essence, they have been conducted on the thesis that an expansion of, and improvements in, the services which have proven effective in the past was the way to attack the problems presented by pupils enrolled in culturally disadvantaged schools. In short, more of the best known practices.

These procedures have led to degrees of saturation in the areas of social work, psychological testing, curriculum enrichment, guidance services, remedial programs, counseling and direct encouragement of pupils and their parents. Typically, the approach has been *total*. That is, there was an increased concentration of all available services.

Present Status

To date, the information and program evaluation coming out of these efforts has been more normative than specific. There is little factual information in the form of actual practices for the teacher who must face the problems of the classroom. Why has there been little research evidence from these extensive programs designed to support alterations in classroom practice? The possible answers include: (1) It may be that the *total* approach was the determining factor. So many services and aids were added simultaneously that the influence of any one factor became obscure and impossible to distinguish. While the general feeling was that pupils benefited from the total program, there was no way to tell which service helped most, or how much any one factor contributed to the overall program. (2) Also, the lack of any clear-cut evidence supporting certain classroom practices over others and the resulting lack of a listing of procedures common to any successful classroom in depressed areas was based on the absence of a behavior model against which to evaluate the programs.

At this time, the writer favors the second explanation. There is a growing lack of confidence in the *more of the same* method. In part, this distrust is based on the conflicting results of the research on teaching. By working through the maze of teaching research, with its false starts and blind alleys, we will better understand the shortcomings of the attempted solutions to our present problems.

Research on Teaching: A Source of Confusion

Some of the more obvious early fallacies were caused by investigators examining a single facet of the classroom and thus isolating it from the total teaching context. Results of these early studies have become so entrenched that they are now stereotypes in the educational literature. To summarize, autocratic teachers were identified, they were then made democratic; teacher-centered classrooms were identified, they were shifted to pupil-centered; the grouping of pupils was investigated and found to be heterogeneous, homogeneous grouping was attempted. This is not to mention the many lists of teacher personality characteristics developed to determine and evaluate the *good* teacher.

With time and sophistication, the single factor attacks were put together and the research model became more complex. By combining the various possibilities, relationships and interactions were found. A general conclusion from the newer more complex model was that each variable must be studied only in relation to all other variables before the contributions could be understood. To help grasp the implications of this generalization, consider that a democratic male teacher in a pupil-centered classroom grouped heterogeneously has a different *effect* on the learning process than a democratic female teacher in a pupil-centered classroom grouped heterogeneously. There are hundreds of possible combinations, as can readily be seen, to confuse our understanding of the pupil-teacher relationship.

The outcome or effect of teaching was also investigated. A better understanding of the many possible outcomes added a new dimension that had to be included to complete the model of "research on teaching." A revaluation of the various teacher-pupil combinations had to be made on the basis of the defined outcomes of teaching. An autocratic teacher might be better able to communicate facts while a democratic teacher might better influence classroom atmosphere. Add to the top of the three dimensional teacher-pupil-outcome model the overriding variable of social class, parental attitude, organizational pattern of the school and the community . . . and the complexity (or perplexity) of this method of research comes into bold relief!

Typical Teacher Attitudes

Taking a moment to look at what might be considered typical practice in teacher behavior and attitude in culturally disadvantaged areas will help to understand a teacher's problems in this situation. Becker, who interviewed teachers in Chicago, found that typically those who were first assigned to culturally disadvantaged schools left for a more desirable school as soon as possible.[1] This transfer pattern is generalizable and consistent with teacher behavior in other metropolitan areas. Generally, the reason for the decision to leave the first assignment is related to the negative valuation placed on teaching in depressed area schools by veteran teachers as well as to the more obvious explanations such as old buildings, poor support, low pupil motivations, etc. Young teachers are influenced by the attitudes of the older teachers.

The sequence of events leading to the decision to transfer follows a pattern. A teacher assumes, when he begins, that students will know how to behave as students, that they will exhibit and value behaviors the teachers feels are typical of students. Further, our new teacher assumes that pupils will know what is expected of a teacher. In other words, the teacher and the pupils will know their roles. They will each show the behaviors expected of teachers and pupils.

These role assumptions carry with them many behaviors, many expectations, that cannot be assumed for pupils in culturally disadvantaged schools. The characteristics of the pupils are such that the expectancies of the new teacher will not be realized. The resulting disappointment often causes a confirmation of the negative evaluation of the teaching situation in disadvantaged areas conveyed to the new teacher by others in and out of the profession. His attitudes change from optimism to pessimism.

The new teacher then expects the worst of his pupils and finds it. A self-fulfilling prophecy is established. The new teacher loses his motivation to improve instruction given to culturally disadvantaged children and the cycle is complete. Working with these children becomes *doing time* until a transfer can be secured. The teacher is eventually replaced by another newly assigned teacher and a new cycle is begun.

Proposals for Changing Teacher Attitude

Attempts have been made to change this situation and to alter the attitudes teachers have about assignments to schools in deprived areas. Experts and laymen have proposed a variety of methods which have met with varying degrees of success. Special service pay, shorter teaching hours, team teaching, smaller classes and appeals to the moral obligations of teaching have been included as possible alternatives.

One of the most unique plans was a peace corps-type program tried in New York City by Haubrich.[2] He appealed to student-teachers to take assignments in difficult schools and worked extensively with those who volunteered. His efforts have met with a relative degree of success and have been highly publicized. But, the number of new teachers involved in the program has been small and the approach has to be considered inadequate on the basis of sheer number of student-teachers willing to participate in the program.

A New Look at the Problem

A more pragmatic effort would not focus on obtaining missionary-type volunteers, but upon the changing of the attitudes and valuations of teachers concerning teaching assignments to deprived area schools. This approach would involve the systematic teaching of specific methods of changing the behaviors of pupils. It would allow teachers to enter the classroom situation with methods and techniques designed to alter pupil behavior and thus reinstate the sense of order necessary for the teacher to experience accomplishment.

The Teaching Situation

There are two questions involved in the teaching situation. The first is concerned with what must be taught while the second focuses on the methods of teaching. These two questions will be treated as they relate to the social learning that must be a part of the education of disadvantaged pupils.

The decision the teacher makes as to how and what to teach in the cognitive area has been well defined. The course of study, tests of achievement, previous grades, and day to day evaluation of pupils all contribute to the decision. Courses in education are designed to assist in making these decisions, but the difference between the theoretical and the actual is considerable.

The Culturally Disadvantaged Pupil

Consider the research on the culturally disadvantaged child. For over a decade, we have been bombarded with psychological, sociological, and cultural-anthropological analyses of the *why* of his behavior. The mores of his culture have been investigated. The marital patterns of his parents have been followed. The female domination of his household has been detailed. The lack of a proper male identification figure has been hypothesized. But, as in the case of the research on teaching, few recommendations in the form of specific practices to alter the attitudes, values, and beliefs of these children have come to the fore. While the *why* is necessary for a better understanding of a problem, the *how* is necessary for the planning of change!

Pupil Behaviors

We have already discussed the expectations of the typical teacher in our teacher-pupil discussion. Now, the typical pupil will be described. While this procedure is fraught with the difficulties of overgeneralization and stereotyping, it does furnish a set of behaviors against which the principles of social learning can be outlined.

The term culturally disadvantaged child is used here in a broad sense to include the many different groups of disadvantaged. When used in this general way, it refers to children living in depressed areas of the cities. In the schools, disadvantaged pupils present problems of academic retardation, discipline, truancy, transiency, and, with older pupils, dropout. They are insecure, not highly motivated for the tasks of the school; their health is poor, they are often malnourished and in many cases unclean. They can be classified as the lowest socioeconomic group.

Culturally disadvantaged children are also present-oriented, value motor skills, physical strength, manual skills, and are concerned with immediate gratification. They are typically behind in grade level in school, have a negative self-evaluation, have experienced a restricted social environment and do not expect things taught in school to have any influence on their adult lives. Along the same line, their future typically holds reading retardation, learning disability, and increasingly poor discrimination of verbal directions.

A Proposal

This proposal makes only the following assumptions: (1) that teacher characteristics and behaviors do, and should be expected to, vary; (2) that pupil behaviors and characteristics also vary both within and among classrooms; (3) that teaching is a process of interaction between the teacher and the pupils, (4) that teachers and pupils must learn to exhibit the behaviors that are necessary to facilitate the process, and (5) that teachers and pupils desire to improve their classroom relationships.

It is a truism that the teacher is assigned a central role in the learning process. Learning theory provided the research evidence that established this truism. But, the learning theory was based on the non-emotional or cognitive processes. Most of what has been written about teaching methods was also influenced by the same body of evidence and concerned itself with the teacher's role in cognitive learning. Until recently, there has been little systematic investigation of the role of the teacher in the emotional, or affective, learning process. Affective learning is concerned with attitudes and valuations.

Recognition of the teacher's role in the learning of social behaviors is slowly coming out of the research findings in several areas. This new social learning theory has certain postulates that are directly transferable to the classroom. In terms of the teaching process, the principles may be stated as: (1) teaching is a directive process which follows lawful predictable learning principles, and (2) the factors which effect classroom relationships involve reinforcement, modeling, manipulation, shaping, exhortation, vicarious learning, and control. Each factor contributes to both the cognitive and affective learning process and is used throughout the remainder of the discussion. Each factor will be briefly defined.

REINFORCEMENT. The effects of behavior have the power to either strengthen or weaken the behavior. As behavior becomes more complex, the pupil is constantly watching the effect on others of each of his behaviors that make up his total act. This knowledge of results is described as *feedback* and allows the pupil to alter his course of behavior during an act, thus allowing change in the final act. Changes are based upon the observation of the effects of the preliminary steps.

MODELING. This term describes the behavior of the teacher and/or pupil who demonstrates behaviors and the outcomes of behaviors. Modeling is done intentionally or unintentionally. The teacher is acting as a model when he disciplines his pupils as well as when he demonstrates the solutions to an arithmetic problem. In a broad sense, an individual is modeling whenever his behavior is being observed by others.

MANIPULATION. The person who controls the reinforcements in the classroom is in a position to manipulate the behavior of others. In this sense, the term has much in common with teaching. An attempt to alter the response potential of pupils by controlling the reinforcement is defined as manipulation. The devices a teacher employs to manipulate the responses of pupils include among others: grades, awards, praise and reproof, isolation, and pleasant and unpleasant facial expressions. When a teacher manipulates, he attempts to alter pupils responses or to institute new behavior responses judged desirable. To date, emphasis has centered on the manipulation of pupils' cognitive behaviors through reinforcement.

SHAPING. Shaping refers to rewarding in a sequential manner, behaviors that approximate the desired behavior. This is usually done by demanding that the pupil make closer approximations of the desired response with each successive attempt. Verbal behavior serves as a prime example of the shaping of response by successive approximation. An infant utters "Nana" in the presence of the grandmother. This response is reinforced positively by attention, praise, and physical contact on the part of the grandmother. The grandparent models the response by repeating it for the infant. Over time, finer and finer approximations are demanded before the infant is given reinforcement. This, "Nana" becomes "Nama," "Gama," and, finally, "Grandma." In the classroom, the expectancy of a closer and closer duplication of the model in writing, reading, and speaking is demanded by the teacher.

EXHORTATION. This more general term refers to the urging, advising, warning, admonishing, sermonizing, and pleading that goes on in the classroom. Exhortation is the most common method of attempting to control the behavior of pupils. It would be fair to say that most remedial efforts undertaken by parents and teachers in the area of pupil social behavior can be classified as exhortation.

VICARIOUS LEARNING. While most learning occurs by watching the behavior of a model, cognitive learning theory pays little attention to the implications of this method in the learning process. Research on affective learning has demonstrated that the act of observing a sequence of behaviors performed by another leads to the learning of the proper or rewarded behavior by the observer.[3] It has also been shown that observing a model punished for exhibiting undesired behaviors leads to the inhibition and suppression of the punished behaviors in the observer.[4] In the classroom setting, the teacher reinforces many pupil behaviors on an individual basis. The class observes the sequence of events leading to the reward or punishment of a fellow student and in this manner learns many expected classroom behaviors.

CONTROL. The prime requisite to the classroom situation is control. The teacher uses all the variables here defined to maintain control of his class. Factors which contribute to teacher control include his physical size, education, age, possession of the reinforcement system, and social expectations of the pupil. We shall concentrate on the application of these variables which are common to, and controllable in, every classroom setting.

Attitude Evaluation

We have described the tools a teacher employs to alter the behavior of his students. Now, we will present a model for evaluating the attitudes and valuations of students. With this model, a teacher can evaluate the degree to which the "typical" disadvantaged pupil so often described approximates the "actual" pupils in his classroom. This evaluation should be an ongoing process as well as an initial measure of the class.

The teacher, to better understand his role in the process of influencing attitudes, can now look to several theoretical frameworks. Each model describes attitude formation and attitude change. Heider, Newcomb, Osgood-Tannenbaum, and Festinger have all contributed positions that are similar and can be summarized under the more general rubric of *Consistency Theory*.[5]

THE ATTITUDE MODEL. Social learning as a part of classroom learning can be clarified by understanding one of the consistency theories. For our discussion, Osgood-Tannenbaum furnish a method they define as *Congruity Theory* for evaluating an affect laden situation. In congruity theory, there are three variables in an interpersonal situation. The variables viewed through the eyes of the person to be influenced by the situation are the perceptions of the learner. Since we assign the observing, or vicarious learning, role to the pupil, his perception of the source of a communication, the object of a communication, and the tone of a communication represent the three variables in the theory. To make this clear, let us assume that a teacher is attempting to motivate his class by telling them how doing well in English will help them when they grow up.

The congruity principle states that when the observer associates one object or person with another by an assertion, the evaluation of the two objects, ideas, or persons involved is always given the same degree of value. This value can be in the same direction or in an opposite direction for each of the two, but the amount will be equal. An example will help clarify this principle.

AN EXAMPLE OF THE MODEL. An interpersonal situation, as seen by the observer is shown in Figure 1. In the figure, the middle line represents the line of zero evaluation. The plus direction represents the positive evaluation of an object, person, or concept. The space below the base line represents the strength of feeling or the degree of polarization. The person making the evaluation is not represented on the grid, but the placement of the three elements represents the observer's evaluation of the situation.

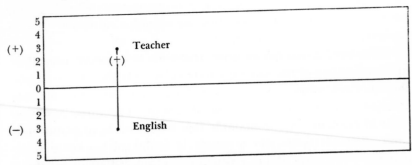

Figure 1. The Evaluation of Teacher Assertions.

In our example, we assume that the teacher is positively valued by the pupil. This assumption is in part based on the age, training, role, and other characteristics of the teacher. Furthermore, English is assumed to be negatively evaluated by the pupil. The reason being that the pupil feels there is no immediate gratification from studying English. The line of teacher assertion is marked as positive since the teacher has told her class the value of English in life. The situation is summarized as a positive teacher making a positive assertion about a negative concept.

ELEMENTS AND CONGRUITY. From the point of view of the observer, two elements (persons, ideas, or objects) of an interpersonal situation joined by an assertion are either compatible or they are not compatible.[6] When congruity exists, there is no tendency for change in the evaluation of any of the elements. Congruity would exist if a negatively evaluated teacher made a positive assertion about a negative concept. Going back to our example, had the pupil positively valued both the teacher and English, he would have expected the teacher to express favorable comments about English. Also, had the pupil negatively valued the teacher and English, he would expect to disagree with the teacher's favorable comments about English. The teacher's positive assertion regarding English constitutes a confirmation of the pupil's negative evaluation of both elements. In either of the above congruous conditions, there is little tendency for the pupil to alter his evaluation of either his teacher or English. Restated, congruity theory postulates that an observer feels comfortable in a situation when two of the three elements are negative or when all are positive.

ELEMENTS AND INCONGRUITY. Incongruity or incompatability exists when two of the three evaluated elements are positive while the other is negative. Our example, Figure 1 is incongruous. This condition causes a tendency toward change. The three combinations of elements in our example that would be incongruous and cause discomfort are: (1) a positively evaluated teacher making a positive assertion about a negatively evaluated concept; (2) a negatively evaluated teacher making a positive assertion about a positively held concept, and (3) a positively evaluated teacher making a negative assertion about a positively evaluated concept.

POSSIBLE SOLUTIONS TO INCONGRUITY. The various consistency theories also describe the possible solutions open to the pupil when faced with an incongruous situation. This unique aspect, that of presenting all possible solutions, is central to understanding the role of consistency theory in social learning.[7] A pupil who is faced with a situation which he sees as incongruous or inconsistent has three courses of action. He can: (1) leave the field; by this we mean that either figuratively or literally a pupil can remove himself from the situation; (2) change his valuation of one of the elements; in our example, he could solve the dilemma by either changing his judgment of the teacher or English, or (3) reinterpret the meaning of the assertion made by the teacher about English. If this solution was chosen, the pupil would in effect reinterpret the teacher's assertion about the English assignment.

USEFULNESS IN CULTURALLY DISADVANTAGED SCHOOLS. If we are willing to make the assumption that teachers do care for their pupils and are interested in obtaining the gratifications of their profession, then the conflicting teacher-pupil expectancy pattern described earlier as the basis of teachers leaving culturally disadvantaged schools can be altered. To accomplish this end, it will be necessary for the teacher to consider himself a social reinforcer. The teacher must define himself as a model with a social stimulus value and systematically present affective learning situations. His social stimulus value is, of course, based on superior age, education, dress, and manner. Primarily though, a teacher's positive stimulus value is gained from his role as the controller and dispenser of reinforcement. The teacher who would implement the social learning model presented must remember that his first task is to teach systematically the necessary social learnings. The reward for this effort comes in providing the proper classroom climate for cognitive learning.

Teaching and Social Learning

The remainder of this paper is devoted to specific ways a teacher can change the social behavior of his pupils. After changing pupils' social behaviors, it is assumed that altered academic behavior will follow. This assumption is based on the belief that a pupil must understand and appreciate the social context of education before the values and attitudes reinforced in cognitive learning situations will have meaning.

After all, gold stars and other educational rewards have little meaning in and of themselves. They are secondary rewards. Their secondary value is gained from association with things that do have value such as praise, attention, and verbal associations. It would be consistent with social learning to concentrate on the learning how to learn aspects of classroom behaviors in the early grades and slowly make the transition to systematic development of positive academic attitudes as the age of the pupils increase.

Consider the first day of school. It is, by definition, in some respects new and novel for each pupil. The responses shown by the pupils are based on past experiences that approximate the experiences of this first day. In situations that are new and ambiguous, pupils look to their peers as models and exhibit affiliatory behavior. Rather than be disappointed that pupils do not know how to *behave* the teacher should consider the first day of school as an ideal situation to step in and demonstrate the proper social behaviors for the class.

Let us say that a fourth grade teacher wishes his class to be favorably inclined toward homework assignments. On the first day, or perhaps the first several days, he would present to his new class, pupils from the previous class to demonstrate homework assignment procedures. The teacher would structure the type of work turned in, the method of collection, the rewards given, and have the older models show their feelings of pleasure and satisfaction with the system. This "programing" of the mechanics would also demonstrate student expected behavior and reward satisfaction. For teacher feedback and also to teach delayed gratification, the demonstrations would be followed by an assignment due the following day. To insure that pupils could accomplish the new "homework behaviors," an assignment that could be completed on paper received in class would be assigned first. The possibilities and examples are endless.

The unique factor of this method centers on the teacher considering each task assigned and each project undertaken as an opportunity to teach social behavior as well as cognitive behavior. Also, it is important to remember that grade level will affect the emphasis placed. The two main divisions of teacher concern would be the acquiring of new social behaviors and the altering of existing behaviors.

Imitation Learning

In the area of cognitive learning the potency of imitation is often neglected. It is forgotten that "to teach" literally translated means "to show." Much of what is learned by pupils in classrooms is acquired by imitation. Again, the use of a model is the basic ingredient for imitative learning and requires that someone do the showing.

Earlier in our history, it was not uncommon for a child to accompany the parent during the working hours and acquire the skills and attitudes that accompanied the parent's craft. Today, it is more common for a child to acquire much of his skill learning through the imitation of symbolic, in contrast to actual, models. These take the form of filmstrips, movies, written directions, verbal instruction, demonstrations and various combinations of these. While the efficiency in teaching cognitive skills has become very sophisticated, the teaching profession has systematically neglected the utilization of the socialization potency of its role. Teaching in culturally disadvantaged areas demands that the prime importance be placed on the affective learning which forms the pre-learning or co-learning experiences.

Teaching How To Be A Student

Culturally disadvantaged children do not expect the things taught in school to have an influence on their adult lives.[8] It then follows that emphasizing the future as a reward for present learning has little value. Since this is the case, and the evidence supports this position, then the teacher must first teach his pupils to value the goal or point toward more meaningful goals.

When we say that we are trying to "raise the level of aspiration" of pupils in culturally disadvantaged areas, are we not saying that these pupils do not value the existing reinforcements of the educational system? Are we not saying that pupil values and attitudes are such that they do not care about the rewards and punishments we have so painstakenly developed in education?

Literally, these pupils must *learn to learn*. The typical culturally disadvantaged pupil does not know how to be a student in the existing educational system. He does not place a value on the controls and rewards traditionally assumed adequate for the learning process. If we are to change the level of aspiration of pupils, it becomes the teacher's task to first teach the necessary social behavior before he can expect that pupils will exhibit and conform to this behavior. Further, this social behavior must be taught, for it forms the basis of cognitive learning in our present educational system.

Methods in Social Learning

Reinforcement and non-reinforcement are the two terms that define the methods best able to establish new behavior and stop the occurrence of undesired behaviors. The operation of these more general concepts is simply one-to-one. Reinforced behavior becomes established while non-reinforced behavior is not established, or is extinguished. The method, or schedule, of reinforcement is more the complex of the two and has been shown to be the determining factor in the establishment of new behaviors and the altering of undesired behaviors.

Learning theory defines three ways to administer reinforcement. It can be: (1) continuous; (2) vary with frequency of occurrence, and (3) vary with time elapsed. Reinforcement can contain elements of all three of the above schedules.[9]

We must remember that the learning of new behavior and the alteration of existing behavior is an entirely separate process from the judgement of the desirability or undesirability of the behavior. Reinforcement is consistent in the learning process and is not related to any judgement of the social value of the behavior. Again it should be pointed out that the pupil can receive reinforcement vicariously and need not be directly involved in the reinforcement process.[10]

Establishing New Behavior

In learning new behavior, the most satisfactory method or schedule of reinforcement for teacher use contains elements of both continuous and intermittent reinforcement. First, new behaviors should be reinforced as soon as possible after they occur. This establishes the new behavior. Then, the newly established behavior should be rewarded intermittently to insure the continued use of the new response. A gradually lengthened schedule would be appropriate in most cases.[11]

When a teacher desires that his pupils learn a behavior which does not have the opportunity to occur in the classroom, he should structure a situation in which it will occur, model the situation, reward the occurrence of the behavior and then, on the basis of time, provide for the reoccurrence of the situation and reward the desired behaviors.

Stopping Undesired Behaviors

Behavior that is judged undesirable can be stopped or extinguished by not reinforcing the behavior when it appears.[12] This is not a simple process as the behavior the teacher judges deviant may not be positively reinforced by the teacher. The other pupils or someone completely outside the classroom setting may be the source of reinforcement for the pupil. In any case, research shows that the nonreward of behavior judged undesirable frequently causes an immediate increase in both the rate and intensity of response.[13] A good instance involving the problems related to ignoring undesirable behavior can be found in attention-seeking behaviors. The sequence which follows is applicable in instances of either an approval or disapproval response on the part of the teacher to the pupils behavior.

A pupil wants the attention of the teacher and/or the class and attempts to gain it by behaving in a way the teacher judges as undesirable. When the teacher ignores the behavior, the pupil then increases both the intensity and frequency of the response. By using the technique of ignoring the behavior, the teacher has actually increased the probability of the occurrence of the behavior immediately after the nonreward sequence.

Although this increase in response is predictable on the basis of learning theory, frequently it causes an increase in anxiety in the teacher. He then deviates from the *ignoring* schedule, pays attention to the pupil and reinforces the occurrence of an increase in intensity of response when the earlier response is ignored. From the point-of-view of the child, the situation becomes one of increasing the intensity and frequency of response when behaviors of lesser degree are ignored.

Even when the teacher does not make the mistake of finally giving in or paying attention to the pupil when response intensity increases, he may still become discouraged when non-reinforced behaviors reappear. It is easy to forget that this is the normal process in eliminating undesired behaviors. Research has shown that behavior presumed extinguished will periodically reappear as time passes.[14] Typically, the recurrence of the undesirable behavior will be less intense each time it recurs once the initial extinguishment period is over.

Also, the teacher can help speed up the process of extinguishing undesirable behavior by providing alternatives for these responses. He is then providing opportunities for the pupils to learn new and more appropriate responses while eliminating older more undesirable behaviors.

Pupils from culturally disadvantaged areas should be expected to show behaviors that are judged undesirable in the classroom. In many instances, the behaviors that teachers judge deviant are behaviors necessary for the pupils to function in the world in which they live. Education, for these pupils, must provide the opportunity to learn and practice the fine discriminations in response necessary to succeed in both the world in which they live and the world in which they learn.

Reinforcement encompasses the rewards and punishments that are at the control of the teacher. Consider that it is the teacher who determines which pupil sits where, who recites, who gets to play, who takes notes to the office, who passes out papers. He gives out the gold stars, the grades, the compliments, the attention. The teacher smiles, frowns, nods, approaches, repeats, paraphrases. In fact, the teacher even controls the medium of expression in the classroom.

Timing in Punishment

Since a paper like this would be incomplete without a mention of punishment, the following represents the authors best understanding of its usefulness in teaching. The term *punishment* has the meaning of inflicting a noxious stimulus to stop an undesired response. It inhibits the occurrence of the response. It does not eliminate the response. In education, punishment is usually verbal. It takes the form of scolding, reprimanding and coercion.

Since a deviant, or undesired, pupil act constitutes a culmination of a series of behaviors, it would help most if a teacher knew the best time to administer a punishment. Research supports the position that early punishment is most effective. That is, punishment administered early in the sequence of events that make up the act judged undesirable. For example, a teacher who wishes to avoid the act of paper-wad shooting would be most effective if he punished the playing with rubber bands.

Conclusion

All that has been written in this paper has been an attempt to refocus attention on the dual learnings of education. Pupils leave our classrooms supplied not only with subject matter competence, they have also acquired a set of fine social discriminations as a by-product. This was an effort to reemphasize the importance of social learning in education.

The ability to make discriminations is probably the most important characteristic of human intelligence. Behavior that shows fine discrimination in response is what is observed in most higher order learning situations. In the context of social learning, discrimination takes the form of altering the response and expectancy of response as the situation alters. This social learning is also a product of education. In fact, a case might be made for its central importance in a democracy. Pupils from socially deprived areas have the right to expect that they too will be taught the social discriminations necessary for achievement in our society.

REFERENCES

1. Howard Becker, "The Career of the Chicago Public School Teacher," *American Social Review*, 17 (7), (July, 1952), pp. 470-476.
2. Vernon F. Haubrich, "Teachers for Big-City Schools" in Passow, A. H., (Ed.) *Education in Depressed Areas*, New York: Bureau of Publications, Teachers College, Columbia University, 1963.
3. Albert Bandura and Richard H. Walters, *Social Learning and Personality Development* (New York, Holt, Rinehart and Winston, Inc., 1963); R. H. Walters, and L. Demkow, "Studies of Reinforcement of Aggression, II. Transfer of Resistance to Temptation," *Child Development*, 34, (1963), pp. 207-214.
4. P. A. Cowan and R. H. Walters, "Studies of Reinforcement of Aggression, I. Effects of Scheduling," *Child Development*, 1963.
5. F. Heider, *The Psychology of Interpersonal Relations*, (New York, Wiley, 1958); T. M. Newcomb, "Individual Systems of Orientation." in S. Kotch (Ed.) *Psychology: A Study of A Science*, Vol. 2 (New York, McGraw-Hill, 1959); pp. 384-422; C. E. Osgood, G. J. Suce, and P. Tannenbaum, *The Measurement of Meaning* (Urbana, University of Illinois Press, 1957): L. Festinger, *A Theory of Cognitive Dissonance* (Evanston, Row, Peterson, 1957).
6. T. M. Newcomb, pp. 384-422; F. Heider.
7. R. Zajonc, "The Concepts of Balance, Congruity, and Dissonance," *Public Opinion Quarterly*, 24, (1960), pp. 290-296.
8. David R. Miller and Gug G. Swanson, *Inner Conflict and Defense* (New York, Henry Holt, 1960); Frank Riessman, *The Culturally Deprived Child* (New York, Harper, 1962).
9. A. W. Staats (Ed.), *Human Learning* (New York, Holt, Rinehart and Winston, 1964): B. F. Skinner, *Verbal Behavior* (New York, Appleton-Century-Crofts, 1957).
10. P. A. Cowan and R. H. Walters; R. H. Walters and L. Demhow, *op. cit.*, pp. 207-214.

11. B. F. Skinner, *Science and Human Behavior* (New York, Macmillan, 1953); A. W. Staats and C. K. Staats, *Complex Human Behavior* (New York, Holt, Rinehart and Winston, 1963); Albert Bandura and R. H. Walters.

12. B. F. Skinner, R. H. Walters, and L. Demkow, *op. cit.,* pp. 207-214.

13. *Ibid.*

14. Albert Bandura and R. H. Walters, *op. cit.,* R. A. Cowan and R. H. Walters, *op. cit.,* B. F. Skinner, *op. cit.,* R. H. Walters and L. Demkow, *op. cit.,* pp. 207-214.

Chapter VI

LANGUAGE ARTS FOR THE DISADVANTAGED

Mildred Letton Wittick*

CHILDREN IN ELEMENTARY classrooms today will be a part of the world of the twenty-first century. It is difficult to forecast the new kinds of communication they will use. Already the world is very small. No nation can afford to have a large segment of population untrained in communication skills. Listening and speaking will probably remain the most frequently used means of communication. The articulate interchange of recorded ideas will demand higher levels of proficiency in reading and writing.

The child disadvantaged in the language arts cannot cope with the world of the twentieth century, much less the one in which he will live as an adult. The task of the school is to identify his problems, to redefine those goals related to his educational needs, and to provide a balanced program through which he can become an effectively participating member of his community.

THE LANGUAGE OF THE DISADVANTAGED CHILD

For a long time, culturally deprived children have been described as antagonistic toward school and disinterested in learning. Recent writers have suggested that the apparent rejection of school and education is probably due to cultural differences and divergent points of view, which children acquire in their families and ethnic groups. In the confusion of trying to reconcile diverse values, they may appear hostile and indifferent toward school.

They may challenge authority in unexpected ways. With minority groups, language sometimes becomes a weapon to exclude outsiders from invading their privacy. "Wherever there is a congregation of people, isolated for one reason or another from

---

*Professor of English, Paterson State College.

the main culture, language seems to become a weapon and a wall, a bulwark for the preservation of dignity and self."[1]

There is a common belief that poorly languaged children are also inarticulate. Eells and Havighurst found that deprived children use many words, even with some precision, but these words are not ones used in the classroom where the vocabulary has been described as *middle class*.[2]

New words that come into a language often appear first in slang expressions, and a large proportion of these have been in the special vocabulary of deprived groups. Gang language includes such colorful forms as *bop*—to fight; *snake*—a spy; *buce*—to shove; *kill*—a severe whipping; and *triflin'*—no good, dirty. The teacher working with disadvantaged children should have word lists with translations of the expressions pupils use at school. These language differences include words with emotional connotations, words with special meaning, colloquialisms and expressions, and peculiar grammar uses.[3]

Loban's study added much to the literature concerned with the language development of children. Among his findings were:

1. During the first seven years of schooling, subjects spoke more words in each succeeding year when they were measured. As they progressed, members of the high group used more and longer communication units than did the low subgroups.

2. The lower group said less than the high group during the first few years of schooling and some had more difficulty in saying it.

3. The low group used many more partial expressions than the high group.

4. Lack of agreement between subject and predicate, particularly in third person singular and consistency of verb tense proved major problems. Difficulty increased for Negro boys in grades one through three and decreased for Negro girls when these children came from homes using a southern Negro dialect.

5. For Negro subjects with southern background, using the verb *to be* appropriately proved to be twelve times as troublesome as for northern Caucasian or Negro subjects.

6. Reading, writing, listening and speaking showed a positive relation.[4]

The culturally deprived child, though he may seem to operate at a very low level, is not necessarily a slow learner. As he is able to overcome the language barrier or paucity of experiential background, he should be able to move along comfortably with other members of his group. The younger he is, the easier it is likely to be for him to master the language patterns for speech and writing.

LISTENING

The disadvantaged child is often severely handicapped in situations involving listening. He may have a short attention span; he may have poor auditory discrimination; he may spend much time daydreaming; he may lack experience to understand what he hears; he may be easily distracted; he may be immature both physically and socially; he may be generally careless and inaccurate; he may be mentally lazy. The poorly languaged child is likely to engage in marginal listening; that is, he may listen part of the time, then let his thoughts wander beyond the classroom. He needs many kinds of listening experiences—listening to stories, to poetry, to records, to class discussions, to jingles.

Importance of Listening

Rankin's early research showed that during the waking day the average person's time is spent: 42 per cent in listening, 32 per cent in speaking, 15 per cent in reading, and 11 per cent in writing.[5] Wilt found that elementary-level pupils spend more than 50 per cent of the school day listening to someone.[6]

Dimensions of the Listening Act

Many of the mental processes involved in getting meaning form an oral presentation are similar to those the reader uses in securing meaning from the written page. The listener uses auditory perception; the reader uses visual perception for the intake.

The listening act includes: auditory perception, grasp of meaning, reaction, and assimilation. As soon as the listener hears the speaker, he begins to try to understand the material. He is influenced in this step by his background experience, his vocabulary, his knowledge of the subject. His reactions to the remarks he hears are colored by his own opinions and attitudes on the subject, his mood, as well as the voice, personal appearance, and methods of presentation of the speaker. He may accept the new ideas he has heard and assimilate them so that his knowledge and attitude toward the topic are broadened and changed. On the other hand, he may reject the speaker's point of view completely.

Listening Defined

Staiger defines the basic characteristics of listening as:

Listening is a learned receptive skill. It is a personal, often private absorption of ideas and attitudes expressed through oral language. To listen implies attention and responsive thinking, sometimes only casual, often quite intent and indeed critical. Listening differs from hearing, which is a physiological process and does not involve interpretation. Listening varies according to the purposes of the listener, his background and interest in the topic, and the situation in which he listens. Listening, like reading, involves the selection of appropriate meanings and the organization of ideas according to their relationships. It also calls for evaluation, acceptance or rejection, internalization, and often appreciation of the ideas expressed. . . . unless it is recorded, it is impossible to relisten to a presentation, while a person may reread at his own pleasure.[7]

Levels of Listening

Strickland has proposed several levels of listening. The teacher of the disadvantaged may find the following check list, adapted from Strickland's material, helpful for recording, at different times, the pupil's progress.[8]

Check List For Levels of Listening
Name _____
Date _____

	Yes	No
Level 1. Is distracted by environment.		
2. Is half-listening; inserts only own ideas.		
3. Is passive, apparently absorbed but with little or no reaction.		

	Yes	No
4. Turns listening *on and off*; *in* when speech is related to own ideas, then *out*.		
5. Tells of own related experiences.		
6. Asks questions or comments.		
7. Appears to participate emotionally or mentally.		
8. Has a meeting of minds with speaker.		

Listening and Speaking

There is general agreement that speaking and listening are best taught together. While the teacher may have specific lessons for emphasizing the separate skills, speaking and listening are inevitably linked in the communication cycle. The speaker must always be aware of his listeners and their reactions. The listeners are affected by the skills of the speaker. One set of skills provide the outgo: the other set provides the intake. Both are linked because of the time element in oral communication.[9]

Teaching Listening Skills

A wide variety of materials and techniques have been developed for improving listening. For young disadvantaged children, the listening situation should be: brief; interesting; related to the child's needs; and require response on the part of the child, first with action then verbal involvement. First listening experiences may give practice in identifying sounds in and out of the classroom and listening to music. Soon pupils can listen to words in stories, poems, on records or tape recorders, and in listening games. (See Russell and Wagner entries in bibliography.) Throughout their school careers children will be listening to each other in conversations, discussions, on the telephone, and in performance situations.

More and more curriculum guides are including specific suggestions for teaching listening skills. These aids give the teacher purpose and direction for planning instruction. A guide described by Turchan outlines the program under the headings: Social, Secondary, Aesthetic, Critical, Concentrative (a study-type listening) and Creative Listening.[10]

To Help the Disadvantaged Listener

The teacher:

1. *Should eliminate distractors, especially potential ones.* (For example, if the class is to listen to a story, have all supplies removed from desk tops so that pencils, books, and pens will not be knocked to the floor during the listening period.)

2. *Must be aware of his own manner of listening to the children.* If the teacher is too busy to listen or "half-listens," the pupil soon ceases to continue efforts to communicate. "I don't recite," said Ted, "because she doesn't listen anyway."

3. Must remember listening improvement can be worked on every day through all areas of the curriculum.

4. Can help children to be aware of the sounds around them, as well as the words.

5. Can guide in the development of criteria for good listening habits.

6. Can help children analyze their own levels of listening.

7. Can prepare teaching materials to develop skill in each of the kinds of listening. The disadvantaged will need help at once with *Social and Concentrative Listening* (i.e., following directions). They should have the pleasure of *Aesthetic Listening* at this time.

8. Should be sure that pupils have directions clearly in mind before they listen. That is, they know why, how, and for what they are to listen in each situation.

9. Must evaluate children's listening skills through teacher observation, informal, teacher-made tests and standardized tests.

SPEAKING

Speech is man's chief tool of communication. He uses it every day, throughout the day, and in a great variety of situations. Speech is the skill we rely upon in our social contacts.

Through conversation and discussion, we express our thoughts and reveal our feelings, we seek and get cooperation from our companions; we inform, inspire, and persuade our listeners; we adjust differences and inconsistencies in purpose and viewpoint; and we bring our social environment under control. Moreover, our listeners tend to evaluate us on the basis of of speech and language patterns and accordingly decide what kind of person we are.[11]

Probably, the poorly languaged child is unaware of his speech until he enters school. He may be frustrated because his teacher and some of his peers cannot understand him. If he speaks another language, he may seek out other children in the school who use it. The older child who locates boys and girls in his own classroom who speak his native language may withdraw from attempts to learn English; he may retreat to the comfortable world which excludes his teacher and peers who do not understand him.

Improving the oral communication of the disadvantaged child is made more difficult because he reinforces his habitual speech patterns in hours outside the classroom. At home with parents and siblings, on the playground at recess and after school, and with his friends over the weekend, he continues to practice oral language patterns that he finds familiar, comfortable, and understood by his listeners.

Changing the speech patterns of the poorly languaged child takes a long time. The older the pupil, the longer it is likely to take, because he may be more resistant to change. It is difficult to prove to him that acceptable speech is desirable when he hears it used only by his teacher. The same problem must be faced when teaching him correct usage.

Speech is learned. It becomes a habit, and it can be taught. When incorrect patterns are practiced, however, it is difficult to eradicate them. One research study showed that children who spent the whole of their school lives in slum neighborhoods tended to retain their old speech patterns, while those who moved to economically better communities quickly adopted the oral expression and usage approved by the people living there.

The school must be prepared to plan in terms of years, not weeks or months, in working out a curriculum to meet the speech needs of the language disadvantaged. As with all speech improvement, practice must go on all day, every day, and there must be constant exposure to acceptable oral patterns.

> Using good speech depends in large part upon the learner's hearing that speech until it sounds natural. The learner, when a baby at home, combines hearing with speaking. All too often the child from the culturally different home hears very little standard speech other than the teacher's. In consequence, he considers what is taught 'school language.' Generous use of recordings, with many voices, can change the situation.[12]

Every classroom should have a tape recorder and a phonograph. Materials prepared by the school make it possible for pupils to hear good colloquial language. The poorly languaged child must hear good speech so often that, even though he may not adopt it for himself in the beginning, he becomes comfortable when he hears it.

Articulation

Most pupils need to improve articulation skills; most disadvantaged children have specific problems in this area. The classroom teacher, with knowledge of the consonant sounds of English and how they relate to speech improvement, can work successfully with children who have articulation problems. Severe problems should be referred to the speech correctionist. The four most common articulation problems of children are: *substitutions, omisions, distortions,* and *additions or insertions of sounds.* Among the poorly languaged, the number of such errors is multiplied.

Speech Activities

The poorly languaged child needs many experiences in a great variety of speech activities. He can learn, too, by being an alert listener as his classmates engage in oral language. He should participate through oral reading, conversations, discussions, story telling, reporting, making explanations, giving directions, and dramatizations.

Two activities that are especially effective with the culturally disadvantaged are *creative dramatics* and *choral speaking.* Creative dramatics can draw upon almost every other school subject for its content. Children have many ideas about how to dramatize a story from their readers or a part of a literary selection. Historical events as presented in social studies texts can become alive and meaningful when the group interprets them in dramatic form. Many children spend free time in dramatic play—being the teacher, running the household, shopping at the supermarket, launching a missle, being an auto mechanic or a jet pilot. The teacher who observes the poorly languaged child in dramatic play can note not only his current interests, but also the extent of his imagination and originality. As he becomes more secure and facile with the *language of the school,* he will use it in dramatic play.

The values of choral speaking in the classroom situation are numerous. This activity can contribute to the enjoyment and appreciation of poetry; to the speech improvement of its participants; to the confidence of the shy or self-conscious child; to cooperative effort on the part of the child who has always been the group leader, perhaps even the bully; to a recognition of the talents of others; and to an understanding of the importance of team work if a reading is to be successful. The disadvantaged child often lacks most of these experiences.

There are five types of choral speaking: refrain, two-part or antiphonal, line-a-child, part-arrangement, and unison speech.[13] *Refrain* is the easiest introduction to choral speaking for both children and teacher. A soloist, teacher or a pupil, reads the narrative, if it is a ballad, and the class joins in the refrain. Some of the Mother Goose rhymes, as well as poems which have a frequently repeated line, lend themselves to the refrain type arrangement. This is probably the most enjoyable way to introduce choral speaking to poorly languaged children.

Two-part, also called antiphonal speaking, uses, as its name indicates, two voices or two groups of voices. Question-and-answer type poetry lends itself easily to such an arrangement.

Line-a-child gives each child a chance to speak one or more lines by himself. The disadvantaged child may not volunteer at once for such an opportunity. Line-a-child arrangements often use a unison beginning or ending, or both.

Part arrangement is difficult to arrange. The inexperienced teacher can find books of choral speaking in which these arrangements have been worked out.[14] Hughes has two anthologies which may be useful.[15]

Unison speech is the most difficult to perfect. It involves all voices speaking as one. This requires "absolute precision in attack, rate of speech, pausing, phrasing, inflection, pronunciation, and emphasis."[16] Teachers who often have the least success with choral speaking think that the term is synonymous with unison speech and begin with this type. Probably the most unpleasant productions are those in which a teacher has directed a class in a twelve-or sixteen-line poem in unison. Children tend to drag the words out after a while, to develop a sing-song pattern, and, because the precision of attack is faulty, words become unintelligible. A safe rule for working with the language disadvantaged would be to avoid using the unison type except for occasional single lines of poems.

The teacher can use the first three types of choral speaking— refrain, two-part, and line-a child—with most groups. Experience with poetry should be pleasurable; children will often memorize parts or all of a poem without having this as an assignment. They can begin to appreciate the importance of words in creating a feeling, describing a person, or establishing a mood.

READING

Most disturbing to those who work with the disadvantaged pupil is the knowledge that his communication skills are minimal. If he is in the first grade, he is likely to not be ready to read when his more verbally experienced classmates are. If he is in the middle grades, he is likely to be two or more years below the reading achievement of his peers.

"The general estimate of reading inability among school children is 15 to 20 per cent, while among educationally deprived children the disability estimate is as high as 50 per cent. The significance of reading cannot be overestimated because all too often the deprived child remains retarded in all subjects due to his inability to read.[17]

Readiness for Learning

Every classroom teacher has long been aware of the importance of a child's readiness for reading at the time instruction begins. However, with the culturally deprived pupil, readiness for learning in the environment presented by the classroom must precede, or parallel closely, the development of readiness for reading. The greatest single handicap these children have academically is lack of facility with language. Usually, they have had little exposure to books and limited personal experiences which would promote and sustain intellectual curiosity.

Since beginning readers enjoy reading about familiar things, the development of (1) their experiential background and (2) their facility with language becomes the major emphasis in the school's initial contacts with the disadvantaged child.

In building learning readiness, the teacher should first observe the child's skill in auditory discrimination since this may be closely linked with his oral language patterns. Through oral language experiences he becomes aware of sentence structure and vocabulary. The length of his attention span and ability to complete a task should be considered. His visual discrimination of word elements is important as well as his level of interest in books and printed words. His health, alertness, and emotional adjustment are factors the teacher must take into account in the general learning situation.

Readiness for Reading

Nursery school and kindergarten experiences can be especially valuable in the development of reading readiness. In the primary grades, special effort must be made to locate reading problems early so that more difficult remedial work later can be minimized or eliminated.

Clark found that the culturally disadvantaged child often lacks the very qualities that are needed for readiness to read: understanding and speaking the language, visual and auditory discrimination, motor coordination, attention and memory, the ability to form concepts, good relationship to adults, order in living, and self and group image.[18]

The speech patterns of many disadvantaged children differ so sharply from accepted English as to impede their learning to read. Their chances for success improve when speech therapy precedes or accompanies reading instruction. Such programs would ideally be concentrated in the primary years, before the pupils' pessimism can crystallize, but in many school districts there are children who need help at all grade levels. Even high schools must sometimes offer regular classes in elementary English. The curriculum should be so organized that children can progress at their best individual rates, and the over-all organization of the school should be flexible enough to allow this kind of progress.[19]

Auditory Discrimination

Perhaps the first impression the teacher has of the child is related to his auditory discrimination. How he pronounces words reveals how he hears them, and how he hears them will often determine how he will spell them. The child who says "gov-er-ment" often spells it this way. Many children say *walk* for the past tense *walked* because they do not hear a difference in endings. Sometimes children confuse words that sound alike and use them incorrectly. For example, a sixth-grade pupil used *antidote* for *anecdote* in oral reporting, but the teacher did not discover this substitution until it appeared in the child's written work.

Errors in auditory discrimination, combined with careless visual discrimination perpetuate the same type of mistakes in oral reading. It is extremely important for the teacher himself to have acute auditory discrimination in order to detect pupils' initial errors so that mistakes are not reinforced through repeated incorrect usage. The pupil must hear such differences as: *ran, rang; then, than, that; thin, thing; bend, band, bond;* and *top, pop,* and *hop.* The teacher who is aware that practice in auditory discrimination provides an excellent opportunity to develop listening skills prepares his lessons to strengthen this interrelationship.

Experience Charts

Experience charts, commonly used to make a gradual transition from the prereading to the actual reading stage, serve an additional purpose for the poorly languaged child. He often has a limited vocabulary, pronunciation patterns unlike those of his more advantaged peers, a special vocabulary of his own not understood by middle-class children or their teachers, and an unconventional sentence structure.

Unfamiliar with many of the common childhood experiences, he also lacks the vocabulary with which to describe them. The school must not only provide experiences which will give him subjects for conversation and dictation, but also must help him build the vocabulary needed to communicate his ideas.

Huus points out how simple activities may build experiences.

Take a trip around the school if you cannot get a bus or make other arrangements to take the children off the school grounds. Let the principal or supervisor tell what he does, what he thinks the school should do, and how the children can cooperate. Visit the librarian, the custodian, or another class, or take a walk around the grounds. Be alert to possibilities for extending the children's vocabulary: talk about the maple tree, the oak, the elm, rather than just "trees," or say "corridor" instead of "hall," and notice how quickly the children follow suit.

When you are back in the classroom, make a chart of each visit, using these later to call attention to such details as the first sentence, "Mary's sentence," to capital letters and their uses, to letters that look alike, to words that are identical or similar, and to the elements that make a story interesting. Illustrate the chart by drawing or making models.

The activity of making the chart lets the children see the language arts as an integrated whole, for they *tell* the story, the teacher *writes* it down, someone *reads* what it says, and the rest *listen*.[20]

The experience chart has many uses in the middle as well as primary grades. It may provide a summary of a topic which has been studied, present a work plan, record a class experience, list words for special study, or indicate standards for performance. It may be helpful for the poorly languaged child in these grades where he can observe correct usage, conventional sentence situations, punctuation and capitalization. He may enjoy making an appropriate illustration for a chart or even writing the content of the experience himself. He should be encouraged to work on charts that: (1) require the use of complete sentences; (2) present ideas accurately and clearly and (3) communicate concepts of interest to the group. These are skills which are needed particularly by the language disadvantaged.

Suggestions for the Use of Experience Charts

1. Begin with very simple sentences which the child or group dictates.
2. Allow space at the bottom of some of the charts for illustrations made by the children. The lower part of the chart is suggested for illustrations so that the words to be read are more easily visible from different parts of the room during the day.
3. Always have at least one old experience chart, along with the most recent one on display where everyone in the room can read it. Encourage the re-reading of the charts as a spare time activity.
4. Occasionally, let the children re-read the old experience charts aloud. This will help them to discover that they *are* gaining command of the English language.
5. For children who have begun to master writing, encourage them to expand the material included on the experience chart by writing a paragraph or two of their own describing the same experience.

Informal Reading Inventories

For the disadvantaged child who is severely retarded in reading, a standardized oral and/or silent reading test may reveal little helpful information for setting up an instructional program. An informal reading inventory may be more revealing. The classroom teacher may find that talking informally to the child about reading is helpful. He may reveal how he feels about reading, what he thinks is involved in learning to read, why he thinks he has reading problems, how he attacks new words, what he thinks might help him. Even young children who have been asked such questions reveal considerable insight into their own problems.

The Dictionary

The disadvantaged reader seldom has the skill to use the dictionary as an aid. More formal dictionary skills are now being introduced in grade three instead of grade four, and picture dictionaries are appearing in kindergarten as well as grade one. For the culturally deprived child, the entries and illustrations may not be very meaningful. For this reason, such children should be encouraged to make picture dictionaries of their own. They may even do the illustrations themselves if there are no magazines or advertising materials that can be cut up. Some of the words that have been selected for personal dictionaries by disadvantaged readers include: wheel, wire, car, stairs, door, shoe, ball, cup, window, cop, and sack. The lack of experience of the pupil dictionary makers is reflected in these words.

Artley suggests that three kinds of readiness are needed in order to make the introduction of the dictionary a meaningful experience: readiness for locating words, readiness for deriving the meaning, and readiness for pronunciation.[21]

Disadvantaged readers in the middle and upper grades often increase their interest in words through the construction of a personal dictionary, usually illustrated. A Spanish-speaking child might be encouraged to make a dictionary of words used in English that are of Spanish origin, i.e., *siesta, patio, tortilla,* and *chile con carne.* For a wealth of ideas for using the dictionary in the elementary school, the teacher should refer to the April, 1964, issue of *Elementary English.* The seventeen articles in this number discuss the dictionary.

The Library

There has been a renewed interest in providing more and better library facilities for the disadvantaged pupil. Librarians are needed. Two recent reports were discouraging. In one elementary school equipped with a library, the principal would not let books be taken home because: (1) they might be lost; (2) they might be damaged by rain or snow; (3) the children would read them with dirty hands and *spoil* the copies. When books are left on the shelves because they look more attractive filled, they no longer serve the purpose for which they were written. A closed book cannot communicate.

Boys must be provided with books that extend their specific interests, like sports, science, automobiles, adventure, science fiction, and biographies. These must carry a low vocabulary load but be written at a high interest level. Libraries in disadvantaged neighborhoods should be kept open all day Saturday and throughout the weekday evenings. Where practical, they might be open for a period on Sunday afternoons. However, having libraries open won't get disadvantaged children into them. Teachers and volunteer workers (in lieu of interested parents) must help these boys and girls "learn the ropes" so that they can feel and handle library visits comfortably. Even *handling* books must become second nature.

> Reading materials and visual aids should take account of the background of the children who will use them. The texts and illustrations should not refer exclusively to the middle and upper classes. In addition, special attention to the history, culture, and contributions of Negroes and of Spanish-speaking people in the United States can foster self-respect, mutual respect, and a sense of identification with the school and the nation among children who are now largely ignored in school materials. Moreover, learning about progress in Puerto Rico or about contributions of American Indians and Negroes is appropriate for children of all backgrounds. And children who have lived in other places can often teach the class something about their earlier homes.[22]

Reading Programs for the Disadvantaged

Several years ago, the Detroit Public Schools developed a set of readers at the primary level in which the stories and illustrations portrayed predominantly Negro families. The first results of a study with first graders indicated that Negro children using these materials appeared to make more progress in reading than comparable children using typical readers. Teachers observed that the children using the experimental materials were more interested in learning to read and in reading books for pleasure. An excellent and detailed explanation of the Detroit Great Cities Project has been done by Washner.[23]

In 1962 in New York City, *Mobilization for Youth* introduced a homework-helper program for 600 elementary school children. Two hundred and forty underprivileged high-school students helped elementary school pupils of similar background. The high school students, who were making satisfactory scholastic progress, spent one or two, two-hour periods a week with their pupils working under the supervision of experienced teachers. Major efforts generally involved reading instruction.

During his initial contacts with formal education, the language disadvantaged child needs more help than schools usually provide. He can profit from supervised study after school, from special help in reading, from individual instruction in speech, and from direct attention to study skills and ways of handling homework. He needs direction in learning to listen, in lengthening his attention span, and in learning to concentrate.

Volunteer workers should be used more often for this out-of-school day direction. As New York City has discovered, there are many adults willing to volunteer their services. Several sources can provide such volunteers. Retired persons, especially teachers, may be secured. Some cities are using high school students who supervise study and give guidance with homework assignments a few hours a week. Unemployed housewives may have time to serve. The government's anti-poverty program will provide funds to pay some of these workers. Research might be profitable to find out whether there are potential high-school dropouts among the disadvantaged who could serve effectively as tutors for primary children of similar background who need help in reading, writing, and speaking. It might effect a change in attitude toward school for both participants and encourage the tutor to gain a higher level of mastery of language arts skills for himself.

WRITING

The culturally disadvantaged are often less interested in writing than reading. After the mechanics of handwriting are mastered, the child is confronted with the annoying realization that he can think faster than he can write. In practical writing, he may resort to copying material verbatim from books or magazines. Once he has hit upon this scheme, he no longer even needs to think. He can perform the task almost automatically.

He will plead "nothing to write about" or "nothing ever happens to me" when the class is engaged in personal (or creative) writing. Of course, this is not true. Observation and imagination are needed for a creative product. Culturally disadvantaged children have both; it simply takes longer to awaken them to what they already know and have seen but have not thought about consciously.

Writing, Practical and Personal

Paucity of vocabulary is a real handicap for the child who tries to record his thoughts and feelings in writing. Even the pupil with some oral skill in English is easily discouraged by problems in spelling, mechanics of expression, and handwriting. Minimize emphasis on mechanics of expression in the initial stages. Teach proofreading even to first-grade writers. If writing activities are short, children can proofread more effectively.

Concentrate at First on the Development of Ideas

1. In personal writing, this includes observations made through sight, sound, touch, taste, and smell. In the classroom, sight and sound are used most often.
2. Encourage children to keep a diary. Entries may be only one sentence in length, but urge the writer to record something he observed during the day.

Make Writing Experiences Meaningful

For example, how can you do this with letter writing? One of the common problems here is related to the difficulty of placing this activity in a meaningful setting. No one is challenged by writing a letter which will never be read except by someone who will correct the errors. There are numerous pen-pal organizations where teachers can secure the names of children, in foreign countries or other parts of the United States, who want to exchange correspondence.

A recent experiment in letter writing within a school system in northern New Jersey has proved very successful. It began when one third grade child during a discussion of letter writing asked if he could write a real letter to his friend who attended a school in another neighborhood. The teacher approved and decided she would contact the teacher of her pupil's friend. After a telephone conversation, the instructors decided that the members of their two groups might be interested in corresponding with each other. The teachers met, discussed the interests and activities of their pupils and paired them as correspondents. When they returned to the teaching of letter writing in their classrooms, they gave the children the names of their local pen pals. All the first letters were sent to the other school in one large envelope. Any communication the children wished to continue beyond the first time was sent by individuals through the mail.

The teachers were not prepared for the deluge of enthusiasm for letter writing which followed. The third graders seemed to have a great many things to say to each other. Four months later, the group which initiated the project decided they wanted to meet the persons with whom they had been corresponding so they planned a party, sent an invitation to the other class, and waited anxiously for a reply. When the acceptance came, the group set about at once to plan an hour's entertainment. The teachers were apprehensive about whether the children might be shy and silent upon meeting these peers for the first time. However, their fears were needless; the children, through their correspondence, already knew a great deal about each other, and simply seemed to begin where they had left off in their last letters. There was so much conversation and showing as well as explaining about projects in the classroom that there was hardly time for eating the refreshments—cupcakes. At last report, the host group was expecting to be the guests at the other school.

The advantages of this kind of letter-writing activity for culturally disadvantaged children are numerous. The child can be matched to his correspondent: in sex, in present level of writing ability, in current interests, in nationality, if this child is a recent arrival in this country, or regionally if the child has come from some other part of the United States. The child can be encouraged to write short but entertaining letters and to include illustrations occasionally if this helps him to communicate. He may describe what he looks like; he may discuss his hobbies, his pets, his best subjects at school, his weekend activities, his family, and best friends in his school. If he can eventually meet the child who receives his letters, it may prove an especially rewarding experience.

Make Writing Experiences Enjoyable

The writing of haiku may be an interesting challenge for poorly languaged children in upper-primary and middle grades. The haiku is an ancient form of Japanese poetry three lines in length; the first and third have five syllables, the second seven. There is no metric pattern. Lines do not rhyme although some translators have made the first and third lines rhyme. This should be discouraged among young writers. Children should be aware of the 5-7-5 pattern but should not be limited to so structured a form. If more or fewer syllables express the thought better, this is acceptable. Emphasis should be on the thought and the best way to communicate it.

The purpose of the haiku is to present an observation that one makes at a particular moment. Its structure helps to limit the writer to one main thought. Most haiku deal with nature in some way and indicate the season of the year.

> If to the moon
> one puts a handle—what
> a splendid fan!
> Sokan[24]

How very cool it feels
taking a noonday nap, to have
a wall against my heels!
Basho[25]
A spring day—and:
in the garden, sparrows
bathing in the sand!
Onitsura[26]

Buson (1715-1783), and Basho, who lived earlier, are considered the two greatest haiku writers. Buson wrote more than thirty haiku on the subject of spring rain.

Afternoon shower . . .
Walking and talking in the street:
Umbrella and raincoat![27]

Kindergarten and first grade teachers have found this poem lends itself to illustration. One first-grade artist drew a series of children in yellow coats walking single file in the rain. Each figure held a brightly colored umbrella which rested on his shoulders completely hiding his head. The haiku is especially good to use with children who are easily discouraged with writing. (1) It is very short. (2) It does not rhyme. (3) It expresses one idea. (4) Almost any observation or everyday experience can become the subject of a haiku. (5) This poetic form is the contribution of a foreign culture, unlike our own, but worthy of attention. The disadvantaged of foreign birth may begin to understand how all nationalities contribute to the culture of the world. (6) In Japan today, haiku are widely published, but most people write them for sheer personal pleasure and to share with friends. This sharing-with-friends can help to break down the generally negative attitude many children, not only the disadvantaged, have toward all poetry.

The role of Haiku poetry in creative writing encourages the student to embellish and create according to his own level of experience. In turn, this allows for both spontaneity and the development of ever richer nuances of interpretation. This represents the very essence of the creative act.[28]

Work with Children on the Errors They Make in Real Writing Situations

We have the delicate three-way task of making the writing a learning experience for the child, giving him a personally satisfying experience, and putting aside the temptation of overwhelming him with his errors.

One afternoon the eighth graders in a classroom were asked to describe what they had seen when they walked home from school and back again after lunch. Some pupils wrote descriptions of houses, yards, pet animals, or people. A few children described activities in their neighborhood. Then the teacher came to Michael's paper. If this paper were turned in to you, what would you do?

Me and the Garbageman

During the lunch hour I usually go by my friends store.
He is a photographer named Joe $_____$. It is only two blocks from school so there isn't very much to see.
I was walking to my friends store. In front it was a white Garbage. I was watching him and then noticed a nylon stocking over his head. Because I was looking at him he said, "What are you looking at." So I asked what the stoking was for. He said it was to keep the Garbage of his hair. Now I know what Garbage men wear stokings over the heads for.
Just as I was walking away I stared laughing because he was bald.
As I was to school I saw in the window of the cleaners a sign that said: "Free Goldfish".
So I stopped in and asked about it the man who ownes the store said that if you spend $15 by Dec. 15, 19__ you get 2 goldfish, a goldfish bowl Gravel seaweed and food. I thanked him and kept on walking to school.

Is this paper illiterate for an eighth-grader? What about the content? Surely it has a definite style; it is entertaining. The writer is a keen observer and is in close contact with his neighborhood world.

Can this writing be salvaged? First of all, only a few words are misspelled, only about 4 per cent, statistically speaking. He misspelled *stocking* twice, but he had it correct once. Proofreading would have caught several of the gross errors. Although he had problems in punctuation and paragraphing, he showed some knowledge of the use of quotation marks.[29]

Michael should be asked about his title. Why did he word it as he did? Why did he capitalize *garbage* in the body of his material? How did he know that the garbageman was bald when the man apparently was wearing a nylon stocking on his head? The writer did not give his reader this information.

> In working with Michael it might help to point out the kinds of errors he made interfere with the communication of his ideas to the reader. Often pupils in the upper grades fail to realize that spelling and the accepted mechanics of expression, as well as language itself, are man-made. It is because we have regularized spelling and mechanics that we are able not only to communicate with one another but to understanding the past as well.[30]

Encourage Children to Illustrate Their Own Writing

Whole stories can be told through a series of pictures, i.e., the comic strip. Oftedal, working with a third-grade group at the Laboratory School of The University of Chicago, found that, when pupils used 12" x 18" drawing paper and folded it into parts, they could use these parts in planning a sequence of pictures.[31] When stories were developed using this technique, the children recorded more ideas and even wrote more words and sentences than when they expressed themselves in writing alone. This plan is especially helpful for the disadvantaged child who lacks minimal skill in writing.

Remember that writing skills develop very slowly. Patience and willingness to reteach are necessary assets of the language arts teacher of all children, not only those who are culturally disadvantaged.

THE DEVELOPMENT OF GAMES

Culturally disadvantaged children are "games"-oriented. Riessman points out that these games usually involve extra-verbal communication and are not word-bound. "Also, most games (not all, by any means), are person-centered and generally are concerned with direct action and visible results. Games are usually sharply defined and structured, with clear-cut goals. The rules are definite and can be absorbed. The deprived child enjoys the challenge of the game and feels he can 'do' it; this is in sharp contrast to many verbal tasks.[32]

However, culturally different children are not familiar with word games. Davis reports that "by the time they are two years old, the children from the lower socioeconomic groups already are inferior in verbal skills to those from the middle class. . . . Moreover, after the primary grades, the superiority of the middle-class child in verbal skills and academic habits *increases* faster than that of low-status children.[33] This is brought about through parental pressures on the middle-class child, the pace set by the school, and his opportunities to reinforce his language experiences through trips and reading.

When the teacher feels that a game would provide motivation in language learning, as in vocabulary development, sentence building, phrase reading, punctuation, or correct usage, he should develop a game whose content is geared to the specific needs of the children who will play it. The pattern may follow some familiar game. Here are examples developed by the author.

Lost Word. Use the rules for Old Maid. Each player matches words in pairs and discards these face up in the center of the table. The dealer allows the player on his left to draw one card from those remaining in his hand. If it makes a pair with a card already in his hand, this player discards and play continues in the same way. The player left with the misspelled or "Lost Word" loses the game.

In selecting words for the pack, use (1) words currently being studied in spelling by the class; or (2) words currently being used in writing in content area subjects; or (3) spelling demons; or other words needed in the writing activities at the particular grade level. The number of pairs of words may vary according to the grade level and the number of players. Suggested words for a pre-primer first-grade pack might include: *run, ran, on, in, go, up, down, and, stop, pop, top, one, the, under,*

over, two, three, big, little, dog, dogs, look, and sun. Using 3"
x 5" cards, write, in manuscript, two cards for each word except
one. Make only one card for the word you have selected as the
"Lost Word" which had no pair and becomes the equivalent for
the "Old Maid" card.

The teacher can develop playing packs for *Lost Word* to
meet the special needs of small groups of pupils. With young
culturally deprived children, this game may also be useful for
developing visual discrimination if the words are selected for
this purpose, i.e., *run, ran, big, bag, top, stop, on, in, dot, doll.*

Tip Top. This is a game to give practice in correct usage.
It follows the general rules of Old Maid except that the odd
card becomes a bonus. The cards use sentences, one correct and
one incorrect, to be matched. When a player gets a pair of sentences, he announces his discard when it is his turn. He must
discard with the correct sentence on *top* of the incorrect one. If
other players agree that he has made the correct choice, he
keeps the pair of cards in front of him and scores one point. If
he is wrong, the two cards are put in the center of the table in
a discard pile. Play passes to the person on his left. Examples
of sentences that might be used:

1. They is late. They are late.
2. Jane and me are going. Jane and I are going.
3. Jack come yesterday. Jack came yesterday.
4. I and John went. John and I went.
5. Fred, Tom, and me were late. Fred, Tom and I were late.

When all the sentences have been matched, one player will
be left with the odd card, marked *Bonus.* He scores an extra
point. Since there may be tied scores and playing time will be
short as pupils gain proficiency, more than one game may need
to be played to determine a winner.

In *Tip Top* a number of sets may be made, each giving practice in a different phase of correct usage. For example, one
whole set could be designed to give practice in the use of *I* and
me.

Capunct (for first grade children). Two to six players. Each
player has a numbered 5" x 8" card with two or three sentences
written in manuscript or typed on it. These lack punctuation
and capital letters. A number of one-inch squares are placed
face down between the players. On some of these squares are a

large C (to make a letter a capital) ; on other are periods. Each player draws a square at his turn and places it on the sentence to make it correct. The winner is the player who gets his card filled correctly first. To check his score there should be a colored 3" x 5" card correctly completed and numbered to correspond with the number on a player's card.

Set A   Number 1

1. i saw mary [.]
    [C]   [C]

2. she is at school [.]
    [C]

When the class is ready, the teacher may add cards required, the use of question marks and commas. For middle-grade players, more difficult uses of capital letters and other marks of punctuation should be added. Again, each set of sentences should have a colored 3" x 5" answer card numbered to correspond with the number on a player's card.

Set C   Number 7

1. when jack came [,] we began the game [.]
    [C]

2. he bought batteries [,] wire [,] tubes [,]
    [C]
    and an extension cord [.]

3. wherever she goes [,] her friends [,]
    [C]

    betty and sue [,] tag along [.]
    [C]   [C]

4. "ouch!" cried ted [.]
    [C]   [C]

If each set has sixteen player cards, four players can play four games without using the same cards again. Sets may be coded A, B, C, etc., according to the kind of practice each provides.

Suggestion: With older players, the size of the square may be reduced to ¾". In typing the sentences, double space the lines and leave two spaces between each word.

Note: When a game includes quotation marks, it may be played faster if a set emphasizing this usage is made providing an ample supply of squares showing beginning and ending quotation marks.

Def (Definition) Bingo. Each player has a card with nine squares on it, each of which contains a word. These squares may be about 2" x 2" or 3" x 3". The card may be of light-colored construction paper. The words should be ones which the children are adding to their speaking, reading, or writing vocabularies. On each small square of a stiff white paper 2" x 2" or 3" x 3", whichever size was used on the playing card, is typed or written the definition of a word that appears on a playing card. The purpose of the game is to draw a white square from the center pile and, if possible, to match the definition to a word on one's card. If they match, the definition is placed on the word. The game is won by the player who first covers all his words. As in bingo, the same words may appear on several cards and there are several copies of the same definition among the white squares.

Sets of such *Def Bingo* games may be made up for science units, geography, health, the new math, and reading.

Player's card for social studies vocabulary:

mountain	lake	gulf
island	inlet	ocean
peninsula	river	sea

A narrow strip of water running into the land or between islands.

This kind of game is especially appropriate for pupils in the middle and upper grades. Since they understand the construction of bingo, members of the group can make up the cards and definitions themselves as soon as the words to be defined have been selected.

One of the advantages of the use of language arts games with the culturally disadvantaged child is that the learning can take place in a small group situation. He can be placed with children who have had wider experiences if the teacher thinks this is advantageous.

Because culturally disadvantaged children are often interested in mechanical devices, the use of teaching machines, tape recorders, phonographs, and other audio-visual aids can provide motivation for improving language skills.

EVALUATION

Because the culturally disadvantaged child may not be school-oriented, the usual methods of evaluating his initial progress in the language arts are likely to produce disappointing results. The teacher may wish to use a guide similar to the following check list at intervals of six to eight weeks to chart each child's progress. Each teacher should develop his own material.

Name _____

Date _____

	Yes	No
I. *General Attitude Toward School*		
A. Is his school attendance pattern satisfactory?		
B. Does he arrive at school on time?		
C. Does he turn in assignments promptly?		
D. Does he respect		
1. School property?		
2. Other children's property?		
E. Does he daydream, seeming to remove himself from the school environment?		
II. *Progress in Listening*		
A. Does he give his attention to the person making announcements and/or giving directions?		

	Yes	No

1. Can he follow oral directions:
    a. Involving 1 direction?
    b. Involving 2 directions?
    c. Involving 3 directions?
2. Can he follow oral directions that have been given only once?
B. Does he understand the oral reports of classmates?
C. Can he reconstruct the sequence of events in a simple story he has heard?
D. Can he recall some of the details he has heard in an oral presentation?

III. *Progress in Speaking*
A. General
    1. Does he use English (rather than a foreign language) and/or more acceptable English on the playground?
    2. Does he cooperate with those who are giving him speech instruction?
B. Mechanics
    1. Does he continue to improve in use of correct pronunciation of words?
    2. Does he speak in phrases rather than isolated words?
    3. Does he use whole sentences with increasing frequency?
    4. Does he place the accent on the correct syllable in common words which he uses often?
    5. Is he learning to group words so that there is rhythm to his speech?
    6. Can he hear the errors in speech that other children make?
        a. Can he indicate the correct form?
C. Activities
    1. Does he occasionally participate in class discussions?
    2. Can he make a brief oral report to his group?

	Yes	No

3. Can he describe a personal experience orally in a few sentences?
4. Does he take a solo part in choral speaking sometimes?
5. Can he tell a joke or story to his class satisfactorily?
6. Does he volunteer to participate in creative dramatics?
7. Can he dictate a story of his own on the tape recorder or for the teacher to record?

IV. *Progress in Reading*
A. Can he read a very short paragraph orally so that his classmates will understand it?
B. Does he ever read aloud at home to other brothers and sisters, or parents?
C. Does he have a growing sight vocabulary?
D. Can he use a simple dictionary or glossary?
E. Is he adding useful words to his reading vocabulary?
F. Can he reconstruct the sequence of events in a story he has read?
G. Can he recall some of the details in material he has read?
H. Does he comprehend what he reads?
I. Can he identify the author's purpose?

V. *Progress in Writing*
A. Content
  1. Is it interesting to the reader?
  2. Does it reflect the interest of the writer?
  3. Does it show careful observation by the writer?
  4. Does it show the imagination of the writer?
B. Mechanics
  1. Does he write in complete sentences?
  2. Do his sentences show variety in structure?

	Yes	No
3. Does he begin sentences with capital letters?		
4. Does he use a mark of punctuation at the end of each sentence?		
5. Is he improving in correct usage?		
6. Does he use legible handwriting?		

WORKING WITH PARENTS

For culturally disadvantaged children and their parents, the school represents a world which values reading and writing. When one has these skills at a very low and inadequate level, why willingly put one's self in this hostile environment?

The teacher of such children plays a double role. He must not only endeavor to reach the child, but he must make special efforts to communicate effectively with the parents.

Those mothers who are not employed should be urged to form small study groups organized by the school to (1) explain what the school is doing and (2) show the parent how she can help her children at home by knowing how to reinforce the school's curriculum. Often this means teaching the parent first what the child will study later. A successful experiment was carried on in 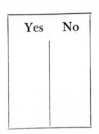 Chicago where a group of mothers met twice a month for two-hour afternoon sessions in which they learned what the children would be studying in reading and English. The adults were supervised in making a number of simple games such as "word bingo," using the vocabulary the children were using in school. The mothers learned how to pronounce spelling words correctly, had instruction in correct usage, and were shown how to judge their children's progress in handwriting.

The school that attempts such a project must solve the problem of how to staff it. Adult volunteers, especially retired school teachers, could possibly do this successfully. However, to be efficient, such a program must have an enthusiastic and informed liaison officer between the classroom teacher and the volunteer worker. Certainly there are times when the teacher himself should be a working member of the group.

The classroom teacher may also make a contact with the home by writing an occasional *Guide for Parents* which can be duplicated and sent home. Ideally, it would be explained at a meeting of room parents so that questions could be answered and samples of acceptable work shown. Realistically, one must admit that parents of the children who need the most help are likely to ignore the entire project. However, the plight of the disadvantaged child can only be improved one child at a time, so if the duplicated suggestions are responded to in even a few homes, the effort is worthwhile.

Guides for Parents to Use at Home

I. To improve *listening*

    A. The teacher can explain to parents, preferably in a face-to-face situation, the role they play in teaching children to follow directions the first time they are given without hearing them repeated two or three times. There are a number of games that children and parents may play at home:

        1. **Do This-Do That.** This usually involves a leader who makes a series of motions (i.e., hands on hips, hands over head, arms straight ahead at shoulder height), and with each motion says, "Do this," and the participants follow directions. When the leader says, "Do that," it is a signal for the group to remain still. Those who follow the directions on the signal "Do that," are out of the game.

        2. **Do It the First Time.** If parents and teachers can, in the initial stages, make a game of following directions the first time they are given, perhaps children can learn to hear instructions the first time they are given. In this game, the score should be kept by the child. For example, the kindergarten teacher or the parent tells the child to put away his blocks and come to the table for his juice. If he does this promptly, without the adult repeating directions, he scores one point. If directions must be repeated, he

receives no score. If he has a chart on a bulletin board or door on which to make his tally mark, he can see how well he has listened during a given period. Emphasis should be placed on listening, not obedience.

II. To improve *handwriting*
   A. The teacher can run off a duplicated copy of:
      1. Manuscript alphabet and numbers and/or
      2. Cursive alphabet and numbers (whichever the child uses)
      3. Samples of words the child must write often, as days of the week, names of the months, names of subjects, i.e., spelling, reading, handwriting, science, and geography. These also would be written in whichever alphabet the child uses.
   B. The teacher can write the child's first and last name on the duplicated alphabet sheet so the parent and the child have an example of acceptable handwriting.
      1. The teacher can show the parent how to use old newspapers for practice in manuscript writing. The want ad section is best for this. Cut the newspaper into four quarters. Turn the paper so that the lead lines between the columns become horizontal guide lines for manuscript writing. The lines of print then become guides for letters that are formed with vertical lines. For the child who likes to use crayons this height for manuscript writing (about 1⅞ inches) is not too large.

CONCLUDING STATEMENT

Our knowledge of how to meet the individual needs of the disadvantaged child is still minimal. We know that he cannot succeed in his school career without skill in each of the language arts areas: listening, speaking, reading, and writing. We know that he will get along better if he has parents who understand the goals of the school and have some idea of how the instructional program is designed to reach them. We know that many agencies must work beside the school to reinforce its efforts. We know the job takes patience, and it will not be completed in one generation.

MATERIALS FOR THE CLASSROOM TEACHER

The publications listed below may help the classroom teacher who wants ideas for the teaching of language arts. Although all discussions are not concerned exclusively with the language-disadvantaged child, their content is easily adapted for use with him.

I. *General*

Ching, Doris C. "Methods for the Bilingual Child," *Elementary English* XXXXII: 22-27, (January) 1965.

The author describes several methods that have been tried in teaching bilingual children to speak, read, and write the English language.

Frazier, Alexander. "Helping Poorly Languaged Children," *Elementary English*, XXXXI: 149-153, (February) 1964.

This material is adapted from a guide developed for use in a pilot study in elementary schools in Akron, Cincinnati, and Toledo, Ohio. The author considers who is poorly languaged and presents a framework for language development.

Jewett, Arno, Mersand, Joseph, and Gunderson, Doris V. *Improving English Skills of Culturally Different Youth in Large Cities*. Washington, D. C.: U. S. Department of Health, Education, and Welfare, Office of Education, 1964.

While this bulletin is designed especially for high-school English teachers, it offers suggestions for successful classroom practices that can be adapted for elementary classrooms.

Lloyd, Donald. "Intonation and Reading," *Education* 84: 538-41 (May) 1964.

The writer points out the values of intonation in reading instruction. Intonation may improve the oral language patterns of the child disadvantaged in speech.

Loban, Walter D. *The Language of Elementary School Children*. National Council of Teachers of English, Research Report No. 1. Champaign, Illinois: National Council of Teachers of English, 1963.

Reports a longitudinal study (1952-1959) of the use and control of language and the relations among speaking, reading, writing, and listening.

Strickland, Ruth G. *The Language of Elementary School Children: Its Relationship to the Language of Reading Textbooks and the Quality of Reading of Selected Children*. Bloomington, Indiana: Bureau of Educational Studies and Testing, School of Education, Indiana University, July, 1962, Volume 38, No. 4.

This study was designed to analyze the structure of children's language in the first through the sixth grade, to compare it with the structure of language in books in which children are taught to read, and to investigate, at the sixth-grade level, any apparent differences of quality of children's reading skill.

Wittick, Mildred Letton. "Selected References on Elementary-School Instruction: Language Arts," *Elementary School Journal*, 65: 103-108 (November) 1964.

This annual, annotated bibliography regularly contains current significant publications related to language arts instruction. Seventy entries appear in this list.

II. *Listening*

Blake, Howard E. "A Code for Teachers of Listening," *Elementary English*, XXXIX: (January) 1962.

The code includes twenty items which teachers may use as a check list to improve their teaching of listening.

Canfield, G. Robert. "How Useful Are Lessons on Listening?" *Elementary School Journal* 62: 146-51 (December) 1961.

The investigator compares the effectiveness of two types of instruction for developing the ability of fifth-graders to understand the spoken language.

Duker, Sam. *Listening Bibliography*. New York: The Scarecrow Press, Inc., 1964.

This annotated bibliography, with its 880 entries, is probably the most extensive one on listening.

Russell, David H. and Russell, Elizabeth F. *Listening Aids Through the Grades—One-hundred Ninety Listening Activities*. New York: Teachers College, Columbia University Bureau of Publications, 1959.

Practical ideas for the teaching of listening are presented.

Wagner, Guy, Hosier, Max, and Blackman, Mildred. *Listening Games—Building Listening Skills with Instructional Games*. Darien, Connecticut: Teachers Publishing Corporation, 1962.

In addition to games, the authors have included an "Index of Listening Skills" which summarizes the wide range of skills needed in the development of good listening habits, skills, and attitudes.

III. *Speaking*

Anderson, Paul. *Language Skills in Elementary Education*. New York: The Macmillan Company, 1964, p. 45-71.

The chapter devoted to speaking suggests a variety of activities which may appeal to the poorly languaged pupil.

Books, Charlotte K. "Some Approaches to Teaching Standard English as a Second Language," *Elementary English*, XXXI: 728-733 (November) 1964.

The author points out the difference between the language problems of the culturally different and the culturally deprived.

Dawson, Mildred A., Zollinger, Mariar, and Elwell, Ardell. *Guiding Language Learning,* Second Edition. New York: Harcourt, Brace & World, Inc., p. 126-146, and p. 200-255.

Presents a rich variety of speech activities for elementary-level classrooms.

Eisenon, Jon, and Ogilvie, Mardel. *Speech Correction in the Schools.* New York: The Macmillan Company, 1957.

The teacher may get help for handling specific speech problems here.

Language Arts for Today's Children. Commission on the English Curriculum of the National Council of Teachers of English. New York: Appleton-Century-Crofts, 1954, p. 106-143.

This chapter presents a careful discussion of speech and an extensive bibliography.

Mellencamp, Virginia. *Play and Say It.* Magnolia, Mass.: Expression Company, 1962.

This is a manual for an organized program of articulation training. The lessons and games should interest both the young and middle-grade disadvantaged child who has articulation problems.

IV. *Reading*

Figurel, J. Allen, Editor. "Sequence VIII—Teaching Reading to the Disadvantaged," *Improvement of Reading through Classroom Practice,* Vol. 9. Newark, Delaware: International Reading Association, 1964, p. 24-26 and 160-64.

These articles represent the suggestions made by several speakers at the IRA annual conference, 1964.

Mingoia, Edwin M. "A Program for Immature Readers," *Elementary English* XXXXI: 616-621 (October) 1964.

The author, a reading consultant, has worked out, in

considerable details, techniques especially appropriate for use with culturally deprived readers in the primary grades.

Monroe, Marion and Rogers, Bernice. *Foundations for Reading.* Chicago: Scott, Foresman and Company, 1964.

While this book deals largely with informal pre-reading procedures, it should give the teacher help in instructing the language-disadvantaged child.

Reading Teacher. "Reading Instruction for Disadvantaged Children," The *Reading Teacher,* Vol. XVIII. (March, 1965), The entire issue is devoted to the topic.

Robinson, H. Alan. *Reading and the Language Arts.* Supplementary Educational Monograph No. 93. Chicago: The University of Chicago Press, (December) 1963.

The interrelationships of reading and the other language arts are clarified, and suggestions for helping the culturally disadvantaged child with reading are made.

Robinson, H. Alan. *The Underachiever in Reading.* Supplementary Educational Monograph No. 92. Chicago: The University of Chicago Press, (December) 1962.

A number of authors have written about methods of teaching and the preparation of reading material for the culturally disadvantaged.

V. *Writing*

Applegate, Maurel. *Easy in English.* Evanston, Ill.: Row, Peterson and Co., 1960.

This volume describes a variety of techniques that teachers have used successfully in developing the writing skills of pupils.

Applegate, Mauree. *Freeing Children to Write.* New York: Harper and Row, 1963.

This expands the author's earlier discussions of children's creative writing and includes many examples of their work.

Burrows, Alvina T. *Teaching Composition*. What Research Says to the Teacher Series, No. 18. Washington, D. C. Department of Classroom Teachers, National Education Association, 1959.

Emphasis in this publication is on items which promise to be of most help to classroom teachers of composition in elementary schools.

Burrows, Alvina Trent, Ferebee, June D. Jackson, Doris C., and Saunders, Dorothy O. *They All Want to Write*. Englewood Cliffs, N. J.: Prentice-Hall, Inc., 1952.

Although the first edition of this book was published in 1939, it still remains a definitive report of written English in the elementary school. The discussion of individual differences in writing is useful for the teacher of language-disadvantaged pupils.

National Conference on Research in English. *Children's Writing: Research in Composition and Related Skills*. Champaign, Illinois: National Council of Teachers of English, 1960-1961.

The authors consider not only composition in the primary and intermediate grades, but also discuss grammar, handwriting, spelling, and evaluation.

Wittick, Mildred Letton. "Correctness and Freshness—Can Children's Writing Have Both?" *Elementary School Journal* 60: 295-300, (March) 1960.

This article points out the advantages of teaching children to proofread and analyzes the personal writing of several poorly languaged children.

REFERENCES

1. Charles J. Calitri, "The Nature and Values of Culturally Different Youth," *Improving English Skills of Culturally Different Youth*, Washington, D. C.: U. S. Department of Health, Education, and Welfare, Office of Education, 1964, p. 2.
2. Kenneth Eells, *et al.*, *Intelligence and Cultural Differences* (Chicago: University of Chicago Press, 1951), p. 43.

3. *Unique Language Differences* from duplicated material developed for the public schools in Decatur, Illinois.
4. Walter D. Loban, *The Language of Elementary School Children,* Champaign, Illinois: National Council of Teachers of English, 1963, pp. 82-89.
5. Paul Rankin, "The Importance of Listening Ability," *English Journal,* XVII, (October, 1928), pp. 623-630.
6. Miriam Wilt, "A Study of Teacher Awareness of Listening as a Factor in Elementary Education," *Journal of Educational Research,* XLIII (April, 1950), pp. 626-636.
7. Ralph C. Staiger, "Examining the Basic Characteristics of Listening and Speaking: Defining the Terms," *Children and Oral Language,* Helen K. Mackintosh (editorial chairman), Washington, D. C.: Association for Childhood Education International, also ASCD, IRA, and NCTE, 1964, p. 3.
8. Ruth G. Strickland, *The Language Arts in the Elementary School* (Boston: D. C. Heath and Company, 1957), p. 119.
9. Mildred A. Dawson, Marion Zollinger, and Ardell Elwell, *Guiding Language Learning,* 2nd Ed. (New York: Harcourt, Brace and World, Inc., 1963), p. 128.
10. Norman R. Turchan, "An Evaluation of a Program in Reading and Listening," *Reading and the Language Arts,* Alan Robinson, compiler and editor (Chicago: University of Chicago Press, 1963), pp. 218-219.
11. Mildred A. Dawson, Marion Zollinger, and Ardell Elwell, *op. cit.,* p. 127.
12. Lou LaBrant, "The Goals for Culturally Different Youth," *Improving English Skills of Culturally Different Youth,* Washington, D. C.: U. S. Department of Health, Education and Welfare, Office of Education, 1964, p. 25.
13. Louise Abney, *Choral Speaking Arrangements for the Upper Grades* (Magnolia, Expression Company, 1952), pp. 7-34.
14. *Ibid.*
15. Rosalind Hughes, *Let's Enjoy Poetry—An Anthology of Children's Verse for Kindergarten, Grades I, II, and III with Suggestions for Teaching,* (Boston: Houghton Mifflin Co., 1958); Rosalind Hughes, *Let's Enjoy Poetry—An Anthology of Children's Verse for Grades IV, V, and VI with Suggestions for Teaching* (Boston: Houghton Mifflin Co., 1961).
16. Louise Abney, *op. cit.,* p. 21.
17. Frank Riessman, *The Culturally Deprived Child* (New York: Harper & Row, 1962), p. 115.
18. Kenneth Clark, "Discrimination and the Disadvantaged," *College Admissions 7: The Search for Talent,* New York: College Entrance Examination Board, 1960, pp. 12-18.
19. Educational Policies Commission: *Education and the Disadvantaged American,* Washington, D. C.: National Education Association, 1962, p. 17.

20. Helen, Huus, "Developing Reading Readiness," *The Instructor,* (March, 1965), pp. 59-60.
21. Sterl A. Artley, "Readiness for Dictionary Usage," *Elementary English,* XXXXI, (April, 1964), pp. 348-350.
22. Educational Policies Commissions, *op. cit.* p. 17-18.
23. Clarence W. Wachner, "Detroit Great Cities School Improvement Program in Language Arts," *Elementary English,* XXXXI, (November, 1964), pp. 734-742.
24. Harold G. Henderson, *An Introduction to Haiku* (Garden City, Doubleday Anchor Books, Doubleday & Company, Inc., 1958), p. 11.
25. *Ibid.,* p. 49.
26. *Ibid.,* p. 79.
27. *Japanese Haiku,* (Mount Vernon, Peter Pauper Press, 1955), no page given; other haiku publications by this company include: *The Four Seasons* (1958), *Cherry Blossoms* (1960), and *Haiku Harvest* (1962).
28. Salvatore M. Messina, "Haiku and Creative Writing," *NJEA Review,* XXXVII, (April, 1964), pp. 458-459.
29. Mildred Letton Wittick, "Correctness and Freshness-Can Children's Writing Have Both?" *Elementary School Journal,* LXI (March, 1960), pp. 297-298.
30. *Ibid.,* p. 298.
31. Laura Oftedal, "Picture Writing: A New Tool in Creative Expression," *Elementary School Journal,* XVIX, (September, 1948), pp. 37-46.
32. Frank Riessman, *op. cit.,* p. 71.
33. Allison Davis, "Society, the School, and the Culturally Deprived Student," *Improving English Skills of Culturally Different Youth,* Washington, D. C.: U. S. Department of Health, Education, and Welfare, Office of Education, 1964, p. 14.

Chapter VII

MATHEMATICS FOR THE DISADVANTAGED CHILD

Kathryn A. Graham*

"WE'VE GOT MODERN MATH. It's fun," enthused the second grader. For those arithmetic teachers who are used to attitudes ranging from boredom to disinterest to almost overt hostility, comments such as the above are both unexpected and exciting. Can we, through a different approach, make the unexpected, expected. Can arithmetic, or as it is now called even in the primary grades, mathematics, be taught so that children will find it challenging, exciting, and even fun? Can only the very gifted child ever really enjoy the beauty and the logic of the structure of mathematics? These are some of the questions which we will discuss within the limitations of this chapter.

Mathematics has been used as a tool by man since the earliest days of civilization. It is an integral part of our everyday life. It is a study of structures in which all is related, in which all is logical. It can be found in the works of the masters, in philosophy, in the arts, and, of course, in the sciences. It encourages individual thinking, scientific problem solving, rigorous logic, and critical evaluation. The layman has always needed mathematical knowledge to buy his food, shelter his family, and manage his everyday finances. The learning of mathematics is obviously a necessity for every child in every school.

During the past twenty years, technological changes have made mathematical understanding a prerequisite for many occupations of the future. Now, more than ever before, the school must expend every effort toward giving quality education in the field of mathematics. Dr. Bernard H. Gundlach expresses this view in commenting:

It is not exaggeration to say that mathematics has become

*Principal, William Bishop Owen Elementary School, Chicago.

150

modern man's second language and is rapidly becoming as indispensable as the first. Fluency in this second language is today a definite asset commanding status, good compensation and interesting jobs. But in the world of tomorrow . . . fluency in this language of mathematics will become an essential prerequisite for every citizen in every walk of life.[1]

MODERN MATH

With the advent of Sputnik and the resultant changes in our own scientific research, a "new" kind of mathematics burst out in a revolutionary manner which rocked curriculum makers, disturbed many classroom teachers, and confused parents. The term *modern mathematics* was heard throughout the land. It was an unfortunate term at best, for modern mathematics is not new in chronological age nor in content. Aspects of it can be found in some arithmetic texts of forty years ago. It is modern, at the elementary school level, only in its approach. It has not replaced the traditional or classical mathematics, it "generalizes it, supplements it, unifies it, and deepens our understanding of it."[2] According to Adler, the distinguishing characteristics of modern, or as he terms it, contemporary mathematics, are the following:

1. Contemporary mathematics is classical mathematics grown mature.
2. Contemporary mathematics is classical mathematics grown self-conscious and self-critical.
3. It is also modern mathematics which developed as a more efficient way of dealing with the content of classical mathematics.
4. Finally, it is mathematics that is more and more intimately related to man's activities in industry, social life, science and philosophy.[3]

Modern mathematics is structured in form, and abstract, having as its cornerstones the qualities of simplification and unification. While some mathematicians believe that modern mathematics with its emphasis on discovery will do away with rote learning, drill and memorization, most educators agree that drill in its proper perspective has a place in the new mathematics. Modern mathematics may be further characterized as the mathematics which incorporates the integration of mathematical ideas and procedures, a continuity of sequence and experience, more precise definitions, terminology and notation, distinction between objects and names of objects, and emphasis on deductive proof and problem solving.[4]

Modern mathematics began at the college level, moved down to the high school, and gradually filtered down into the upper elementary grades. Within the past few years, many programs have been published for the primary grades. The "squeeze" is on the intermediate level at the present time with research centers and publishers working on materials for the fourth, fifth, and sixth grades. A study of such materials by the teachers can lead to confusion. They find that set symbolism should be taught at the primary level, and that set symbolism should *not* be taught until at least the fourth grade; precise vocabulary should be required from first graders, and should *not* be required until the intermediate grades. The proponents of the first view stated in each case argue that children in the primary grades have the ability to accept and use correctly such terms as *equal, equivalent, commutative, associative, distributive, subset, union,* and *intersection.* They aver that children should be taught the precise term at the time a concept is learned instead of having to learn the vocabulary at a later date. It is their contention that children like to use big words, and that when the correct terms are taught as the child masters the idea, he accepts and retains these terms.

The proponents of the more conservative position might use the oft quoted phrase, "just because a child can do trigonometry in kindergarten doesn't mean it should be taught there." Ever increasing numbers of articles are appearing in mathematics journals urging caution in the requirement of formalization in the elementary school. Dr. David Rappaport fears that "the new emphasis is bringing sophisticated mathematics to children at too early an age."[5] It is his contention that such sophisticated mathematics will "take away [from the pupil] the meaningful understanding of basic arithmetic concepts needed in his everyday practical experience and also in his preparation."[6] This opinion is sustained by many educators who believe that the idea of a deductive system is too abstract for young children; that though the child may have the necessary intelligence, he does not have the experience with numbers to use as a basis for building the concepts. If too much importance is placed upon the deductive structure of the mathematical system, the kind of formalism, abhorred in the traditional mathematics, will return in the new system of contemporary mathematics.

Discovery and Mathematics

Every teacher knows that each child is an individual and that each new class is different; that what "strikes a responsive chord in one pupil may leave another completely untouched. Moreover, it is possible that a given stimulus may fail to stir a pupil at one time whereas earlier, or perhaps later, this same stimulus might have been effective."[7] There are classes and individual children who can readily accept the formalistic structure which occurs as a result of previous *discovery* learnings; there are also those classes and children for whom this acceptance will occur late, if at all. This does not mean that modern mathematical theory cannot be taught to the latter group. The *discovery* method as modified to the individual class is still the best way for children to learn. The child can, for example, understand the ideas of union and intersection, even though he may continue to call them "and-or" concepts. Discovering the answer for himself, as every teacher is aware, gives a feeling of success to the child and a confidence in his ability which is needed in all content fields for a good learning situation.

Does this mean that the child must discover every concept which has been discovered through the ages of man? Does it mean that he must be able to express those concepts in precise form? Does it mean that the teacher should not give help to the child in the form of suggestions and clues? Of course not. It is the teacher's role to present situations with the adequate materials and aids necessary so that the child can *discover* that $a+b=b+a$ and that $3(x+2)=3x+6$. Every teacher has said at least once or twice in his career, "If you can't explain it, you don't understand it." In general, such a statement is true. Yet, Van Engen cautions us that "the existence of concepts on the sub-verbal level is a condition that should be of utmost importance to the teacher of mathematics."[8] Children can be aware of generalizations without necessarily being able to give them names or precise language. Concepts are not developed easily or quickly. They usually "develop slowly out of precepts, memories and images, aided greatly by a variety of language and other symbols."[9] Dr. Rappaport likens conceptual construction to "an ever enlarging web of information. New expression opens up additional directions for growth that are related to previous strands and integrated into more complex, interlocking conceptual patterns."[10] All conceptual understandings proceed first from the sensory qualities, then to the generalization, and finally to the rationalization; that is, the explanation of the generalization. There are times when this process is almost instantaneous. These occurrences are, however, infrequent. In general, conceptual development is a gradual process which must be developed by the teacher through as many approaches as may be necessary.

It also needs to be emphasized that every child will not develop to the rationalization stage. Most children will be able to work at the first, or operational, level and proceed after a while to the level of generalization; only the brightest children can be expected to reach the level of rationalization. The aim of the classroom teacher is to help each child realize realistic goals by developing his ability to the highest level of his capacity.

Attitudes Toward Math

One of the biggest hurdles which the classroom teacher of traditional arithmetic has had to overcome is the widespread negative attitude toward mathematics. Parents influence their children with remarks, such as, "I never understood it when I was in school either," or "I always hated arithmetic, too." The teacher, who often had similar feelings, was sometimes poorly prepared to teach the subject. Arithmetic became a dull, rote subject to be endured.

Was there ever a subject so often used for punishment homework as arithmetic? Should we be surprised that children came to school disliking arithmetic, and after eight years, left the elementary school with the firm decision to elect any subject in high school except mathematics? If this is the case for most children, how much more can be said for the child of the disadvantaged neighborhood? A boy who has had no breakfast and is cold because of the lack of clothes would find it difficult to concentrate on or care about the rules for long division. A change of attitude can only be brought about by a teacher who uses proper motivation. He needs to build the child's self-esteem, his need for approval. He must help him to experience successes, not a series of failures in arithmetic. The pupil must become involved personally with the problems. It is only when the problem becomes *his* that he will attempt a solution.

The teacher must have the same qualities as the teacher of any other subject, and he must love mathematics. He must bring to the child a love of subject, a delight in the child, a positive attitude toward his successes and be able to communicate this feeling to him. He must give him a reason to learn. The problems used in the lessons can be related to class, school or home activities, or to future occupations. The mathematics of shopping, wage earning, installment buying, budgeting; i.e., the mathematics of human life, should be included in the curriculum. Instead of measuring Farmer Jones' barn, let the children measure their classroom, the desks, the door, the gymnasium, the playground. Use newspaper clippings to demonstrate how mathematics can be found in almost all facets of our environment. Plan as many activities as possible in which the children can personally participate. Make sure that there are at least little successes along the way, always remembering to praise progress at any level, for, as Bernard Gundlach notes:

> To bring about an attitude of deep-felt pride in one's own work and of growing reliance upon one's own reasoning power, together with the joy and satisfaction that results from them— that is really the deepest aim and purpose of the modern approach to mathematics.[11]

Gundlach's aim should be that of every teacher of mathematics, particularly the teacher of the disadvantaged child who, more than any other child, must feel pride in his work and in himself.

Teaching the Disadvantaged Pupil

As we mentioned previously, many modern mathematics programs have been published recently by book companies and research centers. While some of these programs are specifically written only for the gifted or accelerated student, most are written for the average child. None of these programs deal with the below-average child. It is unfortunate, but true, that due to environmental factors, the child from a disadvantaged family is usually below-grade in arithmetic. Yet, modern mathematics experimental programs being carried on in many of the large city schools in disadvantaged areas seem to show signs of success. It is not the proper role of this writer to recommend programs by name for use in such classrooms, only to say that modern mathematics is not beyond the grasp of these pupils, provided the material is presented and developed properly.

In developing an abstraction, one always begins with concrete examples. This is true regardless of the cultural or environmental background of the child. However, Henderson reminds us that:

> Slow learners need more repetition, more concrete development, more trial and error experience and simpler reasoning. They need help with their reading and vocabulary. They need more help in making generalizations.[12]

The child's senses—his sight, his hearing, and particularly his sense of touch, should be utilized. Some years ago it was said that all a teacher needed to teach arithmetic was a blackboard and a piece of chalk. Perhaps this is why so many children left school without the mathematical understanding they should have received. The disadvantaged child, even more than most, must be exposed to many experiences with concrete materials, and perhaps for a longer period of time, for as Silberman discovered:

> The non-verbal atmosphere of the home also means that lower-class children have a limited perception of the world about them: they do not know that objects have names (table, wall, book) or that the same object may have several names (an apple is a fruit, red, round, juicy). They also have very little concept of size or time.[13]

This does not mean that his arithmetic should consist of a series of games and puzzles. There is a danger that the beauty and logic of mathematics will be lost in the fun. Games, puzzles, and many varied activities are necessary for the below-grade youngster.

Activities for the Disadvantaged Pupil

The list of some suggested activities which follows is at best a limited one. Most of the activities listed have been culled from many sources; however, a few are credited to Lois Rapp,[14] and Henry W. Syer.[15] They are not listed according to grade level, for some which might be considered primary activities in average classrooms might well be used at the intermediate level in a disadvantaged area.

Patterns

1. Weave strips of two colors into mats.
2. Using pre-cut drinking straws, have the children string colored circles and squares, separated by the straws, into various patterns, making a daisy chain.
3. Use jigsaw puzzles for sensory contact.
4. Yarn designs can be stitched on construction paper.
5. Make abstract cut-outs or painting designs.
6. Cover a sheet of construction paper with an all-over design of squares, circles, and triangles.
7. Have several children work on a stained glass window.

Geometry and Measurement

1. Have the children handle geometric forms while blindfolded. The forms can also be placed under a sheet of newspaper and the children can take turns guessing the correct form through their sense of touch.
2. Let the children handle thick and thin objects, such as, paper and carboard, pencil and marking pen.
3. Fill a box with objects of assorted sizes, shapes and colors. Have the children sort them into groups of large or small, by color, by shape, or into pairs or identities.
4. Use circus animals and the circus rings in teaching inside and outside.

5. Using large circles, have the children cut one in halves, another into fourths, another into eighths, etc. These can be kept in an envelope made by the child. Another set can be made for thirds, fifths, etc. Use the same size for the circles.

6. With a sheet of $8\frac{1}{2}$"x$11\frac{1}{2}$" paper representing one gallon, quarts and pints may be cut to size. As in the previous suggestion, the children may practice making up problems with the figures.

7. Bring a gallon milk carton and four quart cartons. Demonstrate that the contents of the four quart cartons can be placed into the gallon carton. A responsible child may fill the gallon carton with water by re-filling one quart carton four times.

8. Construct five boxes of the same dimensions. Paste weights of varying degree on the bottom or within each box. Have the children determine the lightest or heaviest. Ask various children to arrange them in order of their respective weights.

9. On the bulletin board place cut-out circles, squares, and triangles of varied sizes to help to develop the idea of "greater-smaller."

10. Make transparencies for geometric figures.

Numeration

1. Buttons, chips, tooth picks, or tongue depressors can be used for counting or place value.

2. In teaching consecutive numbers, some of the following may be effective devices. Ask the children to:
   a. Name the next three numbers greater than 8.
   b. Name the next three numbers smaller than 12.
   c. Fill in the sets of numbers between 5 and 9.
   d. Fill in the sets of numbers between 862 and 885.
   e. Use tongue depressors having one numeral printed on each. Ask each child to select one. One pupil is called on to stand in front of the room holding up his number. The children who have numerals which precede and follow the number shown walk up to

stand beside him. This may be continued until the desired number of children are in a row with their numerals in consecutive order.

   f. Rearrange numerals in the order of their size.

   g. Name the sets of numbers between 211 and 197 which have no tens.

3. In teaching large numbers, use statistics found in the newspapers such as, how many years it would take to reach the amount of national debt if a man counted it a dollar a second, twenty-four hours a day.

4. Read high and low degrees from a demonstration thermometer.

5. Using a map can aid in teaching directions, north and up, south and down, etc. (Remember that in polar maps, however, north is not up.)

6. Place a number line on the floor of the room from 0-20. Play the "Cricket Game." The children in teams hop spaces up and back. At some time during the game, a child who has hopped backwards will find he has hopped off the number line and has no numeral to express his position unless he uses negative numbers.

7. A "puzzler" can be placed on the bulletin board each Monday, the solution given on Friday.

8. Posters can be made of base 10 and bases other than 10 for comparison.

9. A monthly calendar on poster board whose numerals are base 5 can be very effective.

10. Construct simple computers with upper grade classes.

Estimation

1. Use a straight edge instead of a measured ruler for estimating.

2. Request a child to place two books at what he estimates is five feet apart, then measure the distance.

3. Have each child place two pencils six inches apart on his desk, then measure.

4. Provide each child with a yardstick. The teacher holds her hands one foot apart. The children hold their hands

at what they estimate is the same distance, then measure it with the yardstick.

5. Have a child pace off the length or width of the classroom, then measure it.

Miscellaneous

1. Plot points in graphing which result in pictures of animals, Christmas tree, etc.
2. Use crossword puzzles with mathematical terms or numbers, or use cross-number puzzles.
3. The abacus is an effective device in teaching place value, and addition.
4. The cuisenaire rods have almost limitless possibilities for use in size, shape, color, counting, and the fundamental operations.
5. On 4"x6" cards, paste one or two problems either from cut up old workbooks or teacher made for individual use. These can be kept in a coded file for use by the child for a few minutes every day.
6. In some upper grade classes, children enjoy making "daffynitions" with the mathematical terms.
7. The use of the flannel board, the magnetic board, the hundred and the place value board, and the peg board cannot be recommended too highly.
8. Add many childrens' mathematics books to the room library.

Added to the above list should be topics in budgeting, banking (deposits, withdrawals), installment buying, rates of interest, and taxes taught with the use of actual forms, for unfortunately, there will always be a dropout problem. The dropouts need practical mathematics before concluding their school experience. Books, films, filmstrips, pictures and records are a necessary and desirable part of every good mathematics program. These act as multisensory aids.

In all activities concerned with learning, give the child a clue, help him to search for patterns. If he finds the way difficult, suggest that he shift his approach. Use conversation as much as possible in teaching in order to facilitate communication and understanding. Accept his child-like definitions. The boy who describes a circle as consisting of a "line that turns around until it meets and is the same distance all the way around" has the idea of a circle. Use the objects of the home and school as much as possible. According to Howard Fehr:

> The teacher who has made more or less use of the sensible world, the school room environment; that is, of strings, rubber bands, watches, shadows, alignment of books, grouping of objects . . . knows the richness of mathematical situations which they suggest.[16]

Teachers' Role

Every child has the right to good instruction in mathematics. We have said little about the teacher. It is obvious, however, that in order to teach a subject well, one must not only be interested and enthusiastic but must also know the content. Many teachers need in-service work, either through attendance at workshops or college courses. For the teacher who finds neither of these possible, there are literally hundreds of worthwhile books which have been written on modern mathematics; films produced by research companies and lectures are available; consultant help can be obtained in most school systems; TV presentations are helpful.

The children from disadvantaged areas are everyone's problem. They are our future citizens and voters, our future working force. They will require good mathematical instruction just to live a normal, productive life, just to retain the dignity which is the right of every human being.

REFERENCES

1. Bernard H. Gundlach, "Modern Mathematics Education," Curriculum Council, Education Research Council, Cleveland, Ohio, p. 1.
2. Irving Adler, "The Changes Taking Place in Mathematics," *The Mathematical Teacher,* LV (October 1962) , p. 449.
3. *Ibid.,* p. 441.
4. A. B. Evenson, *Modern Mathematics* (Chicago, Scott Foresman and Company, 1962) , pp. 4-7.
5. David Rappaport, "Does 'Modern Math' Ignore Learning Theory," *Phi Delta Kappan,* XLIV (June, 1963) , p. 445.

6. *Ibid.,* p. 447.
7. Robert F. DeHaan and Ronald C. Doll, "Individualization and Human Potential," *Individualizing Instruction, 1964 Yearbook,* Association for Supervision and Curriculum Development (Washington, D. C.: The Association, 1964), p. 17.
8. Henry Van Engen, "The Formation of Concepts," *The Learning of Mathematics: Its Theory and Practice, 21st Yearbook, National Council of Teachers of Mathematics* (Washington, D. C.: 1953), p. 82.
9. David A. Rappaport, *op. cit.,* p. 446.
10. *Ibid.,* p. 446.
11. Bernard H. Gundlach, *op. cit.* p. 6.
12. Kenneth H. Henderson and Robert E. Pingry, "Problem Solving in Mathematics," *The Learning of Mathematics: Its Theory and Practice, 21st Yearbook, National Council of Teachers of Mathematics,* (Washington, D. C., 1953), p. 277.
13. Charles E. Silberman, "Give Slum Children A Chance: A Radical Proposal," *Harper's Magazine,* CCXXVIII (May, 1964), p. 38. Reprinted from *Crisis in Black and White,* Random House, Inc. 1964.
14. Lois Rapp, "Arithmetic is Fun," *The Arithmetic Teacher,* X (May, 1963), p. 257.
15. Henry W. Syer, "Sensory Learning Applies to Mathematics," *The Learning of Mathematics: Its Theory and Practice, 21st Yearbook, National Council of Teachers of Mathematics* (Washington, D. C.: 1953), p. 117 ff.
16. Howard F. Fehr, "Modern Mathematics and Good Pedagogy," *The Arithmetic Teacher,* X (November, 1963), p. 405.

Chapter VIII

SCIENCE FOR THE DISADVANTAGED CHILD

ILLA PODENDORF*

"THERE IS JOY IN THE search for knowledge" is a sentence from an article discussing objectives for elementary science which appears in the *Journal of Research in Science Teaching* for March 1964. These objectives were written by William Kesson of Yale University and a committee which was appointed by the Commission of the American Association for the Advancement of Science. For purposes of this discussion let us consider briefly three words which appear in the sentence—joy, search, and knowledge. Every child is endowed with the right to joys and pleasures which he finds in the environment into which he was born. He will pursue and elaborate upon the activities which he finds most satisfying to him. He will search for more opportunities to experience the joy and satisfaction of activities which bring him pleasure. It is satisfying to have knowledge and as a child pursues activities and enjoys new experiences, he is building toward a store of knowledge. This is, indeed, basic in science education. It is this joy in the search for knowledge that has been very largely responsible for the march of scientific progress throughout the world.

CHANGING TRENDS

The last twenty years have brought about a trend toward more emphasis on elementary science in the total elementary school curriculum. War, advances in technology, discovery, and invention have all influenced the directions which the trends have taken. As the environment has changed due to the impact of scientific advancement, it has become clear that in some way

*Chairman of the Science Department at the Laboratory Schools at the University of Chicago.

children should be provided with the science education or background which is essential for a citizen to be scientifically literate.

For many years, the curriculum provided for an organized program which would equip children with many facts, concepts and principles which it was thought would prepare them for participating as informed citizens. There has been a definite change within the last five years in the beliefs and understandings about what children should learn in a worthwhile elementary science program.

Today, science is recognized as more than a body of facts and supporting information. Some say it is the way scientists go about doing the things which they do in their search for new knowledge. Others say it is not only the way that scientists do things but that it is also the never-ending search for descripions, patterns, explanations, and new knowledge of the phenomena in the environment. It is increasingly clear that the road to becoming scientifically literate is a long and continuous one. It is a road of many experiences—activities, discoveries, successes, failures and much repetition.

No attempt will be made to list all the elements of a child's world which should be in a science curriculum, except to say that it draws from all the broad areas of science—biological, physical and earth sciences. It should also be pointed out that the quantity of scientific information has increased beyond measure the last ten years and will doubtless increase in a comparable way in the future. It is unrealistic to consider teaching children *all* the knowledge that might be suitably selected and organized into a curriculum. They would remember only that portion which they used enough to internalize or to make a part of themselves. On the other hand, children cherish information and *knowing things* and they should not be sold short.

What is the thinking about what a child must be able to do to be a searcher for knowledge? If the trend is away from compounding a knowledge of facts, concepts and principles, then what characteristics or skills are considered to be essential? Some of the more recent elementary science programs are being developed around what are called scientific processes. One of the developing programs is called *Elementary Science—A Process Approach*. Others stress the process in the development of the topic or unit.

Observation is thought to be one of the basic and important processes. A child must be able to use his senses—to see, hear, feel, smell, and taste—more than in a superficial way. What they see and hear is likely to be the dramatic or the trivial, leaving the important unnoticed and not recorded in their thinking. It is for this reason that they need instruction which will sharpen the powers of observation in all the senses. The child must be able to observe in enough detail that he may evaluate, describe and communicate to others what he has observed. The child who has problems with communication will be more able to overcome these problems if he has collected, through observation, that which he has interest in describing. To describe accurately he must have some ability to measure. To say that something is larger or smaller, faster or slower, heavier or lighter, hotter or colder conveys no meaning in a real sense. These are all relative terms. It is important that size, speed, weight, and amount of heat be expressed in meaningful terms, which are the result of precise measurement. Classification is also an important process.

The trend, then, in teaching elementary science today is to give children a great deal of practice with what is being called the processes of science—observing, communicating, measuring, classifying, experimenting, predicting. Such experiences will help a child feel the satisfactions which may come with the activities of science.

Changing emphasis from a content-oriented program to a process-oriented program does not deny the importance of carefully selected content. It is generally agreed that both processes and an organized body of content are fundamental as one functions profitably in scientific activities.

It is not the intent that every child be made a scientist, but it is recognized that every child is a potential scientist. More important, every normal, healthy child can be a searcher for knowledge and be able to function as a citizen in a society rich in scientific heritage. Not every child will ask the same kinds of questions or look for the same kinds of answers but almost every child is curious and more or less experimental. These characteristics need to be protected, nurtured and directed. This can be done by helping him to be successful in answering his own questions about his environment. Learning how to find answers and confidence in this ability make for responsible, contributing citizens in a democratic society.

A DISADVANTAGED CHILD WHO IS ACADEMICALLY ABLE

It is said that all children are disadvantaged in some respects. However, some children are disadvantaged in more ways and to a greater extent than others. A disadvantaged child may be one whose academic potential is low mainly for genetic reasons. We are, in this article, concerned chiefly with the child who is academically able but is disadvantaged for other reasons. In many cases, this child has not been taught nor encouraged and even more often has not been permitted to think for himself although he has the potential. He has not been helped to make and carry out plans of his own. He has not had occasion to enter into discussions; indeed, he may not have heard discussions carried on— only short commands. He is familiar with one- or two-word questions and answers and many of these short statements have not involved him. He has seen and moved in a limited environment, very often economically deprived and socially unacceptable. The environment may have been not only limiting but frightening— one which has fostered deep feelings of insecurity.

Since the academic potential is adequate, the self motivation may still be sufficient for a considerable amount of investigation, self discovery, and exploration. These children may have advanced in some areas beyond their counterparts in a more advantaged environment. For example, exploring a "dump" and finding wire, wheels, boards, boxes, and other things from which to fashion a functional wagon of sorts have much more educational value than receiving a beautifully designed wagon with a price tag on it. A mechanically capable boy might build a telegraph set or a motor or a steam engine from scrap materials which he finds among other peoples' discards, with resultant incalculable learnings and growth of self. The student of history of science can cite a number of examples of scientific achievement coming from persons who began their lives in what may have been considered deprived or disadvantaged areas.

However, it is more often true that disadvantaged children have not had such fortunate experiences. Many have never created anything, nor even learned to ask questions.

SCIENCE CURRICULUM

As has been pointed out earlier, an examination of newer directions in teaching elementary science reveals an emphasis on the skills which are particularly basic to science. These skills have been referred to as the processes of science. Not all people completely agree upon the identification of these processes, although certain of them are generally accepted as basic. There is generally agreement that it is not possible to teach in an organized way all the scientific knowledge which is a significant part of a child's environment. There must be selections made and children must be trained to be able to use techniques and skills to fill in the information as the need arises for it. It is here that skill in the use of scientific processes becomes important.

Any curriculum may be said to be culture-free if it is not dependent upon previously developed communication skills such as reading, writing, spelling or upon certain bodies of background experience. A curriculum may be culture-free and at the same time emphasize skills in the use of processes as well as the content or organized subject matter. Whether or not skill in the use of processes comes through to children in a classroom depends very largely upon the teaching methods which are used. That the values of an elementary science program rest not only with the objectives set up but upon the methods used to achieve the objectives is not a new idea. *Science Instruction in Elementary and High School Grades,* written by members of the faculty of the Laboratory Schools of the University of Chicago and published in 1939, says:

"The values of the intermediate-grade course in science are thought of in terms of knowledge acquired, abilities and appreciations developed, attitudes changed, interests widened, and personality development directed along desirable lines. It is axiomatic that many of the values of the course are inherent in the method of presentation, not in the subject matter itself."

Disadvantaged children with adequate academic potential will profit equally with their counterparts in the more advantaged social structure if the series of activities or curriculum is culture-free and appropriate methods of instruction are used. If the curriculum does not depend upon reading, diagrams, discussion of past experiences or any of the accepted communication skills, they will have few handicaps. Indeed, the communication skills can be further developed *through* science activities. Children who were non-readers have become interested in reading and received satisfaction in reading through the use of science-oriented materials. Any science curriculum should not be static but should rather be modified and expanded as children are able to cope with it.

An example of an activity and the methods used in the kind of science program described above may serve to amplify and clarify. Classification is a basic process in all areas of science. Plants and animals are classified according to their structure and function; rocks and minerals are classified according to ways in which they are formed; chemists and physicists talk about solids, liquids, and gases. Children, regardless of environmental background, use classification schemes. They refer to brothers, sisters, parents, pets, dogs, cats, and things which are theirs and things which are not theirs. Adults use classification in day-by-day activities as do scientists in their professional work. Children are called upon to make intelligent groupings not only in science but in many other activities.

It is important that they receive a considerable amount of experience with making classifications beyond that which would normally come their way. Most science curricula or textbooks include lessons or a series of activities dealing with the classification of animals. For example, the emphasis may be upon which animals are mammals, birds, or reptiles, and upon the characteristics of each group considered. The emphasis is not likely to be on classification as a process. In many situations, students are required to read and are then tested upon the information which they read, with little or no consideration for the grouping. A suitable and practical classroom activity could be developed which would not be based upon the textbook or the reading skill. Reading materials would be used only as enrichment. Pictures of familiar animals can be used. If possible, several sets, each consisting of about twelve pictures, should be assembled. The sets should all be alike. If it is not possible to have more than one set, then the set should consist of larger pictures so that they may be viewed by the whole class at one time. A series of activities similar to the following can be planned:

Activity 1. Present the collection of pictures to the class as a whole or in small groups, depending upon the number of sets available. Ask them to plan a way to divide the pictures into two groups. Suggest only that they be sure that the plan will not leave any pictures out. They are likely to suggest any or all of the following groupings:

1. Those which live in water and those which live on land.
2. Those that fly and those that cannot fly.
3. Those which have fur and those which do not have fur.
4. Those which have feathers and those which do not have feathers.
5. Those which have four or less legs and those which have more than four legs.
6. Those which have backbones and those which do not have backbones.
7. Those which make good pets and those which do not make good pets.
8. Those which are farm animals and those which are not farm animals.

Any suggestion which seems reasonable should be tried and considered acceptable if it can be used according to the directions.

Activity 2. Ask the children which of the plans which were tried in Activity 1 they consider to be the most useful. Through discussion, decide upon one of the plans and divide the pictures according to this plan. Ask the children to suggest a plan to divide each of the sub-groups into two groups. The sub-groups can be divided and subdivided as many times as is possible with this group of animal pictures.

Activity 3. (Optional) Follow one of the suggestions which is almost sure to be made concerning animals with fur, animals with feathers, or animals with backbones. The words *vertebrate, mammal, bird, reptile, amphibian,* and others can be introduced, if appropriate, to stress vocabulary. Whether or not the vocabulary is stressed should be determined in part by the readiness of the children for it. In the opinion of the writer, the experience with classification and the observations which must be made to support the classifications are much more important learnings than the building of the vocabulary; however, if the children are ready for the vocabulary, then it should be introduced.

THE DISADVANTAGED CHILD IN A WORLD
OF SCIENCE

Many of the materials which are used in scientific study are in every child's environment. Air, water, rocks, tin cans, empty bottles, and boxes are but a few of them. A child may or may not be able to use the words *wind, air,* or *sounds* in his everyday conversations. None of these elements of a child's environment is likely to offer an academic challenge to the child who has been unguided or untutored. For many children, they mean only discomfort or unpleasantness.

If the instructions can be provided, these same children are able to learn quickly that wind makes a pinwheel turn, that water makes things wet, and that sounds are different from each other. The three-or four-year-old child can learn readily to watch snow melt and to make some pertinent observations concerning it. He can see that a glass full of snow will melt into only a fraction of a glass of water. He can learn to distinguish colors from each other and may be able to give names to colors, including shades and tints. He is able to distinguish sounds and to understand the importance of listening for sounds. In a home environment, a child's attention is not likely to be on any of these phenomena until after he has had guided experiences with them. After instruction, a child is likely to repeat such experiences and extend them to further observations in the home environment. He has something positive and pleasant upon which to fix his attention.

The primary children from disadvantaged homes are able to succeed in science activities to the extent that they are not called upon to use any certain set of experiences or skills which they are almost certain not to have adequately developed. They get the same satisfactions from experiences which extend their abilities to observe—to see, hear, and feel—as do other children. They, too, can practice their observation skills outside the classroom in their home environments. They will probably not get the same recognition from their family members as their more privileged counterparts receive, but they may spend more time with their new-found interest because the home furnishes less to occupy their time in the way of toys or other interests.

Activities which are designed to stress observation skills should be built in part around the commonplace in the home environment in order that children may carry the activity outside the classroom into their leisure time. These activities should also gradually offer experience with the less commonplace to help the child fill in his barren background and extend his interests. Such activities may be built around color recognition, using materials such as crayons, pieces of construction paper, bits of ribbon, cloth or felt. The activity could be expanded to give children experiences in classification as they are encouraged to try grouping these colors. Small boxes of pieces of ribbon of different sizes, colors and shapes might be prepared for individual children to have, to handle, to cherish as their own and to take home with them if they wish. Children who see much of need, discomfort, and crowdedness can profit a great deal from having what each can claim as "my own" in a classroom. This may be a space, a desk, a locker, a box of crayons, a box of small pieces of ribbons, or anything which can be claimed as one's own.

Activities designed around the shapes, feel, and sizes of these things can promote much of what is basic in science. The names of the shapes of the things may be taught to the children and thus become a part of their vocabularies. This activity may be expanded to include the names of the shapes of toys in the classroom such as balls, blocks, and boxes. Children can also be taught to make comparisons. They may be encouraged to describe in a more precise way by saying "the red ribbon is wider than the blue ribbon" instead of saying "the red ribbon is wide and the blue ribbon is not" or "the red ribbon is thicker than the blue ribbon" instead of "the red ribbon is thick and the blue ribbon is not."

A live animal in the classroom is a good hub for many worthwhile activities. For instance:

1. Children should learn to recognize the needs of living things.
2. Children should learn to assume the responsibility for something beyond themselves.
3. Children should have opportunities to observe the behavior of the animal.
4. Children should have practice in describing their observations in an appropriately precise way.
5. Children should be encouraged to make a record of their observations in ways suitable to skills previously established and to appropriate objectives.

It should be pointed out that most disadvantaged children have had little or no experience with caring for small animal pets properly.

The weather conditions provide opportunities for learning to read thermometers and to record conditions from day to day.

Organizing a day into blocks of time is a new experience for many children. Putting order into a part of their lives provides an opportunity for teaching measurements of time such as hour, day, week, month, etc.

The middle grade level science will offer no difficulty for the academically able child if it can be presented culture-free. Here again, this means that the activities must be built around first-hand experiences with materials, things, or ideas. Instead of reading about them, a fourth-grade child should have opportunities to look at materials, handle them, manipulate them, describe them in whatever way is appropriate—perhaps in terms of color, size, shape, speed, sound, etc.

In any one activity there will necessarily be several processes or skills basic in science which should be stressed. Many of the science curricula and textbooks deal with heat conduction, stressing the idea that some materials conduct heat better than others. An activity designed to answer the question, "Do some materials conduct heat better than others?" and similar to the following may be set up to be demonstrated by the teacher, with provisions made for the children to do it individually or in groups. In order to make group or individual participation possible, it is necessary to provide several glass stirring rods and metal rods of the same diameter and length, also several marbles of uniform size and material. Fasten a marble with melted candle wax about one inch from one end of a glass rod and fasten another identical marble in the same way to the metal rod. Hold the metal rod so that the end which is near the marble is in a flame from a candle or alcohol burner and note the time it takes for the marble to fall. Make a record of the time. Now hold the glass rod in the flame and note the time. To verify these results, the experiment should be repeated several times. Individual or small groups of children should try the same experiment. An examination of the results should show a pattern but variation. Such questions as the following could be used to direct the discussion:

Which of the materials is the better conductor? (metal)

Can it be said that metal is the best conductor? (No. This experiment shows only that metal is better than glass.)

Can it be said that glass is the poorest conductor? (No. This experiment shows it to be poorer than the metal used.)

Why were the results not always the same? (Differences in the way it was held, amount of wax, flame, where marble was placed.)

What assumptions had to be made? (Same amount of wax used on each, same kind of marble used, rod would be held equally steady each time, etc.)

An activity such as this one offers opportunities for questioning on the part of the students and planning of ways to find answers to the questions. For example, the question of whether all metals conduct at the same rate may be raised and answered through additional planned experimentation.

The author believes that methods similar to those discussed briefly in this chapter are suitable and desirable for all children. The so-called disadvantaged child has little or no handicap in this kind of science program. One might infer from the discussion to this point that the author believes that reading has no place in a science curriculum. This, however, is not the case. Reading is essential to pursuing any scientific inquiry or knowledge. To the extent a child is able to read he should be encouraged to include reading in his activities. It is only that the child who cannot, or for some reason is unwilling to read should not be considered incapable of profiting from experiences in science and for this reason, isolated from them. The reading disadvantage may cause emotional blocks or intense dislikes to be generated if the only approach to science is through reading.

A rich school environment will help in a substantial way to make up for the lack which may exist in many home environments. This school environment should include many resources, such as plants, animals, toys, multiple pieces of simple equipment, charts, films, and books. The child who has never traveled to the seacoast has a chance through films to view the expanse of water, some of the animals typical of the salt water environment—starfish, sea anemone, crabs, lobsters, and many others. The child who has never seen the mountains has a chance to view the mountains, with close-ups of some of the plants and animals which live there. The value of such films is much enhanced if basic skills in science are clearly kept as objectives. Book shelves in a classroom and library should include many titles of text and trade books carefully selected and of varying degrees of difficulty. Children may read to check, to verify, to compare, and to supplement their information. It has been the experience of the author that sometimes children who had resisted reading put forth an effort to read because they have found reading for a purpose and using reading materials which were suitable to their level and interests rewarding. As has been pointed out before, science vocabulary may become a burden to children if it is not handled thoughtfully. Many of the so-called *new* words are new to all children. Some are new only to some children. The disadvantaged child will doubtless carry a somewhat heavier vocabulary load than others, but his enthusiasm for using *new* and *big* words may compensate for this handicap.

A CHILD DISADVANTAGED FOR ACADEMIC REASONS

There is another kind of disadvantaged child. These children come from all kinds of environments and social backgrounds and are handicapped because of low academic ability. There is the question of whether science should be included in the curriculum of these children. The contention has long been that the abstractness which is characteristic of such science material makes it almost impossible for these children of all ages—elementary and high school—to learn science. Many people feel that these children are not able to generalize, to make appropriate applications, to comprehend major concepts, or to make precise measurements. It is doubtless true that these children would have more difficulty with a great deal of science material than children who are academically able. This does not mean that they would have difficulty with all of it or that material could not be selected which would pay good educational dividends. The children who are less able will grow up in the same world as the others. They will use the same electrical equipment, push the same kinds of buttons, and vote in the same society. It seems that it would be totally unwise to keep science experiences out of their lives.

The experience of the author leads to the belief that less able children learn in much the same way as other children. They profit best from firsthand experience—opportunities to do things repeatedly for themselves, to discover on their own and to pursue their own interests. They may proceed at a slower rate but they often succeed at a higher level than was thought possible. It would be a great mistake to keep science out of their program of studies. The critical problem is one of selection of materials. The materials may be in some respects much the same as for other children and, again, they may profit from materials which are totally unnecessary for other children. The materials should be selected to provide motivation, interest in learning, interest in doing, and in sharing. These children are entitled to the same joys in discovering for themselves and in learning as are other children. The child who can do birdcalls and win recognition for himself by a short demonstration of birdcalls but can gain almost nothing from a discussion of characteristics of birds should have the joys of practicing the bird calls and sharing his success with other children.

Many Children Are Disadvantaged

There are many disadvantaged children in science classrooms who are not disadvantaged because of poverty, persecution, or lack of academic ability, but rather because they have not had the opportunity to question, to discover for themselves, to pursue their own special interests, or to share their own discoveries or interests. In short, they have not had the opportunity to feel the joy which comes from successfully searching for knowledge. What does this mean to parents, teachers, administrators, and scientists? It means that every effort possible must be made to support and extend programs which are developed and carried out to find ways of improving elementary school science curricula for all children. Involved is the improvement of:

1. Curricular materials (text and trade books, films, equipment and other laboratory supplies).
2. Methods of instruction (individual and group participation).
3. Preparation of teachers to teach science (in-service and pre-service training).
4. Classroom situations (reducing class size to a manageable number and providing individual help for children who have need for it).

The last ten years have seen much change in the attitude toward science as a substantial part of the elementary program. Most school systems are actively instituting programs if there was not one previously in progress. Much credit goes to the men and women of vision who laid early foundations upon which people are working today.

All children have a right to the joy which comes with successfully searching for knowledge. Our schools have the responsibility of providing the appropriate environment. Our society could not but profit.

Chapter IX

TEACHING THE SOCIAL STUDIES TO CULTURALLY DISADVANTAGED PUPILS

Lillian Dimitroff*

CULTURALLY DISADVANTAGED people may be defined as those persons who are not a recognized part of the mainstream of American life. These Americans include Indians, Puerto Ricans, Mexicans, Negroes, and rural Southern whites. At this time, large numbers of these people do not participate successfully in American life. On the one hand, many lack the needed preparation; on the other, some of these groups are not motivated to seize the existing advantages in our society. In some types of employment, they face a lack of opportunity as well as prejudice and discrimination. With this background, disadvantaged adults do not provide a good supportive atmosphere for their children's education and the schools.

Inasmuch as many of the children attending public schools in our major cities are classified as culturally disadvantaged, should they have special curricula? The author has not observed this to a large extent in any cities consulted. Flexibility in degree of mastery, depth, and quantity are required. Teacher freedom to select suitable portions of subject matter and adjustment of coverage to suit the slowness of the culturally disadvantaged pupil are needed. The studies which have been reviewed furnish a background for considering what any children, including culturally disadvantaged, should study. Authorities in curriculum and the social studies do not agree on the sequence. Their divergent views follow. Leonard Kenworthy considers the idea of concentric-ever-widening circles as an outmoded curriculum theory.[1] Dorothy M. Fraser subscribes to "sequence in sequential development of basic concepts, values, and skills in organizing the social studies programs."[2] She feels that television, radio, movies, and travel have

---

*Professor of Education, Chicago Teachers College South.

widened children's horizons to the point that the expanding geographic areas approach is no longer sound. Ralph Preston, on the other hand, adheres partly to the "expanding environment" principle, but he too feels it is "restrictive of children's intellectual interests."[3] There can be no doubt that new and complex external stimuli affect all children. As for the culturally disadvantaged, moving outward from their limited environment seems a good approach.

CURRICULUM PROPOSALS

There are several proposals which will undoubtedly gain much notice. Two of these have been included. The plan of the American Council of Learned Societies follows.

Grade One.   Study of the Netselik Eskimo.

Grade Two.   Study of Bushmen (Australian aborigines and a Kalahari Desert people of Bechuanaland.

Grade Three.   Study of free-ranging bands of primates (baboons and chimpanzees) and of prehistoric cavemen. These foci would be involved with the subject matter of the first two grades.

Grade Four.   Origins of husbandry in the Near East and in Middle America.

Grade Five.   Origins and development of urban life in the Near East and elsewhere.

Grade Six.   Beginnings of the Western tradition in the Aegean world of Minoan Crete, Myceanean Greece, and Troy.

Grade Seven.   Western developments from about 500 B.C. to about 1600 A. D. which stress man in community.

Grade Eight.   Series of case studies on seventeenth and eighteenth century England and America with stress on the transition from subject-to-citizen.

Grade Nine.   Western developments from about 1800 to the present.[4]

To this author such a highly anthropological curriculum suggestion seems unsuited to all children and especially to the culturally disadvantaged. Subject matter should be closer to children's everyday experiences, television viewing, interests, and feelings.

The Harvard-Lexington proposals have developed considerably since 1960. Although some of the units have been tried in the Lexington pilot schools, most of them have not been used in a classroom. The Harvard-Lexington proposals are noted below.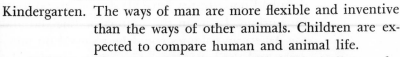

Kindergarten. The ways of man are more flexible and inventive than the ways of other animals. Children are expected to compare human and animal life.

Grade One. Men have different ways of meeting similar needs: work, learning, celebrations, art, and play.

Grade Two. Human groups and institutions involve various patterns of norms, interactions, and feelings. Such subjects as healing, medicine, markets, factories, and courts in one or two foreign countries are to be compared with the same in their community.

Grade Three. Primitive societies have adapted to a variety of natural habitats. This would include a study of horticultural people (Hopi Indians), herding people (the Masai), hunting and fishing people (the Copper Eskimos), and rice-growing people (the Tanala of Madagascar).

Grade Four. Man finds new ways to control his relationships to his environment. The units would emphasize modern beliefs and practices in contrast to primitive living in respect to water, agriculture, metals, fishing, whaling, and textiles.

Grade Five. The industrial revolution has changed the production and distribution of goods and services and has created new opportunities and problems for human society. Units on power, technology, natural resources, trade, food, population, and cities have been suggested.

Grade Six. Man's acts of inquiry, creativity, and expression evolved from and influence his total way of life. Units on these subjects could evolve from this generalization: writing and measurement associated with the Fertile Crescent, drama related to Greece, architecture connected with Rome, universities related to Europe, and exploration linked with the Renaissance.

Grade Seven. The need for law and order in community life, man's ambition for power, and his desires for freedom and opportunity have all shaped his political institutions. Units in the context of England and the American colonies could be planned on monarchy and parliament, colonies and territories, the frontier, towns and plantations, and revolution.

Grade Eight. The government and economic development of a nation are interrelated. Units would pertain to the Americas on such topics as the national constitution, migrations, and settlement, Civil War, industrialization, and modern regions.

Grade Nine. There are a variety of patterns of rivalry and cooperation among the nations of the world. In a context of United States involvement with other nations since around 1910, units could be prepared on warfare and military alliances, world government, cultural and technological exchange, economic interdependence, modern science.[5]

This interdisciplinary plan moves quite early away from the child's firsthand experience; it does, however, establish bases for relating to children's daily lives. It does not observe a chronological approach but attempts to move gradually into more complex concepts.

Typical Topics

What are the usual curricular offerings? Units on the topics which follow are common in our schools today.

Kindergarten. Holidays, school life, home, immediate neighborhood, pets, store, garden, safety, health, circus, boats, transportation, community helpers.

Grade One. Life at home and at school, family helpers, community, helpers, farm life, food, clothing, shelter, pets, transportation and communication, pioneer days, children of other lands, holidays.

Grade Two.   Community helpers.

Grade Three.   Expanding community life; food, clothing, shelter.

Grade Four.   Ways of living in other lands.

Grade Five.   History and geography of the United States.

Grade Six.   Geography of the western hemisphere or history and geography of the eastern hemisphere.

Grade Seven.   World geography, geography of the eastern hemisphere, United States history, civics, history and geography of the home state, old-world backgrounds for United States history, and social living.

Grade Eight.   United States history, geography, state history, civics, and social living.[6]

Although research indicates that children have interests beyond their own communities, this traditional plan has some advantages for culturally disadvantaged children in that it does not move out of the immediate community too fast. Small children from culturally disadvantaged homes need opportunity to develop with the familiar as a starting point. They cannot cut themselves off completely from the familiar and move into an area which is foreign to their experiences.

Chicago Curriculum

The new curriculum guides for the social studies in Chicago are cognizant of children's interests, which, research indicates, go beyond the immediate community. The subject matter seems to be within the capacities of the learners. This plan follows:

Kindergarten. At school and at home.

Grade One.   At school and in the neighborhood.

Grade Two.   Our community and other urban areas of the world.

Grade Three.   Our city and other metropolitan areas of the world.

Grade Four.   Living in regions of the United States.

Grade Five.   Cultural patterns in the western hemisphere.
Grade Six.   World cultures.
Grade Seven.   Background and beginning of the United States.
Grade Eight.   Living together in the United States.[7]

For culturally disadvantaged children, the topics through the fourth grade are exceptionally good. These guides do not make the mistake of moving too rapidly from the familiar. There is time for culturally disadvantaged pupils to build a bridge of experience to compensate for what they have missed and to have some instruction on what a good home, family, and community are. For children whose world has extended only a few blocks in any direction from their residences, starting with the familiar is necessary. But at the same level there is opportunity, even in kindergarten, for children to learn something about faraway places.

One of the criticisms made of curricula in the social studies has been a dearth of attention to metropolitan areas. In both the second and the third grades, the Chicago Guide has overcome this deficiency. In the fourth grade, the expanding environment theory continues in operation, inasmuch as the pupils study first about living in Illinois, then in the Middle West, and finally in other regions of the United States. From the standpoint of the culturally disadvantaged, "Cultural patterns in the western hemisphere" is excellent; however, the United States is not treated in the same manner as Canada, Mexico, Central America, and South America. There are units on exploration, settlement, establishing a new nation and westward expansion. In the past, this additional effort on our national history in the fifth grade has not brought satisfactory results. There are, moreover, many Spanish-American children in these classes. Treating the United States in the same manner as the other Americas would permit fuller treatment of the other countries in this hemisphere. Moreover, in the Chicago curriculum, the fifth grade is the only place where all the Americas are treated; adequate treatment of the cultural patterns of our neighbors would seem to be necessary here. In the sixth grade, this curriculum has in its treatment of world cultures emphasized Africa, the Middle East, India, the Chinas, Japan,

The story of our country, moreover, is presented with the United States playing a glorified and perfect role; this is unhappily in direct conflict with the experiences many children have in everyday life. To them, this seems unreal. The culturally disadvantaged are present oriented and to them textual material concerned with the past seems dull and unimportant. The social studies are not utilitarian in the narrow sense of the word; this certainly reduces their appeal. The very nature of the subject makes this content frustrating to these pupils.

Social Studies Skills

With a background of nonparticipation, learning the skills associated with the social studies is somewhat bewildering. These pupils have few good adult models to which they can relate. Map work is among the least frustrating of social science skills. Maps are semi-concrete in nature, and thus they have more appeal; but these children sometimes misinterpret their purpose as a picture.

Critical thinking requires careful examination of premises and factual data; conclusions are to be reached on the basis of careful consideration of all pertinent information. Such a procedure is not a part of the background of culturally disadvantaged children. Teaching critical thinking is frustrating to the teacher because she is faced with apathy, disinterest, indifference or hostility. This situation creates difficulties for the formulation of a premise; in addition, some background in content must precede it. Poor skills, poor attitude toward learning, and an inclination against organization and postponing conclusions until all data have been evaluated make the teaching of critical thinking very difficult indeed.

Group Work

For the survival of our way of life and for playing a role in a democratic state, children need practice both in leading and in following. They can get this training by group work. Lack of a sense of responsibility and an image of the role to be played by each participant makes group work difficult too. As stated above, these children come to class with poor informational and experiential backgrounds. Participating in a panel discussion is, therefore, very difficult because of the necessary grasp of subject matter and reorganization of content required while discussion is proceeding. Foundational to the success of this type of group work are library skills. Too many of these children want only to look at pictures in magazines or books in the library. If they go to the library with a serious purpose, most of them have problems in locating, collecting, and organizing material for presentation. Even if the research in the library has been successful, there is still the problem of presentation. Some of these children are very reluctant to speak before a group, even a group of their peers. One source of this problem seems to be a lack of a participating model and a feeling of personal inadequacy. As a result of so many frustrations in attempting group work, many teachers discontinue it.

Insight

Two skills requiring both imagination and organizational ability, as applied to facts, are seeing cause-and-effect relationships and graphic interpretation. Children often cannot fathom how certain events occurred. They fail to get the connection between events in the past and those of the present. These children seem not to have learned that every person's actions are rooted in the past and that all deeds have consequences. They need to be shown that historical events are like personal events on an enlarged scale with roots in the past and having an influence on the shape of the future. Seeing relationship between an event, its cause, and its effect requires imagination and organization of facts in order to achieve a complete mental picture of the situation. Teaching this can be accomplished only by the analysis of many examples; this is a laborious and time consuming procedure.

Interpretation of graphic materials requires the same skills. Whether information is to be extracted from a picture, a chart, or a graph, the learner needs a creative imagination, foundation of factual information, and practice as a springboard to gaining an interpretation from such a representation. All children have some problems with mastery of social studies skills; owing to the paucity of suitable background materials and experience, the culturally deprived experience difficulty in these learnings to a much greater degree.

Reading and Study Skills

Vocabulary and Concept Development

The reading level of many social studies textbooks seems to be higher than the average reading skills of pupils for whom the book is intended. For culturally deprived pupils, this is unsuitable. These pupils need intensive work on vocabulary development. The language they hear in their neighborhoods is not the same as the formal English of textbooks; the vocabulary used in the home is frequently quite limited. The pupils need help in a social studies skills period. These steps have been found useful in attacking words and enlarging the vocabulary:

1. Place a vocabulary list on the chalk board daily.
2. Apply diacritical marks to letters to aid pronunciation.
3. Pronounce the words.
4. Divide the words into syllables.
5. Place the accents on the words.
6. Find the root word.
7. Add prefixes and suffixes to the root word and explore changes in meaning.
8. Find the word in context.
9. Try to define the word from the context in which it appears.
10. Check the definition in the dictionary.
11. Let pupils use the words in sentences of their own. For variety the teacher can give a short multiple choice exercise.
12. Review frequently.
13. Let the children prepare personal dictionaries of especially troublesome words or devote a section of their notebooks to vocabulary. Small children may enjoy making a picture dictionary.

Disadvantaged children are said to be physically oriented; they are *thing minded* as some authorities have stated. If children cannot understand the concepts, they have not really learned. Words may be spoken, but if there is no understanding of the concepts, nothing but empty verbalization has taken place. Mere memorization is dull, and children soon forget. This is the level at which some social studies classes operate. Only if learners can use concepts and facts to make generalization do they remember.

The hints which follow have been helpful to some pupils. Classroom human relations can be explored for concepts which a teacher is attempting to teach. When children discuss concepts in relationship to situations which occurred in the classroom, in school, or on the playground, they are exploring experiences in their immediate environment. These have meaning for children. The community, a field trip, a movie, a filmstrip or pictures can be utilized in the same way to reveal the meaning of abstract concepts. Children can sometimes comprehend abstractions from stories which have been read or told by teacher or pupils. Current events, radio, television, and comics can serve the same purpose.

Purpose for Reading

In order to gain the maximum meaning from what one reads, there should be a definite, established purpose so that the reader is expectant and receptive. In too many cases in classrooms of culturally deprived, pupils are merely instructed to read. They should have a definite purpose for reading. Different types of reading are needed for mastery of the social studies. These children need to be instructed in these techniques. Some useful types of reading follow.

1. Reading for details requires concentration and slow reading for the purpose of noting and remembering many facts. Listing details in answer to definite questions helps children to concentrate on the content. These answers should be used in preparing for a lesson or a quiz—for a definite purpose.

2. Skimming is rapid reading to locate a date, a name, a place, or a definite fact. The teacher can teach this technique as well as use it in classroom work, such as, finding the significance of a list of key words.

3. Predicting outcomes is that type of reading by which the reader guesses at the outcome of a situation before he has actually completed reading about it. This is highly motivating and speeds up reading. To introduce and illustrate the technique, the teacher can tell a human relations story and let the pupils finish it. From this example, the pupils can use the same technique on textbook material.

4. Seeing relationships between facts is important to comprehension of cause and effect. The teacher can demonstrate this by writing two lists of facts on the chalk board, asking the children to read a few paragraphs, and then permitting a child to draw lines to facts which have a relationship to each other.

5. Drawing conclusions from a set of facts about a situation is a necessary ability to give meaning to historical events. Pupils can be introduced to this by letting them act as detectives with definite questions and a set of classroom events from which they are to draw conclusions. After pupils learn this technique, they should be able to apply it to historical problems.

6. Perceiving the main idea requires the ability, while reading, of eliminating extraneous information. It is a reading skill which is necessary in judging the relative importance of events. Children may be introduced to this by letting them write a caption for a bulletin board display. After this experience, they can capsulize the content of a paragraph in one sentence.

7. Recognizing and organizing supporting information is needed to construct an outline. The bulletin board may again be used as a point of departure. Select several good captions which members of the class have previously written. From the bulletin board display, let the class write the details supporting the main idea. Starting with the bulletin board would attract more pupils to this activity than the textbook would. From this exercise, move to the textbook. Boys and girls should write the main idea or ideas of a section with supporting details listed below in a logical order.

These need to be discussed for applicability to main topic and logical sequence.

8. Following directions is an important reading skill for solving any kind of problem, whether it is connected with the lesson, activities, map work, etc. Using a "help wanted" advertisement would be attractive to culturally disadvantaged young people and should impress the importance of sequential steps and retention of information.

9. Critical reading requires the pupil to relate what he is reading to his experience and to compare his reading with information which he has read elsewhere. Since the pupil must recall and compare information while he is reading, his rate of reading will be slow. This is a valuable type of reading because the reader is mentally organizing the information and will, therefore, remember it.

Handicapped Readers

Inasmuch as many culturally disadvantaged pupils are so seriously handicapped in reading, it is possible to borrow a method from the primary grades. The successful use of the experience chart with older boys and girls for teaching vocabulary and reading has been observed. Events which can be employed for background information for the experience chart are teacher or pupil stories about an adventure, emergency, or other exciting event, a field trip, picture explorations, viewing a film or a filmstrip, and realia organized about a major event or striking personality. After having listened or experienced, pupils will tell what impressed them. The teacher can write this story on the chalk board or on wrapping paper.

The vocabulary and the approximate sentence structure of the learners should be used. This material uses the experience of children and their language. It is simple, but it is not a primary book (much resented by older children). This technique has been used to teach reading to intermediate grade children who were practically nonreaders. It is an excellent starting point for the culturally disadvantaged child who cannot read and is already quite large. When children are defeated by reading problems is the time to teach the skills which are needed, regardless of where they are usually taught.

Study Skills

The learner should be made aware in a social studies skills period that there are definite procedures for mastering this subject. This is one of the times that he should be required to practice these skills. Experience with varied rates of reading when using different social studies reading techniques will acquaint the learner with the need for adjusting the rate of reading to purpose and content. The *SQ3R* technique—survey the material, formulate questions, and then read, recite, and review—should be a regular part of the social studies skills period until the learner comprehends. Outlining and summarizing should be practiced on a small scale at first to enable the teacher to check thoroughly and immediately on the learner's organizational skill. Reorganizing a scrambled outline is helpful in teaching organization. Summarizing current events is a helpful step toward learning to organize selected textual materials for learning or review purposes.

Additional essential study skills are the proper use of textbooks, encyclopedias, dictionaries, and the library. The teacher in elementary school should acquaint the pupils with the tools through problem situations. With the teacher's help, children should practice preparing lessons by using services available in a textbook. These include the table of contents, maps, pictures, glossary, index, chapter headings, section headings, topical headings, and finally questions, tests, suggested activities, and word lists at the end of a chapter. Finding needed information in the textbook should be practiced constantly so that the child does not feel that a textbook is to be memorized. A textbook is a source of information—an attitude many children do not have. The dictionary skills of locating words by the use of the alphabet and guide words should be practiced by using the dictionary, not just talking about it, for solving specific problems. Giving general instructions on the use of the textbook and the dictionary are of as little value as giving general hints on the use of the library and the location of materials. Pupils should be sent to the library to solve specific problems, such as, using the card catalogue and the *Reader's Guide* or locating information in encyclopedias. Only through helping pupils use these sources of information can frustration be reduced. Culturally disadvantaged children need more time and practice to develop skills for obtaining information and presenting it.

Techniques

As stated earlier, reading is the key to the social studies. Reading skills and library skills needed in the social studies have already been discussed. In the lower grades in culturally disadvantaged areas, the social studies lesson can profitably become a reading lesson part of the time. Furthermore, if the content of readers were more closely correlated with content of the social studies in second and third grades, the change would be mutually beneficial. This would give definite purpose to reading, but it should also provide a sounder foundation for the social studies by allotting much more time to the exploration of the content of the social studies. The primary grades are the place to begin teaching the social studies skills. This is a period when children are more cooperative, uninhibited, and more receptive to the idea of participation. This plan would seem also to provide opportunity to gain some experiential background to compensate for lack of experiences.

In appealing to culturally disadvantaged pupils, emphasizing the problems, controversies, and struggles that individuals and nations have undergone would touch on a daily experience in their lives. The use of biography and careful structuring of units would be helpful in this emphasis. Current events can be given this slant; using current events as a flashback technique, from the present to the past, brings out the similarity of events or at least the connection between the happenings of present and past. Culturally disadvantaged children are also more interested if they have realistic goals, and if they are aware what their goals are. The skillful and enthusiastic teacher can carry children along to plan their goals. Certainly, techniques which enrich and enable children to be more successful in mastering this area are helpful.

Activities bring subject matter to life by building a background of experience, encouraging participation, and enabling children to learn responsibility. Field trips provide opportunities to escape the limitations of their neighborhoods and to lift their horizons by experiencing in a museum, an art gallery, or a factory what has been the subject of their lesson. Because these pupils are not highly verbal, graphic material is frequently better understood. Charts, pictures, cartoons, graphs and maps can be prepared by pupils; if these materials are placed on display, the self-image of the participants is indeed improved. Enthusiasm and competition are generated by this recognition. Contests are another technique for generating enthusiasm. Dramatization has high appeal. Elementary children enjoy acting out what they learn in classrooms and in assembly programs in the form of dramatic play, puppets, and dramatizations, depending upon their age. The sociodrama is a type of acting out, but the purpose is to gain perspective and solutions of people's problems by looking at them through the eyes of someone else. This method can be applied to personal or to historical problems; this activity enlarges the understanding of people. The interview technique, modeled on television, is a motivating and informative activity.

Teachers are often disappointed with the results of a round table discussion, a panel, a debate, a report, etc. The results are usually better if children are brought into group work gradually and afforded much supervision in preparation. The first step is to teach pupils how to prepare and present a report. Even an individual activity with all responsibility resting on one pupil requires much follow-up work by the teacher to make sure that the preparation of the report is progressing by collecting materials. After materials have been collected, a conference between teacher and pupil is necessary to organize the material. The next step is to instruct the child how to present the report. Many culturally disadvantaged children have no mental image of such an activity. If they understand their role, they will more likely respond. For any kind of group work, starting on the most structured activity first is wise; a debate is a structured activity, whereas a panel is less structured and much more difficult for culturally disadvantaged pupils. Setting standards for participation, defining roles, assisting with preparation, and evaluating efforts do help. Because a group project does not meet a teacher's expectations does not make it a failure. Much may have been learned from a clumsy effort. Only repeated attempts at group work, followed by a sympathetic evaluation, will bring improvement. To break the pattern of passiveness, apathy, and indifference requires much more time and effort on a teacher's part.

A number of other activities and methods aid culturally disadvantaged children with learning. Audio-visual materials largely circumvent the reading problem; when properly used these devices are effective. One of the big problems of these children is listening. In their home environment, they have learned to shut out noise; this habit carries over into the classroom. Teachers have taught listening with exercises and games which require pupils to listen for some definite point. The room library is especially useful to pupils of this type because they need much supervision and assistance by the classroom teacher in preparing projects. These children solve many environmental problems. In upper grades, they need to be taught the steps of problem solving which include the following stages:

1. Recognizing and defining a problem.
2. Analyzing a problem and organizing it into its basic elements and forming tentative hypotheses.
3. Collecting relevant data.
4. Evaluating data.
5. Organizing and interpreting data.
6. Forming conclusions.
7. Verifying conclusions.
8. Applying conclusions.[11]

If pupils can be personally or emotionally involved in problem solving, this technique can be rewarding.

A new technique in the social studies is known as the *discovery* method or figuring out clues. It has been used in the secondary schools. The author can see no reason why this technique should not be used on a limited scale in the elementary school, especially for motivation. If realia were arranged on a table, the culturally deprived would likely be attracted and would try to figure out from the clues what kind of people used these items. It would seem that this could be a very stimulating technique.

Not all pupils classified as slow learners are really slow learners; some are underachievers. The fact remains, however, that there are many culturally disadvantaged children who have difficulty in learning. Some helpful methods include the following: cutting the subject into small bits so that essentials can be taught on a one-day basis; units should be very short; each day's work must begin with a review of previous work because much repetition is essential for retention of limited amounts of content; all nonessential content must be excluded. The pace of learning must be slowed to fit the pupils, reading materials must be kept at a level at which pupils can read them; outlining subject matter simplifies it and reduces the reading task; work sheets of one-half page of reading and one-half page of exercises based on the reading; workbooks; duplicated reading sheets on which the content has been simplified and the reading level is reduced several years. The author has observed all of these methods in operation with varying degrees of success.

An essential ingredient to learning is motivation. For the culturally deprived, this is probably the most important prerequisite to learning. Here are some motivational techniques used by teachers in New York City: unscrambling words, compiling a who's who for review, newspaper articles dealing with subject matter under consideration, stick figure charts to follow progress of important historical figures, interpret pictures, reading interesting excerpts from books, cartoons, tape recorder, sociodrama, roving reporter, poll taker, mock campaign, drawing up a budget, your wardrobe 100 years ago, flannel board, newspaper headlines related to study of history or geography, map work.[12] These motivations should appeal to all children, culturally disadvantaged included.

The Social Studies Teacher

To teach in a socially disadvantaged area, a social studies teacher needs both a good background of subject matter and an orientation to teaching in such an area. There is no one type of teacher who is successful to the exclusion of other types. To make progress in such a school a teacher must develop empathy for these children. Such characteristics as a sense of humor, tolerance, warmth, dignity, decisiveness, consistency and sincerity are essential to survival. One of the greatest fears of teachers entering culturally disadvantaged schools in discipline. Describing reasonable limitations on conduct and enforcing restrictions provides psychological support needed by these pupils. Helpful, too, is a somewhat formal, routinized, and structured procedure. Applying all of these suggestions, the teacher must still expect days for which she needs high frustration tolerance. Never forgetting the importance of being an example and developing empathy with these children, in time the teacher can earn the respect of his class.

Additional Services

Additional services are required to assist teachers of the social studies in culturally disadvantaged areas. At best, these teachers are exhausted from their efforts with large classes of difficult pupils. They lack the time and energy to assemble the types of illustrative and supplementary materials so necessary for motivation and learning in the social studies. The author proposes the establishment of a school-wide materials center from which materials could be loaned to teachers as needed. This room could be a repository for pictures, projectors, films, filmstrips, tape recorders, record players, records, slides, posters, charts, statistical data, graphs, cartoons, art work, drawings, maps, murals, flannel boards, free and inexpensive materials, clipping files, models, mock-ups, diorama, booklets on special subjects, novels, magazines, periodicals, reduced reading sheets, work sheets, workbooks, costumes, realia, etc. These materials should be circulated by a materials center coordinator who does not need to be a professional. Teaching with only a textbook is drab; from my observation culturally deprived children respond to the types of materials noted above.

Teachers should have the assistance and leadership of a social studies master teacher. There should be one for every 200 teachers. In the slums, the school day should be lengthened with a definite time, such as from 8:00-9:00 a.m., set aside for planning Every Thursday, for example, could be the planning day for social studies.

The social studies have been short changed in regard to time. In many schedules, the social studies classes command only three periods per week. The program necessary to improve the teaching of social studies in the elementary school cannot be accomplished in three periods. The author suggests daily social studies classes with a minimum of 200 minutes per week, plus a compensatory social studies skills period of twenty or twenty-five minutes per day. Such a program would go far in laying a foundation which would enable both elementary and secondary social studies teachers to function as they should.

Is there a key to solving the problems of teaching the social studies to culturally disadvantaged pupils? Are there methods which work magic? From the viewpoint of the author, the answer is *no* to both questions. Should culturally disadvantaged children have a special program and special activities? Inasmuch as these children will grow to adulthood to make their contribution in a democratic state, they should be exposed to the same curriculum; how the curriculum is implemented for culturally disadvantaged would be different. For these children, activities must be more structured, materials must be written at their level of performance, and there must be enough time for them to function. They must have plenty of time to practice the roles they are to learn. The teacher's attitude is all-important in establishing a climate for learning; the teacher must be warm, accepting and respectful toward these children. He should have great emotional stability and self-control. To implement an effective social studies program for all of our children is a paramount responsibility of all educators today. The relationship between the world's unsolved human problems and the social studies requires no elaboration.

REFERENCES

1. L. J. Alitunas, "An Analysis of Social Studies Content in the Middle Grades," *Social Studies,* 52 (November, 1961) , p. 215.
2. *Ibid.,* p. 215.

3. *Ibid.,* p. 216.
4. Joseph C. Grannis, "The Framework of the Social Studies Curriculum," *National Elementary Principal,* 42 (April, 1963), p. 23.
5. *Ibid.,* p. 25.
6. Dorothy M. Fraser and Edith West, *Social Studies in Secondary Schools* (New York, The Ronald Press Company, 1961), p. 23.
7. Chicago Public Schools, *Curriculum Guides for the Social Studies* (Chicago, Board of Education, 1964).
8. Curriculum Bulletin, vol. viii, Milwaukee, Wisconsin: Board of Education, 1951.
9. At the Burns Elementary School in Chicago, Mrs. Helen Saunders, a student teacher, taught this work successfully to a seventh grade.
10. Helen Huus, "Reading," *Thirty-third Yearbook of the National Council for the Social Studies* (Washington, D. C.: National Council for the Social Studies, 1963), p. 96.
11. James Quillen and Lavone Hanna, *Education for Social Competence* (Chicago, Scott, Foresman and Company, 1948), p. 128.
12. Lillian Howitt, Suggested Motivations in the Social Studies," *High Points,* 40 (October, 1958), pp. 40-54.

Suggested Readings

Alexander, Albert, "The Gray Flannel Cover on the American History Textbook," *Social Education,* 24:11-14, January, 1960.

Alilunas, L. J., "An Analysis of Social Studies Content in the Middle Grades," *Social Studies,* 52:210-218, November, 1961.

Cammarota, Gloria, "New Emphases in Social Studies for the Primary Grades," *Social Education,* 27:77-80, February, 1963.

Davis, O. L., "Children Can Learn Complex Concepts," *Educational Leadership,* 17:170-175, December, 1959.

Della-Dora, Delmo, "The Culturally Disadvantaged, Further Observations," *Journal of Exceptional Children,* 29:467-471, January, 1963. Curriculum Bulletin, vol. VIII. Milwaukee, Wisconsin: Board of Education, 1951.

Dimitroff, Lillian, "A Quantitative-Qualitative Analysis of Selected Social Science Generalizations in Social Studies Textbooks in the Intermediate Grades." Unpublished Doctor's dissertation, Northwestern University, Evanston, Illinois, 1958, pp. 580.

Dimitroff, Lillian, "Small Group Training for Spanish-speaking Pupils," *Chicago Schools Journal,* 45:71, November, 1963.

Farrell, Muriel, "Understanding of Time Relations of Five, Six and Seven-year-old Children of High IQ," *Journal of Educational Research,* 46:587-594, April, 1953.

Fraser, Dorothy M. and Edith West, *Social Studies in Secondary Schools.* New York: The Ronald Press Company, 1961, pp. 476.

Grannis, Joseph C., "The Framework of the Social Studies Curriculum," *National Elementary Principal*, 42:20-26, April, 1963.

Havighurst, Robert J., "Conditions Productive of Superior Children," *Teachers College Record*, 62:524-531, April, 1961.

Howeitt, Lillian, "Suggested Motivations in the Social Studies," *High Points*, 40:40-54, October, 1958.

Huck, Charlotte S., "The Nature and Derivation of Young Children's Social Concepts." Unpublished Doctor's dissertation, Northwestern University, Evanston, Illinois, 1955. 298 pp.

Huus, Helen, "Reading," *Thirty-third Yearbook of the National Council for the Social Studies*, Washington, D. C.: National Council for the Social Studies, 1963. pp. 94-115.

Ingraham, Leonard W., "Programed Instructional Materials in Social Studies: 1962," *Social Education*, 27:15-17+, January, 1964.

Kenworthy, Leonard S., "Ferment in the Social Studies," *Phi Delta Kappan*, 44:12-16, October, 1962.

Krug, Mark M., "Needed: New Frontiers in the Social Studies," *Chicago Schools Journal*, 43: 7-12, October, 1961.

McAulay, J. D., "What Understandings do Second Grade Children Have of Time Relationships?" *Journal of Educational Research*, 54:312, April 1961.

McAulay, J. D., "Interests of Elementary School Children," *Social Education*, 25:407-409, December, 1961.

McAulay, J. D., "Social Studies Interests of Primary-grade Child," *Social Education*, 26:247-248, May, 1962.

Mugge, Dorothy J., "Precocity of Today's Young Children: Real or Wishful?" *Social Education*, 27:436-439, December, 1963.

Norton, Monte S., "The Use of Self-Evaluation in the Social Studies," *Social Studies*, 51:3-9, January, 1960.

Oliver, Donald W., "The Selection of Content in the Social Sciences," *Harvard Educational Review*, 27:271-300, Fall, 1957.

Pistar, Frederick, "How Time Concepts are Acquired by Children," *Educational Method*, 20: 107-112, November, 1940.

Chapter X

MUSIC FOR THE DISADVANTAGED PUPIL

Dolores Nicosia*

Music is an important segment of every child's training and for the culturally disadvantaged it is an absolute necessity. Through music, intellectual achievement is sensed; cultural traditions recognized; group interdependence accepted. Music sustains dreams; reinforces concepts and skills learned in other subjects; and stabilizes the pressures inherent in a competitive, academically oriented classroom. Besides, it's fun!

In a too short (from one point of view) workday, teachers ask how can music help to vitalize and interpret the curriculum for the culturally disadvantaged? What activities and concepts can either the teacher with a limited background or the music specialist provide to extend the experiences needed to balance the child's total development? This discussion is divided into three classifications: (1) the acculturation and socialization of the child through music; (2) linguistics, literature and music, and (3) the classroom teacher and basic music concepts.

ACCULTURATION AND SOCIALIZATION THROUGH MUSIC

"Acculturation refers to the group's taking on elements from the culture of another group."[1] Socialization is "the process of building group values into the individual."[2] For the purpose of this presentation, acculturation pertains to the activities which *ease* the newcomer into a strange environment, and socialization relates to the activities which assist the child in creating a self-school-community image, as well as the development of linguistic skills. Often, both terms will apply to the examples cited and the suggestions given. It is assumed that the preceeding chapters have

---

*Music supervisor, Chicago Public Schools.

made readers knowledgeable about the socio-psycho-economic factors which contribute to the behavior of the child.

Self-image

School had been in session for one week, yet enrollees still filed into the auditorium for registration.

"Number 74," called the registrar.

Mothers, aunts, an older brother and two shy girls responded. All helped answer the questionnaire and all agreed that placing the girls in separate second grade rooms was unreasonable and portentous.

"You'll see," taunted one mother, "they won't be back this afternoon."

The entourage followed the registrar to the classroom door, and peering in listened to the introduction of one small girl to thirty strangers.

"Each of you remembers your first day at school—how frightened you were and how much you wanted to make new friends," coached the teacher. All nodded in unison.

"Who, as a new friend, will help Sonia during her first days at school?" Several hands waved in the air. Sonia was smiling but the registrar could feel a trembling hand within her clasp. A busy little helper ran for some paper, pencils and crayons and then pulled Sonia to an empty seat near her. So began a very belated first day of school for a ten year old Gypsy.

Similar incidents occur hundreds of times during the school year. Like Sonia, transients are insecure, and fearful of rejection and loneliness (Sutton, p. 23-26). In one school where the turnover is so great that the front door should be on a revolving hinge, the principal asked a teacher to write a welcome song to help minimize this feeling of strangeness. "How Do You Do! A Friendly Introduction" would have been an ideal audio-aid to establish rapport between Sonia and her classmates. It would also indicate that the resident students were prepared to receive recent arrivals (Sutton, p. 35).

With little coaching from the teacher and an assigned 'buddy' the newcomer can easily participate in the song.

How Do You Do!
A Friendly Introduction

KRAWITZ '62

Greet ev-'ry-one (*Name* ___) Won't you stand up? { Here I am / Here we are / Stand up } How do you do, ev-'ry-one! Glad to be here, hav-ing fun! How do you do, ev-'ry-one! Wel-come t you, wel-come t you!

ritard *a tempo*

D.C.

Fine

School Image

Because the population explosion has reached the high schools, eighth grade graduates often are required to remain in the elementary school as a ninth grade division. Disappointed, a negative attitude towards the high school branch soon becomes apparent among those displaced freshmen. What they seek is a status symbol to help create an identity distinguishing them from the elementary school pupils. What they need is school spirit.

The music teacher from DuSable Branch can tell you that school spirit is a flesh and blood creature not subject to conjuration.[3] Her suggestion for a school song was unanimously vetoed by the school body. As a motivational device she used poetry by prominent Negro poets, e.g., Frank Home's *Kidstuff*. Owen Dodson's *Counterpoint*, and Clarissa Scott Delany's *Solace* to spark a discussion of the differences between the ideas expressed in the poems and life as it is in school. Student suggested ideas and opinions were adapted to a rhythmic chant. Musical selections and chord tuned pop bottles were used as background or harmonic accompaniment. A gifted boy accepted the subtle challenge and composed a calypso school song.[4] Encouraged by his success, other students brought their bongos to school and created a rhythmic accompaniment for the school song which they sing and play with gusto and pride.

Community Image

An impact upon the community can manifest itself in the most unexpected ways. As part of their routine class work, the sixth and seventh graders of the Farren Elementary School used a simply structured play as a vehicle to create a positive school image to the community. The classroom teacher incorporated local gangism into a twenty minute musical playet, *Be a Bond,* based on the theme of *West Side Story*, by Leonard Bernstein.[5] Two groups, the Black Jackets and the White Jackets become involved in a street fight, are apprehended by the police, brought to trial and sentenced to one year of "getting along." At the end of the year, they were bound in brotherhood. The press didn't review the playlet, yet, overnight the performers became "cele-

Forrestville, Hey! Forrestville!

Words and Music by
JAMES HATCHER, 9th Grade

Calypso beat

We work in school 'til day is done, We
leave from home in the morn-ing sun; Play-ing games and
Cho. hav-ing fun, But no-bod-y goes 'til the work is done.
For - rest - ville, Hey! For - rest - ville,
Ev-'ry-bod-y talk-in' bout For-rest-ville. For-rest-ville,
For-rest-ville, Ev-'ry-bod-y talk-in' bout For-rest-ville.

2. Now reading' writin' and 'rithmetic
   can be fun, we learn this quick.
   In the noon we dash for food
   Drinkin' milk in a happy mood.
         Chorus:

3. Then after lunch we head for the door,
   Got to go back and work some more.
   My hands they burn, my head it aches,
   And forty-five minutes is all it takes.
         Chorus.

4. In the noontime when the sun is low,
   Got to get moving it's time to go,
   Gather up the books and we're on our way
   Start out again the same each day.
         Chorus:

brities" giving command performances for the PTA and the housing authority personnel of the local settlement houses.

A more direct and as effective method for developing a positive school image is inter-school and inter-community programing. The special summer schools strategically located throughout the city enroll pupils from several communities. Dr. Angeline Caruso and her staff designed and presented two programs to overcome the parochialism of the child's world, to promote school unity and to create a community image.[6]

A warm and inviting climate for the first program, Music-in-the-Round, was achieved by the welcoming committee of students and teachers. They decorated the school, rolled out a red carpet and flanked it with drummers and cheerleaders who greeted the bus loads of visiting pupils. More than 650 pupils sat on the floor in a circle, four deep around the multi-purpose gymnasium. The piano, microphone and master of ceremonies were in the center of the floor. A hearty, boisterous parody, "Hello Mason, Hello Hefferan," opened the program. Guests from the central office, district office, PTA and community were introduced to the assembly. Even though school had been in session only two weeks, each class was able to present a short musical selection.

In response to a request for some instant harmony and group singing, the music consultant used the familiar *Swing Low*, with two descants that required one minute to learn.

A comparison was made between the children around the room and children around the world singing songs which have similar themes. In England, the song is called *Looby Loo*, in the United States it's the *Hokey Pokey*, but in Liberia it becomes *Peter Works with One Hammer.*[7]

Five weeks later, Folk-Dances-in-the-Round was presented as a school-community culminating activity. The children paraded around the school in costumes illustrative of the dances which were to be performed outside. Pupils from the Dumas arrived and were given the same rousing welcome as the Mason and Hefferan schools. Parents came to the program equipped with their own chairs and camp stools. Groups of twenty-five, fifty, one hundred, and even 650 performed typical American folk

Peter Works With One Hammer

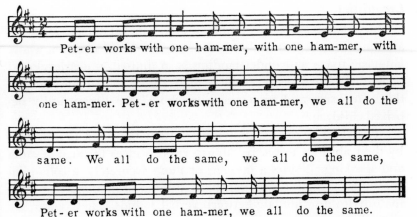

Pet-er works with one ham-mer, with one ham-mer, with one ham-mer. Pet-er works with one ham-mer, we all do the same. We all do the same, we all do the same, Pet-er works with one ham-mer, we all do the same.

Printed with permission of the collection Marian A Gerlach; Glenbrook North High-School, Northbrook, Illinois.

Peter Works with One Hammer

1. One hammer   move right hand in pounding motion

2. Two hammers   move right and left hands in alternating pounding motion

3. Three hammers   move both hands and scuff right foot.

4. Four hammers   move both hands and scuff left and right foot.

5. Five hammers   do above motions while nodding the head.

dances. "These special events established morale and identification for the children as well as the staff not to mention the happy dividends of reinforced public relations."[8]

LINGUISTICS, LITERATURE, AND MUSIC

Linguistics

Inept language facility dominates the long list of characteristics attributed to the culturally disadvantaged. "Those children whose language usage and understanding is so limited, underdeveloped or wrongly developed as to limit their ability to communicate, to think, to learn and to succeed in school" are linguistically deprived children.[9]

The level of success individuals attain in school is measured by their abilities to receive and to express ideas through reading and speaking. Besides a meager, or more accurately, a colloquial vocabulary, linguistically deprived children are hampered by the inability to discriminate between verbal sounds. They cannot see what they hear nor can they hear what they see. Auditory perception not only affects a child's reading skills but his speech skills as well (Russell and Fea, Bloomfield). "The melodies of speech are a subtle and elusive music which requires as much ear training as singing for clear reception of the finer details."[10]

In a second grade classroom demonstration of an approach to creative music through speech, a music consultant suggested to the children that they play an echo game. To be certain that they understood what she was referring to, she asked them to define "an echo." Unhesitatingly, a Negro girl replied "An echo, why that's five pennies."

After the consultant illustrated an echo with a loud and soft "hello," one little fellow from Appalachia, leaped to his feet and beamed, "That's like in the mountains."

Neither of these children was mentally slow as they later demonstrated, but their answers do reflect serious differences in speech patterns and experiences. "The psychology of a second language development (for many Americans, formal English is equivalent to a second language), indicates that hearing words, phrases and sentences as they are spoken in situations which the pupil understands, is fundamental to learning how to use the language meaningfully."[11]

An approach which provides meaningful experiences both in language and in music is the *Orff-Schulwerk*. Prior to World War II Carl Orff, and an assistant Gunild Keetman, formulated and developed his theory of music education at the Gunterschule in Munich, Germany. In the late forties, Orff, prompted by friends, resumed his work with children through a series of radio broadcasts from which have evolved the five volumes of *Music for Children* (Orff).

The principles underlying Orff's doctrine are: (1) music is the natural outcome of speech, rhythm and movement; (2) the purpose of education is to free the child's creative ability which manifests itself in improvisation, and (3) performance should precede the theoretical (Orff, Col. I). In other words, rote learning should precede notation just as speech precedes reading.

Correlating Orff with the language arts curriculum is simple and fascinating. Begin with something as familiar to you as the chanting of the ABC's to the rhythm and tune of "Twinkle, Twinkle Little Star." Easier still, is the chanting of the roll call,

e.g., Juan, Ma-ri-a, Hen-ry, Lil-i-mae. Have the children echo by repeating their names or the proper speech pattern, "I am here" rather than "I'se hereah." Try chanting a row of words borrowed from Bloomfield's *Let's Read,* or names of objects in the room, or the reading-spelling vocabularies, e.g.,

pin, pan, pun

sit, sat, set

window, floor, door.

Observe how the diction becomes more precise the moment you

chant a group of isolated words, phrases, rhymes or riddles. In order to maintain the rhythm, the final consonant sounds must be pronounced.

Use the following chant as an example for making apparent the mood and tonal qualities of words. Call the children's attention to the differences in the sound of the words blue and black, the crispness of bob-o-link and the softness of whippoorwill. After the children have learned the chant, have one section of the class stamp and clap the pulse and another section clap the rhythmic pattern.

Orff's emphasis on physical response, i.e., clapping, stamping, knee-slapping, and finger snapping as well as dance movements support Riessman's concept that the culturally disadvantaged child is more responsive to tactile or motor experiences (Riessman p. 29).

Rhythm, which includes accent, meter, pattern, and tempo is only one element of music or language. Another equally important element is intonation or pitch. Together these elements comprise what Lefevre refers to as the "melodies of the printed page."[13] While rhythm can stand alone as in a chant, a melody must have both pitch and rhythm. Both Lefevre and Orff recognize the importance of melody each in his own special way. Lefevre advises that the best method to develop consciously the signals and structures of language a child should, "practice speaking and oral reading of familiar patterns with emphasis on native intonation."[14] Orff introduces rhythmic patterns and tonal patterns simultaneously by encouraging children to set to music various rhymes, riddles, and ballads. He begins with the falling minor third, g-e and successively adds the following tonal patterns a-g-e, a-g-e-c, and a-g-e-d-c. These patterns comprise the pentatonic scale. The advantage of the pentatonic scale is that any combination of tones will be correct. Some combinations may be better than others but none will be wrong. What a relief for children who find it difficult to come up with the right answers!

To avoid monotony, vary both the dynamics and the tempo. Divide the class into groups of high-low, dark-light voices or solo and chorus. When using familiar rhymes, add a second or third verse to make the experience more contemporary. For example the "muffin man on Drury Lane" is not as realistic a verbal experience as the "mailman on Kenmore Avenue" or the "baker on Halsted street."

To summarize the Orff approach, let's apply the process of chant-clap-sing-play to the following rhyme:

Only My Opinion[15]
Is a caterpillar ticklish?
Well, it's always my belief
That he giggles, as he wiggles
Across a hairy leaf.

Step One. Chant words rhythmically
Step Two. Clap the pulse (beat).
Step Three. Stamp or patschen (knee-slapping) on first beat and clap the remaining beats.
Step Four. Divide the class into two groups. Have one group clap and stamp the meter and the other group clap the rhythmic pattern.
Step Five. Make up a tune based on the pentatonic scale, c-d-e-g-a-c. Be sure to end on 'c'. Go ahead and try it. You can't make a mistake.
Step Six. Play your tune on resonator bells, melody bells, xylophone or even the piano. If necessary put markers on the keys to indicate the pentatonic scale.

Step Seven.   Try improvising an accompaniment by playing two or three tones over and over. This repeated figure or pattern is an ostinato.

One possible rhythmic analysis is as follows:

Of course, Orff incorporates the aspects of notation into his approach. However, our major objectives at this level are (1) the improvement of speech and (2) building a repertoire of performing experiences.

Literature

In *Heal the Hurt Child,* Hertha Riese indicates that the environment in which many culturally deprived children exist is not conducive for the creation of poetry. Rhythmic flow of speech is scarcely within the scope of an inharmonious household. Regardless of the background, children enjoy the imagery and rhythmic flow of poetry. This is one reason why the Orff approach has such extensive appeal.

When presenting a poem to children, keep in mind the same elements that prevail in the artistic interpretation of a song, namely, articulation, tempo, dynamics, intonation, tone quality, mood and harmonic blending of voices. The suggested procedure can be done in one forty-minute period or extended over several days.

1. Help the children select a short poem from their readers or an anthology.

2. Write the poem on the board in syllables.
3. Read the poem for its metric pattern, i.e., strong-weak or strong-weak-weak pulses.
4. Mark the accented (strong or stressed) syllables with a long vertical line; mark the unaccented (weak or unstressed) pulses with a short vertical line.
5. Place a measure bar in front of the accented pulse.
6. Reread and mark the syllables for their long and short duration of their sounds. Use horizontal lines, first, and then substitute the proper notes e.g., ♩ ♩ ♩ ♪♪
7. Have individual children create a tune for the first phrase. Select the best and most suitable tune.
8. Continue the procedure for each phrase.
9. Indicate the pitch levels by line, number or syllable.
10. Teacher selects the key most appropriate for the song.
11. Teacher writes the notation on a staff.
12. Class improvises a rhythmic accompaniment.

Frequently, the procedure is done in reverse. Most teachers and children find it easier to begin with a familiar tune and then create verses to fit the rhythm of the song. At an Open House meeting, a second grade class of the LeMoyne school entertained their parents and guests with a program on *clothing*, which was an outgrowth of their science and social studies units. Interlacing the script were several songs, the words of which were created by the children under the guidance of the teacher.[16] The theme song, "Clothing's Not What It Appears To Be" to the tune of "Baa, Baa, Black Sheep" and "Rubber" to the tune of "This Old Man" were two of the children's favorites.

> "Clothing's Not What It Appears To Be."
> Clothing's not what it appears to be.
> It comes from such strange things you see.
> Growing things like plants and trees,
> Provide much clothing for you and me.
> Ladies find nylon hosiery
> Comes from black coal, yes siree.

Sheep, cows, rocoons and rabbits
Are some of the animals from which clothing comes.

"Rubber"

Rubber comes from a tree,
It makes rain coats for you and me.
We're very lucky that rubber we get
Or we'd be so very very wet.

Mary Austin suggests that teachers help children to read in technicolor and to hear the sound of words (Austin, p. 2). Why not vitalize literature with the sound of music? Teachers can achieve a stereo dimension through songs, records, and dramatizations.

If the story includes a reference to a song, first teach the song, then as you read the story with the children have them sing rather than speak the verse.

Then the one in the center chooses someone in the circle to skip with him, and everyone sings:

Yes, I know the Muffin Man,
The Muffin Man,
The Muffin Man,
Yes I know the Muffin Man
Who lives on Drury Lane.

Woodrow almost never was chosen because he always skipped so hard his partner tripped and sometimes bit a lip.[17]

Other suggestions are: Bulla, C. R., *Secret Valley*; Bulla, C. R., *Songs of Mr. Small* to correlate with Lenski's *Songs of Mr. Small*; Chase, R., *Grandfathers Tales*; Conger, Marion, *A Day at the Zoo*; Credle, E., *Here Comes the Showboat*, and Politi, L., *A Boat for Peppe, Juanita Pedro, Angel of Olvera Street*, and *Song of the Swallows*.

Opportunities should be given to the culturally different child to contribute information, and material peculiar to his culture. When studying or reading about Spanish speaking peoples, have the children who are able to perform a Spanish song or dance or play the guitar present their talents to the class (Shapiro). A vehicle which would provide such an outlet is Fern's *Pepito's Story* (Fern). Pepito's greatest ambition is to be a dancer. After the children have read the story suggest that they listen to recordings of flamenco guitarists and discuss the differences in Spanish dances and American dances. Have the class learn a Spanish dance, *La Raspa* and an American Dance *Shoo Fly* (Tobett). This story could easily be adapted into a playlet using narrator and simple dialogue. Add a few Spanish singing games, dances, songs, recordings and you have an ideal culminating activity or program to which other classes might be invited.

Not only do disadvantaged children enjoy singing and dancing, they take great delight in play acting. They need more opportunities to pretend or to do a bit of unsophisticated role playing. Start with something simple like imitating the movements and sounds of a train as in the song "The Rock Island Line" (Landeck). Divide the class into boys and girls who sing the verses while two other children pantomime the humorous dialogue song, "The Deaf Woman's Courtship" (Landeck). Then read a story, perhaps *Springtime for Jeanne-Marie* by Francoise, while the children try to visualize all the people and props one would need for a television production. As you reread the story, you are providing the children with ideas for possible dialogue. Create a tune for the verse, select the cast, sketch scenery on the blackboard, designate parts of the room as settings and allow the children to dramatize the story in their own words and actions.

Puppets are ideal for the older child to conceal his shyness, feelings of insecurity and embarrassment. This concept was vividly portrayed in Deutch's *Lili* or the stage production of *Carnival*. In working with a group of Chinese children in the presentation of Tazwell's *The Littlest Angel*, we observed that as they became involved in the manipulation of the hand puppets, they forgot their language handicap and spoke and sang rather fluently. Again, the importance of kinesthetic learning becomes apparent.

At least once a year, every teacher is required to provide a program for an assembly, a PTA meeting or dedication, or some special holiday. The third grade class at Oakenwald School provided an assembly program that was out of the ordinary. The classroom teacher's avocation was ballet which she used to interpret for her class the story of *The Little Match Girl*.[18] This school is located in a community that would hardly enjoy seeing a ballet, let alone participate in one. At first, the boys were skeptical but once they discovered the physical demands of ballet they were vying for parts in the dance-drama. Motivation for a perfect performance was so keen that they offered to give up recess and to come to school early and stay late. Other members of the teaching staff assisted by making the simple sets and providing the special lighting effects. The audience thoroughly enjoyed the presentation for two reasons: it was well done and the story was a vivid, realistic portrayal of their lives, cold, wanting for the simple comforts of food and clothing and above all wanting for friendships.

This program started off a cultural exchange between neighboring schools. Bus loads of children would bring their best program to a school which would later reciprocate with one of its outstanding presentations. On one occasion, the seventh and eighth grades of the Gillespie School presented Hagemann-Jones' operetta based on Dickens' *A Christmas Carol* at the high school. This was attended by seventh and eighth grade pupils of other elementary schools within the district.

In summarizing the values and uses of music with literature, it can be safely said that the purposes of motivation, and correlation are realized and the basic needs of the child are fulfilled by focusing on human relations, by revealing a nation's culture, by encouraging self expression and by providing a means of relaxation and enjoyment (Nicosia) .

BASIC MUSIC CONCEPTS AND THE CLASSROOM TEACHER

Harried by the demands of a bulging curriculum, the classroom teacher has become a hazy montage of Euclid, Einstein and G. B. Shaw, not to mention Chagall and Bernstein. Withstanding the pressures of the subject areas, our stalwart creature is fancied a Mead, Durkheim, and a Piaget engaged in successfully identifying and solving the innumerable problems of at least thirty-five Eliza Doolittles. Faced with the cold realities of handicapped students, insufficient time, and, probably, limited training, what basic musical concepts should the teacher present to his class?

Concepts

"The music class must be recognized as a laboratory whose purpose is to teach by means of physical exposure to music and experimentation with the making of music. The classroom should not be a museum which merely preserves and disseminates correct facts and attitudes."[19]

Certainly, music educators work for musical literacy among our eighth grade graduates but the truth is that there are many law abiding, church going college graduates in the $10,000 plus income bracket who don't know the historical background of *The Star-Spangled Banner* or the key signature of "f" minor.

The objectives of the music curriculum for the culturally disadvantaged should be kept to a minimum of feasible concepts predicated by the students' potential and the teacher's capabilities. The following objectives are suggested for the child who begins with a limited background and who is getting his education on the run, from one school to the next:

Build a repertoire of worthwhile songs, singing games, and dances:

1. For relaxation and enjoyment.
2. For development of an understanding and an appreciation of other cultures (use both foreign and English texts).
3. For development of tone quality, diction and musical interpretation.
4. For the development of specific musical concepts.
   Pitch recognition: the tune goes up or down or remains the same; the tonal pattern is high or low.

   Rhythmic recognition: metric pattern—the song swings in 2's (strong-weak) or 3's (strong-weak-weak); rhythmic pattern—the notes are even ♩♩♩, or uneven ♩♪♩♪,

   long ♩ or short ♫ ; tempo—the music is fast or slow.

Phrasing: recognize number of phrases; kind of phrases—identical, almost alike, or different.

Dynamics: the mood and tonal quality are related to the degree of loudness or softness as well as tempo.

Children engage in attentive and active listening for recognition of a few appropriate selections of a variety of vocal and instrumental recordings. (For suggestions see the Lyons catalogue or other comparable catalogues.) Children should be encouraged to participate individually and in groups.

Role of the Teacher

It should be clarified from the outset that the classroom teacher is not solely responsible for the music program. It is the teacher in cooperation with the consultant and the administrator who, as a team, guarantee an environment conducive to musical growth. The administrator provides the curriculum guide, the time and materials while the consultant provides the leadership in instruction.

The teacher in viewing his role should keep three principles in mind. First, he should forget that he is not a specialist but remember that he needs to be willing to devote adequate time for daily preparation and to continue his own personal development.

Daily preparation involves lesson planning even if the lesson is only fifteen minutes long. Just as a good teacher wouldn't consider thumbing through the science text for an idea five minutes before the class meets, neither should he do so for the music lesson. There is nothing like a well planned lesson to bolster one's confidence.

Also, to overcome a sense of insecurity, the teacher should rely upon the teacher's guide and records to any of the series available. The following are outstanding series:

This is Music. Boston: Allyn and Bacon, 1962.
Music for Young Americans. New York: American Book Company, 1961.

Together-We-Sing. Chicago: Follett Publishing Company, 1960.
The Magic of Music. Chicago: Ginn and Company, 1965.
Making Music Your Own. Park Ridge, Illinois: Silver Burdett, 1965.
Birchard Music Series. Evanston, Illinois: Summy-Birchard Publishers, 1960.

The teacher should disregard the indicated grade level of songs and use his own judgement as to the appropriateness of the text and melodic line for his class. It might be helpful to use an all grades edition such as the Follett's *Together-We-Sing* or several little booklets published by the Cooperative Recreation Service, Inc., Delaware, Ohio.

The teacher should call upon the consultant for practical and professional assistance. "Empirical study indicates that instructional excellence is not the exclusive province either of the classroom teacher or of the special music teacher. Such excellence can result from efforts and skill of either or of both working together cooperatively."[19]

The teacher can continue his own personal development by attending institutions of higher learning, participating in workshops and in-service meetings or studying self-explanatory books, e.g.,

Bergethon, B. and Boardman, E. *Musical Growth in the Elementary School.* Chicago: Holt, Rinehart and Winston, Inc., 1963.

Monsour, S. and Perry, M. *A Junior High School Music Handbook.* Englewood Cliffs, New Jersey: Prentice-Hall, Inc., 1963.

Secondly, the teacher should be sensitive and sympathetic to the needs and feelings of the child. Never ask of a child that which he would not ask of himself or his contemporaries. Thirdly, keep in mind that you as a personality are the sum total of every minute experience that has crossed your life's path. Your musical tastes and abilities are a result of experiences provided you by other teachers. If your teacher was unable to teach music, she undoubt-edly omitted it from the curriculum and from your life's experience. Don't compound the error by omitting music from the experiences necessary for the total development of the children you teach. The teacher who can find neither the time or a significant place in her daily schedule for music is educating children for a monaural existence in a stereophonic world.

SUMMARY

The approach to music for the disadvantaged has been two-fold: interdisciplinary and practical. It has been interdisciplinary in its emphasis on music as an emolient for the acculturation and socialization of the child or as a third dimension in the teaching of linguistics and literature. Although the chapter focused on these areas, it was not the intent of the writer to minimize the importance of music as a self-contained discipline but rather to illustrate the fluidity and diversity of the subject's content. The approach is practical because the suggestions are not theoretical—not a might be done—but examples of activities that have been done successfully with the disadvantaged. As a catalyst, the teacher must endeavor to be informed and to understand her materials both creature and content. The teacher's tools are a personal philosophy, a cultivated intellect and an insatiable desire to change the *status quo*. The ultimate aim of education is excellence. Why not excellence through music?

REFERENCES

1. Leonard Broom and Philip Selznick, *Sociology: A Text with Adapted Readings* (Evanston, Row Peterson and Company, 1956), p. 75.
2. *Ibid.*
3. B. Leslie Ransley, Music Teacher, DuSable Branch in Forrestville Upper Grade Center, Chicago Public Schools, Chicago, Illinois.
4. James Hatcher, Freshman, DuSable Branch in Forrestville Upper Grade Center, Chicago Public Schools, Chicago, Illinois.
5. Marie Holt, classroom teacher, John Farren Elementary School, Chicago Public Schools, Chicago, Illinois.
6. Dr. Angeline P. Caruso, principal, Henry O. Tanner Summer School, Chicago Public Schools, Chicago, Illinois.
7. Printed with permission of the collector, Marian A. Gerlach, Glenbrook North High School, Northbrook, Illinois.

8. Angeline P. Caruso, "Special Summer Schools: Advantages of Size," *Chicago Principals Club Reporter,* LIV (Fall, 1964), p. 24.
9. Milton J. Cohler, A Language Experience Program for the Linguistically Deprived," Chicago: Joint Committee of District 14 Personnel, June, 1960, p. 1, (Mimeographed).
10. Carl A. Lefevre, *Linguistics and the Teaching of Reading* (New York: McGraw-Hill Company, 1964), p. 56.
11. Board of Education, City of Chicago, *Communication Skills: Games, Techniques, and Devices,* Curriculum Guide for Kdg, 1, 2, and 3, Chicago: Board of Education, 1964, p. 27.
12. Doreen Hall and Arnold Walter (trans.), *Orff-Keetman: Music for Children* (New York: Schott's Music Corporation, Associated Music Publishers Inc., 1955), Vol. 1, p. 66.
13. Lefevre, *op. cit.,* p. 41.
14. *Ibid.,* p. 43.
15. From *Goose Grass Rhymes* by Monica Shannon. Copyright 1930 by Doubleday and Company, Inc., Reprinted by permission of the publisher.
16. Frances Biersborn, teacher, John V. LeMoyne Elementary School, Chicago Public School, Chicago, Illinois.
17. Sue Felt, *Contrary Woodrow* (New York: Doubleday and Company, Inc., 1958), p. 17.
18. Lucille Worthy, teacher, Oakenwald South Chicago Public Schools, Chicago, Illinois.
19. Claude V. Palisca, Music in Our Schools: A Search for Improvement. Report of the Yale Seminar on Music Education, Washington, D. C.: U. S. Department of Health, Education and Welfare, Office of Education, 1964, p. 9.
20. O. M. Hartsell, *Teaching Music in the Elementary Schools: Opinion and Comment,* Washington, D. C.: Association for Supervision and Curriculum Development, NEA, 1963, p. 7.

Suggested Readings

Arbuthnot, M. H., *Time for Poetry.* Chicago: Scott Foresman and Company, 1951.
Austin, M. C., *Teaching Creative Reading.* The A and B Reading Bulletin, No. 103, Chicago: Allyn and Bacon, Inc., May 1960, p. 2.
Bergethon, B. and Boardman, E., *Musical Growth In the Elementary School.* Chicago: Holt, Rinehart and Winston, Inc., 1963.
Bloomfield, L. and Barnhart, C. L., *Let's Read: A Linguistic Approach.* Detroit: Wayne State University Press, 1961.
Broom, L. and Selznick, P., *Sociology: A Text With Adapted Reading.* Evanston, Illinois: Row, Peterson and Co., 1956.

Broudy, H. S., "Educational Theory and the Music Curriculum." *Music Educators Journal* 51: 32-36 +, Nov.-Dec., 1964.

Bruner, J. S., *The Process of Education.* New York: Random House Vintage Books, 1960.

Caruso, A. P., "Special Summer Schools: Advantages of Size," *Chicago Principals Club Reporter* 54:9-12, 23-24, Fall, 1964.

Chicago Board of Education, *Communication Skills: Games, Techniques, and Devices,* Kdg. Grades 1, 2, 3. Chicago Bureau of Curriculum, Chicago Board of Education, Chicago; 1964.

Chicago Board of Education, *Curriculum Guide for the Language Arts,* for Kdg., Grades 1, 2, 3. Chicago Bureau of Curriculum, Chicago Board of Education, Chicago; 1963.

Cohler, M. J., and others. A Language Experience Program for the Linguistically Deprived. Chicago: 1960 (Mimeographed.)

Education and the Disadvantaged American. Educational Policies Commission, Washington, D. C.,: 1962.

Fern, E., *Pepito's Story.* New York: Ariel Books, 1960.

Francoise, *Springtime for Jeanne-Marie.* New York: Charles Scribner's Sons, 1955.

Hall, Doreen, *Music for Children:* Teacher's manual. New York: Schott Music Corp. (Associated Music Publishers, Inc.) , 1960.

Hartsell, O. M., Teaching Music in the Elementary School: Opinion and Comment. Washington, D. C.: Association for Supervision and Curriculum Development, NEA, 1963.

Institute on Cultural Patterns of Newcomers: Selected Papers. Welfare Council of Metropolitan Chicago and the Chicago Commission on Human Relations, Jan. 1958, 4th printing, 1961 Chicago, Illinois.

Jenkins, W. A., "Linguistic Trends in Elementary English," *Hexagon* 1:6-19 No. 3, 1964.

Jewett, A., Mereand, J., Gunderson, D. V. (Eds.) , *Improving English Skills of Culturally Different Youth in Large Cities.* Excerpts of speeches given at a conference, May 31-June 2, 1962, Washington, D. C., U. S. Department of Health Education and Welfare, Office of Education, Bulletin No. 5, 1964.

Krone, B. P. and Miller, K. R., *Help Yourself to Music.* San Francisco: Chandler Publishing Co., 1959.

Landeck, B., *Songs to Grow on.* New York: Edward B. Marks Music Corporation, 1950.

Lefevre, C. A., *Linguistics and the Teaching of Reading.* New York: McGraw-Hill Book Company, 1964.

Lefevre, C. A., "The Proper Study of Mankind," *Hexagon,* 1:1-6, No. 1, 1962.

Lloyd-Jones, E. and Westervelt, E. M. (Eds.) , *Behavioral Science and Guidance.* New York: Bureau of Publications, Teachers College, Columbia University, 1963.

Monsour, S., Perry, M., *A Junior High School Music Handbook*. Englewood Cliffs, New Jersey: Prentice-Hall, Inc., 1963.

Nicosia, D. J. "An Annotated Bibliography for the Correlation of Children's Literature and Music." Unpublished master thesis, Northwestern University, Evanston, Illinois: 1951.

Nye, R. E. and Bergethon, B., *Basic Music for Classroom Teachers*, Second edition. Englewood Cliffs, N. J.: Prentice-Hall, Inc., 1962.

Orff-Institute Year-Book 1962: *At the Mozarteum Academy Salzburg*. Published by Thomas, Werner and Gotze, Willibaud Mainz: B. Schott's Sohne, 1963.

Orff, C. and Keetman, G., *Music for Children*. Volumes I-V, English adaptation by D. Hall and A. Walter. New York: Schott Music Corp. (Associated Music Publishers Inc.) 1955.

Orff, C. and Keetman, G., *Music for Children*. Volumes I-IV, English Adaptation by Margaret Murray. New York: Schott Music Corp. (Associated Music Publishers, Inc.), 1955.

Palisco, C. V., *Music in Our Schools: A Search for Improvement*. Washington, D. C.: U. S. Department of Health, Education and Welfare, Office of Education, 1964.

Programs for the Educationally Disadvantaged. A report of a conference on teaching children and youth who are educationally disadvantaged. Washington, D. C.: U. S. Department of Health, Education and Welfare, Office of Education, Bulletin No. 17, 1963.

Riese, H., *Heal the Hurt Child*. Chicago: University of Chicago Press, 1962.

Riessman, F., *The Culturally Deprived Child*. Evanston: Harper and Row, Publishers, 1962.

Rosenberg, B. and White, D. M. (Eds.), *Mass Culture*. Glencoe, Illinois: The Free Press, 1957.

Russell, D. H. and Russell, E. F., *Listening Aids Through the Grades*. New York: Bureau of Publications, Teachers College Columbia University, 1959.

Russell, D. H. and Fea, H. R., *Research on Teaching Reading. Handbook of Research on Teaching*. Chicago: Rand McNally and Company, 1963, 865-928.

School Catalog for Elementary and Secondary Schools. Chicago, Illinois: Lyons Band Instrument Co.

Schoolfield, L. D., *Better Speech and Better Reading*. Boston: Expression Company, 1937.

Shapiro, S. R. and Covello, L., *How the Schools Can Help*. New York: New York City Board of Education (mimeographed.)

Snow, C. P., *The Two Cultures: and a Second Look*. New York: A Mentor Book, The New American Library, 1959, 1963.

Snyder, A. M., *Creating Music With Children*. New York: Mills music Co, Inc. 1957.

"A Survey of Puerto Rican Pupils in the Philadelphia Public Elementary Schools," Philadelphia Board of Education, 1959.

Sutton, E., *Knowing and Teaching the Migrant Child.* Washington, D. C.: National Education Association, Department of Rural Education, 1960.

Timmerman, M. *Let's Teach Music in the Elementary School:* Evanston, Illinois: Sunny-Birchard Company, 1960.

Tobett, J. E., *The Red Book of Singing Games and Dances from the Americas.* Evanston, Illinois: Summy-Birchard Publishing Co., 1960.

Warfel, H. R., "The Language Element in Literature," *Hexagon*, 1:29-35, No. 1, 1962 pp. 29-35.

Wilkins, G. T., *Art, Music and Physical Education—A Basic Part of General Education.* Springfield, Illinois: Office of the Superintendent of Public Instruction.

Woodward, H. H. Jr., *The Southern White Migrant in Lake View.* Chicago: Lake View Citizens' Council, August 1962 (Mimeographed).

Chapter XI

ART EDUCATION FOR THE DISADVANTAGED PUPIL

Jane Neale*

THE ART EDUCATION program in the elementary school can make significant contributions to the education of the culturally disadvantaged child. Such contributions are not set apart in any way from those that serve all children. The values and goals in art do not change; they are the goals of all well-educated people.

If the values of art education and the goals remain the same, perhaps it is in a realization of the conflict in values and attitudes of the culturally disadvantaged child that we may find the implications for developing a program in art to meet the special needs of these children. If an art program is based on an understanding of the general characteristics of the culturally different, then the differences in structuring and implementing such a program might lie in varying the *emphasis* of the methods in guidance, instruction, motivation, and evaluation rather than in any radical departure from a well-organized art program.

For the teacher of the self-contained classroom three fundamental concepts are needed: (1) understanding of the culturally disadvantaged child; his educational deficiencies, his positive and negative interests and his abilities; (2) understanding of values in art; what they can achieve and how they can be used as objectives in re-educating, expanding, and enriching the culturally limited world of this child, and (3) understanding of general guideposts in constructing, organizing, and teaching art; and the ability to develop specific objectives to implement the art program.

THE GOALS OF A CREATIVE ART PROGRAM

Conant believes that "In its broadest expression, art is conceived as an inseparable part of a rich and satisfying life."[1] Art

---

*Chairman, Art Department and Assistant Professor, Chicago Teachers College South.

can be an effective tool in the process of learning and growing, and the implications for an effective art education program are founded on the values inherent in art. As we emphasized at the outset, these values apply to all individuals everywhere, regardless of the socioeconomic factors.

However, the deficiencies in art experiences of the culturally disadvantaged child, in a sense parallel his general educational deficiencies. This implies that to structure a program in art so as to give more meaning to each activity in direct relation to the child's needs, and to help in his re-education, we must know and understand the fundamental values of a creative art program.[2]

Art education is varied and flexible in its nature. The bodies of knowledge and understandings, the techniques and skills, and the appreciations and attitudes in part, allow the teacher to meet many of the special needs in the education of the disadvantaged child. The teacher of art is in a unique situation to work with the disadvantaged pupil and should develop a philosophy accordingly. The teacher must structure the art program and adapt it to new conditions and needs. The art program should give rise to situations which help the child cope with those problems which have affected his creative and cultural growth.

Most of the recent research of the culturally disadvantaged child in art has emphasized cultural enrichment, involving such programs as museum visits, the showing of appreciational type art films, artist-studio type lectures, and other forms of enrichment. Very little research is available on projects which have developed classroom practices in the *doing* phase of the subject of art. Activities involving the creative aspects through participation have not been consciously developed to foster and improve the limited and deficit qualities for personality development of the culturally disadvantaged child.

There is a great need for sensitive, perceptive classroom teachers engaged in working with the culturally disadvantaged child to develop programs in art which utilize practical applications to achieve objectives and goals. Much could be learned by a consideration of the achievements in a well-developed art activity program. This does not in any way discount the values derived from museum education, trips, films, and visual aids of the appreciational type that may add to the cultural enrichment program. On the other hand, however, something closer, more personal, and more immediate can be developed in the classroom and in the actual participation in creative activities. The educational gains which may be attained through such an art activity program may have unexpected and far-reaching effects.

Organizing Elements for an Art Program

What, then, are some of the contributing factors in art for the education of the culturally disadvantaged child? How can the values inherent in an art program serve and foster those cultural aspects in developing maturity for worthy citizenship? How can the classroom teacher attain goals which cultivate cultural-social growth through art activities? If we consider four developments which are unique contributions to the school program possible through the teaching of art, we may use them as guideposts to structure an art program and to develop classroom art activities. It is generally agreed among art educators that the philosophy of art education is especially concerned with: (1) the development of individual differences and the fostering of uniqueness; (2) the development of imaginative resourcefulness and the creative potential of every child; (3) the development of perceptual awareness and sensitivity through emotional expressiveness, and (4) the progressive development of improved attitudes and appreciations.

Taking each of these separately and considering it as an objective, the teacher can develop a program by structuring appropriate art activities to foster and enhance growth in each area. In doing so, however, the teacher must be aware of the limitations and deficiencies in the art background of the culturally disadvantaged child in order to build an effective art program.

Art education is concerned with the recognition, development, and the encouragement of the uniqueness of every individual.

The discovering and expressing of the "self" is a dynamic and forceful concern in the education of the culturally disadvantaged. Art, as a visual means of communication, has always concerned itself with the expression of the individual. The varied program in art allows, encourages, and recognizes the qualities that are unique and different in each child. Because every child is encouraged through his art activities to make a personal statement about his feelings and thoughts and to do so *in his own way*, we find that this subject area, perhaps more than any other, places a premium on individuality and fosters a consciousness of the "self."

The art activities developed with this value kept foremost as an objective, may be able to act as an antidote to the conformity and to the materialistic pressures found in mass communication media. More importantly, these art activities can encourage in the child a sense of personal worth. The child knows that he as an individual is important and that he, as well as his work, is recognized, encouraged, and appreciated for his *own* sake. The child must be made aware that in art there is no absolute right or wrong way to express his personal thoughts or feelings and to say what he wants to say. The child must have confidence, knowing that his personal statements will be accepted if they are honest and sincere.

The teacher recognizes each child and honors uniqueness as he also esteems and encourages the differences between students in the classroom. Such practice can do a great deal to create a sense of satisfaction and security by removing the fear of failure or of being different. The culturally disadvantaged child's sense of failure is based very often on fear, or equating being different as not being accepted. By respecting and encouraging differences, the teacher may enable the child to develop a more positive self-concept. The child can be helped to see himself as a valued member of his group, as a worker, a producer, and a consumer.

The culturally disadvantaged child often seeks respect rather than affection. The teacher, in recognizing his individuality in art, may see a gain in self-respect as he helps the pupil to experience success. The teacher's role is to aid the pupil to succeed by structuring activities in which the pupil can accomplish his goal and gain a sense of satisfaction and security.

The culturally disadvantaged child is characteristically lacking in self-direction and self-expression. He has had little opportunity to develop these qualities, therefore, in most cases he does not like to do individual work and may appear passive. He fails to identify with art problems and displays a lack of skill in handling art materials and tools due to the meager opportunities afforded him.

The teacher, in order to develop individuality and uniqueness, must be sensitive to these fears, feelings, and conflicts. He must speak the child's language. He must formulate a guide for developing simple art experiences—activities in which a successful end-product can be attained and which are sequentially developed to result in continuous growth.

The teacher should help the child resolve conflicting attitudes the child has regarding the value of art in his everyday life; he must find and present logical activities that will stimulate a will to learn. Ideas which are common to the child's daily habits; ideas for making useful things; ideas which appeal to the immediate, to desires, to dramatic action, to novelty, curiosity, or suspense should form the basis for projects and problems in art. An excellent series of articles which have case studies on teaching art in difficult schools can be found in the June, 1963 issue of *Art Education*, a journal of the NAEA.

Art activities should be planned to develop a concept of the "self," to remove the fear of failure, to give a feeling of security and satisfaction, to aid in successful achievement and to develop a respect for the child's own work as well as that of his peers. They must be the type of activities in which the subject matter revolves around the events, things, and people that are found within the child's personal experiences. The child should be encouraged to tell of experiences which are most common and familiar to him. He should be encouraged to have respect for his *own* ideas and feelings and be motivated to record them visually. Some children like to paint, draw, construct or model about how they "feel" about things, others about how they "see" things. Either approach has value and the teacher should encourage the child to create and record in the way he works best.

The teacher can help the child gain respect for his own work and for that of his peers by examining the work of great artists, especially those artists who make use of visual impressions which are common to everyday life. Helping the child become aware of the experience which the artist goes through in the act of creating, what the artist has said and how he is able to communicate his thoughts and feelings in visual form, draws a parallel between the mature artist and the child's own creations. While the child may realize he cannot achieve the same skillful results, he can recognize that the process of creating is essentially the same.

If the child becomes discouraged, the teacher needs to help him re-examine his work, to talk over what he did and suggest how he might tell his story so that its message is conveyed in a better way. This is a great aid in bolstering confidence, for the child must make his own evaluations and do his own discovering. This implies, for the teacher, that there is no place for criticism based on adult standards of perfection. Criticism must be of a positive nature, the kind that helps the child analyze and discover his own mistakes and make his own decisions, changes, or corrections. The child needs help in thinking things through and if he honestly makes an effort, the result should be honored and respected. The teacher has the opportunity to develop in the child a sense of pride and achievement in "doing" which may have more far-reaching and important results than by achievements which can be tested objectively.

Subject matter should include aspects of his personal life, his everyday activities, ideals, aspirations, his world of work, play, school, family, and friends. These, as central starting points for art activities can develop a feeling that, as a person, the child has something of value to say which might interest others. He, in turn, can develop respect for and interest in the visual expressions of others. The teacher of the self-contained classroom may find excellent sources for help in structuring such art activities in books on art education by Gaitskell, De Francesco, and Jefferson. See the chapter bibliography for a complete listing.

The culturally disadvantaged child can be helped to gain satisfaction and security by being allowed to explore new media and processes. Often if the pupil finds a certain area wherein his interest is especially stimulated, the development of skill and dexterity resulting in successful achievement may motivate an improved interest in other areas. The child, as he develops skill in using the varied tools and materials, should be made increasingly aware of the art fundamentals necessary to create and communicate by visual means. He should learn how line, color, values, textures, and shapes can be used to aid him in attaining a fuller expression. He should become progressively involved in his ability to compare, explore, discover, evaluate, and analyze.

An enthusiastic teacher can open a fascinating, dramatic, action-filled world that appeals to this child through art activities within the child's limited world. He can use that background to expand the child's observational abilities and sensitivity, and then begin to extend the limited environment.

The teacher can build sincere interest and encouragement by providing an atmosphere that relieves emotional tension. It is in the satisfaction that comes from creating and self-expression that the child becomes more confident. The teacher of the culturally disadvantaged child has an opportunity in art as in no other subject area for developing interviewing techniques which can aid him in reacting and interacting with his students. The teacher should develop his own listening skill and be sensitive to what the child is interested in. It is in this way, perhaps, via this intense personal contact, that the teacher has the opportunity to learn more about the student, and can develop a rapport which may enable him to discover inhibited attitudes and hidden conflicts so that growth can be fostered. This close personal involvement is perhaps more important than the development of skills or the acquisition of excellent end-products.

Art is rich in the process of developing imagination and the ability to be creative.

Growth in self-expression and creativity depends on the ability to give form to images, insights, and those imaginative faculties which provide the means for enriching experiences. The child who ordinarily lacks self-motivation can be helped by participating in art activities of the more imaginative type where he can proceed at his own pace and create in his own way. There are no hard and fast rules to threaten him, no decision of promotion or failure, and no marks to reflect his progress. He has every opportunity to fail in order to learn and he must learn how to have "successful failures" from which he can build toward more successful end-products.

The types of art activities which use the imaginative abilities can also aid in the development of self-motivation by appealing to the culturally disadvantaged child's liking for physical involve-ment and his motoric impulses. These are factors directly in-volved with the *doing* phase in art, and can be especially meaning-ful and gratifying.

The development of the imaginative qualities of the culturally disadvantaged child and of his creative potential aid in enriching and redirecting emotions and energy into constructive channels. This child usually has had little experience in art and for the most part does not come to class eager and full of ideas. His op-portunity for self-expression has been neglected or discouraged and his lack of imagination may have resulted from an over-con-cern with the immediate and the practical. Since, in most cases, he has had little opportunity to become familiar with fantasy or fairy tales, even those of his traditional heritage in his early child-hood, his imagination is limited. Therefore, the kinds of activities which foster in him the feeling of freedom to do unusual things, to invent, experiment, and explore in structured ways can en-courage him to use his imagination creatively. Some art education books which develop this area in depth are those written by Low-enfeld, Conant and Randall, D'Amico, and especially the *Expand-ing Vision Series*.

Ausubel, writing about the cognitive and motivational prob-lems of the culturally disadvantaged child, believes that motiva-tion for learning is probably derived from curiosity and the pre-disposition to explore, manipulate and cope with the environ-ment.[3] In art, the child has the opportunity to do just this and, in helping the child become familiar with the tools, materials, and processes in art, the teacher can direct energy into useful, satis-fying channels. The teacher must help the child examine all modes of thinking and give him alternate ways to approach his work which are self-enhancing. These factors are important and are certainly a part of the *doing* in art.

Wilson conducted a case study to determine some factors which affect the teaching of art to pupils from low socioeconomic com-munities.[4] He states that these children are limited in their artistic growth and inspiration in relation to their potential. He believes that art should be an emotionally satisfying experience and that the teacher should not evaluate the creative results as products of art or even as mentally challenging exercises.

For the teacher, this means that concepts about the perfection of an end-product have to be discarded or de-emphasized. The teacher must help the child develop the skill and techniques necessary to manipulate the tools and materials at hand. Since accomplishment plays an important part, it is not only possible, but logical that the teacher should eliminate the fear of failure.

Being too demanding, Wilson says, results in confusion, demoralization and the impairment of self-confidence.[5] Therefore, activities structured to foster imaginative resourcefulness can, by not creating excessive demands, do much to restore self-confidence and develop further the ability to self-express. The teacher can help the child by setting goals consistent with his ability. Moreover, in praising a child's work, even if only for effort, the teacher should ignore minor mistakes. The teacher must be able to see the good in what each student has done and encourage the child to see what he has done well, helping him to select those things that can be developed further.

Linderman and Herberholz, in their book on developing perceptual awareness, summarize a composite picture of creative people by saying that they usually are builders of ideas, are alert perceptually, like to explore new ideas, like to investigate the nature of things, and are very sensitive to aesthetic stimuli.[6] If the teacher is to develop art activities which cultivate the creative abilities of the culturally disadvantaged child, then these activities must aim to amplify the imaginative faculties and establish confidence in the pupil to use these aptitudes.

The teacher needs to help the child to see, to listen, to feel, and to think. From this comes the power to relate and interpret. The child can be aided through lively, verbal discussions that challenge his thinking. By creating visual experiences wherein the exploring of details can be encouraged, the child may be more able to respond emotionally to objects, people, events and things around him. The teacher can help the child experience sensory reactions through listening, tactile and olfactory activities which develop more imaginative art expressions.

Art activities that focus on developing the imagination should emphasize the uniqueness of an idea. Linderman and Herberholz have unusual approaches for developing ideas which are less conventional and less hide-bound in routine thinking which they call "odd-ball" approaches.[7] These types of activities can be very stimulating to children of all ages. They suggest such things as inventing a nonsense machine which the child might produce as a construction problem. Ideas such as the child imagining himself as the smallest, tallest, thinnest, or fattest person in the world, give the child a sense of freedom and stimulation when he conceptualizes his ideas in visual form through a drawing or painting. The teacher has the child imagine an unusual viewpoint or asks him to think in terms of being an object rather than a person. The child can then develop his art expression from this approach, thus releasing inhibited feelings he may have that he must draw and paint things as they really are.

The pupil can be encouraged to work with materials in a curious or unusual way; to combine odd materials such as clay and string; or to paint a picture with glue, string, or other mixed media. He might paint a picture without a brush, using instead found objects such as sticks, wads of paper, combs, or paper clips. The child might be stimulated with music, by modeling or painting to the rhythms of the sounds or by responding to the mood. Another approach might be to hide textural items in boxes or bags and have the child react with words which express feelings about the tactile qualities and then try to reproduce their reactions in paint or clay. Working with materials in inventive ways can often lead toward producing objects which can later be developed into more practical and functional end-products.

Children, as they grow older, want to be able to draw representationally and to make things "look right." At the same time, the fun element, the accidental and the highly nonsensical approach, can be used as a starting point toward the development of ability in forming better end-products. The direction of the physical activity and the promotion of it in using manipulative devices and materials to foster growth however, should be more than just *doing* in art. The *doing* should be related to doing something worthwhile, the final phases of which contribute in some way directly to the doer's person or environment.

The child, in seeking physical involvement, can be motivated, however, the teacher must be sure that the child is not only seeking a goal but knows *what he is doing, why*, and of *what value* it is to him. The quick physical involvement can be directed over a period of time so that self-motivation grows to develop a desire for exploration in depth. Growth in skill and ability enables the child to become more successful and to sequentially use that ability to achieve more.

Imagination plays an important role in making a link between the inner impressions and the external environment. Helen Merritt points out that problems involved in achieving a satisfying expression on paper are not solved by simply stimulating the imagination.[8] But with the culturally disadvantaged child who may lack the ability to use his imagination constructively or who perhaps feels more inhibited, activities of this kind can be most gratifying. Under a skillful teacher's guidance, they can lead the way toward more productive goals. Stimulating and motivating activities might well create the desire for further guidance in art on the part of the child.

In the process of art education, the development of perceptual awareness, sensitivity, and emotional expression can enrich and expand an understanding of the world of nature and man.

The limitations in communication and deficits in perceptual skills of the culturally disadvantaged child whose background is lacking in both quantity and quality of varied experiences, may be improved through art activities in a nonverbal manner. Activities which strengthen the powers of observation and the other sensory faculties can provide a means for organizing ideas, personal thoughts and feelings. They can bring about the ability to see relationships between a personal idea and its conceptualization into a concrete form. The culturally disadvantaged child's limitations in communicating verbally, his short attention span, his easy frustrations and early abandonment of tasks might well become positive attributes through art activities which concentrate on nonverbal means and manipulative skills.

The physical form can be conceptualized verbally or not, but even in nonverbal forming there is growth and understanding in attitudes and appreciations. The culturally disadvantaged child's perceptual awareness is not well developed and he has a verbal difficulty (although he may have a rich language of his own). In art, there is opportunity for him to work nonverbally and still *communicate* his personal thoughts and feelings by putting them into visual form. There is always the further possibility for developing verbal ability by encouraging the child to talk about what he has seen, felt and expressed in his art work.

The culturally disadvantaged child thinks in terms of large, general categories, such as trees, flowers, and nature, when asked about his concept of beauty. He is not usually aware of the special types of beauty in his immediate environment or in the heritage of his own symbolic art forms.[9] The teacher can develop awareness by teaching the child to see details, by relating the child's personal experiences to the visual expression and by fostering identification and empathy with such experiences. Children have to be *taught* to be aware of the visual excitement in their own neighborhood. The child's lack of attention to details and relationships is enlarged and expanded when he becomes personally involved through his artistic expressions.

For the teacher, there should be a realization that all of us are visually ignorant to some extent. Although we are bombarded visually every day by various sights and sounds of mass communication media, we wear blinders to the simple beauties around us. The culturally disadvantaged child has not as many things to see and to experience in quantity but it is the *quality* within things that makes us sensitive and develops our appreciations. Art can open a door through which the child can learn to see, not just look; he can learn to respond with feelings and emotions to the world about him so that he may experience greater aesthetic realization.

Art aids in developing attitudes of appreciation of our cultural heritage and the function of art in our everyday life.

The culturally disadvantaged child brings a varied cultural background to the school. The aggregate of the child's subcultural environment and his interaction with a larger culture may have caused conflicts in attitudes to develop. Art activities should draw upon and implement the child's understanding of his cultural background and promote an interaction with his present social-cultural environment. By learning to observe the world of nature and man-made objects, the child can be helped in the realization of the importance that art plays in his life.

McFee believes it is a false assumption that art is a universal language and therefore, no cross-cultural conflicts exist.[10] In art, children whose cultures use strong colors are often told to refine them and assimilate more American art standards. The ethnic standards and art forms which have been defined by the family are often rejected by well-meaning adults. The teacher should try to preserve the cultural symbols and use them to develop a feeling of what is good in them. These symbols can be used as a basis for exploration of not only the child's own cultural background but as an aid in developing an appreciation of other cultures as well. Excellent sources for help in developing art activities using the study of art forms of the past and present along with creative art activities can be found in books written by Conrad, Conant, McFee, and Ocvirk.

If the teacher consciously incorporates design learning in the art activities, the child can become more competent to make judgments independent from the inherited environment or the dictates of the masses. Although we want the child to improve in discrimination and taste, it is more important to make him feel that he can do so. The teacher must not make him more unhappy about his environment so the child should be encouraged to notice and appreciate those forms in his surroundings that have their own kinds of beauty. Awareness of this type can be built through the study of line, color, texture, and shapes. When the child becomes aware of the design elements and uses them consciously to a more artistic expression, he can recognize how such elements are used to improve our personal life.

The culturally disadvantaged child uses very little of his time outside the school in self-expressive activity and his creative efforts are usually stereotyped in concept. Since there is often a refusal to take advantage of the local resources, the teacher must plan in detail, using exciting visual stimuli, many and varied objects often presented with enthusiastic role-playing. A variety of projects and subject matter choices should be motivated simultaneously so that more students can become interested. The child and teacher both have experiences upon which they can draw. But since the attitudes of the child do not exist in isolation, the teacher must structure art activities which are more likely to appeal to the child because they are in context with the immediate and personal.

Classroom Organization for Art Activities

Freedom—a necessary part of creative expression—does not mean license to do as one pleases! In the art classroom, it is only through well organized sets of rules and regulations, through established routines, and by having materials organized, labeled and accessible that the right kind of freedom can be established. The child must be free to do his own choosing and selecting, to experiment, explore, discover, solve problems, and arrive at his own end-product. This can only be done in an atmosphere that is relaxed, smooth-running, and secure because it is orderly—not chaotic, flexible—not restrained, relaxed—not undisciplined.

McFee, Wilson, and Fass, in articles written about special case studies they have made in art, arrived at some specific ideas for structuring art activities for the culturally disadvantaged child.[11] Since the child may be reluctant to cooperate in classroom procedures and may lack self-discipline, the teacher must make firm demands. The teacher needs to develop orderly distribution and clean-up procedures and do so early in the year. Storage ideas and routines should be developed so that the students themselves are used in positions of responsibility and accept such activity as a part of group sharing and cooperation.

Disadvantaged children seem to need more direction than usual. The oral repetition of words in giving directions should be supplemented by written rule sheets, summaries of lessons, checklists, and other methods. The lessons should be kept simple and short; the goals should be predictable and constant. Deficiencies in work habits should be looked after and excuses removed. The teacher should not condone substandard conduct but instead set clearly defined rules, fix boundaries and be impersonal within these. Nevertheless, the teacher should be flexible, warm, and enthusiastic in adapting his behavior to the individual. The teacher, in the final analysis, lets the child know he likes him and believes in his ability.

The teacher must exert special emphasis in providing motivation; structure activities to meet special needs; offer guidance and instruction in the necessary skills and techniques; teach self-evaluation procedures so that growth and satisfaction may take place and become a part of the learning process.

Riessman recently said that he believes the teacher must make a break-through in two stages; first by winning the child's attention through the development of techniques and routines, and then by developing a *teaching style*.[12] In art, the close and personal contact, the sympathetic and spontaneous atmosphere can serve the teacher to achieve the goals and objectives presented here. A further possibility may be that the atmosphere established in the art classroom may act as a springboard toward achieving such desired results in other subject areas.

The contributions in art that are unique are the same for all children. The culturally disadvantaged child is not potentially different or even disadvantaged in art when compared to most other children. It is that each teacher must find his own method of reaching this child and lighting the spark that is meaningful and motivating. The teacher of art has a colorful, exiciting, sensitive, varied, and aesthetically satisfying subject area in which to work. If the teacher develops a sense of personal empathy with his students, an art activity program planned especially for the culturally disadvantaged child could make significant contributions to his intellectual, emotional, and social growth.

REFERENCES

1. Howard C. Conant, *Art Education* (Washington, D. C.: Center for Applied Research in Education, 1964), p. 106.
2. June K. Mc Fee, "Art Education for the Culturally Deprived Child," *Art Education*, Sixty-fourth Yearbook of the National Society for the Study of Education, Part II (Bloomington, Illinois: Public School Publishing Company, 1964), Chapter VII, pp. 153-175. This reference is an excellent source for understanding the artistic deficiencies and potentials among some ethnic groups.
3. David P. Ausubel, "A Teaching Strategy for Culturally Deprived Pupils: Cognitive and Motivational Considerations," *The School Review*,

Vol. 71, No. 4, (Winter, 1963) pp. 454-463.

4. Delius E. Wilson, "Art in the Difficult School/A Study," *Art Education,* A Journal of the National Art Educators Association, Vol. XVI, No. 6 (June, 1963) , p. 4-8.

5. *Ibid.*

6. Earl W. Linderman and Donald W. Herberholz, *Developing Artistic and Perceptual Awareness* (Dubuque, Wm. C. Brown Company, 1964), pp. 4-6.

7. *Ibid.* pp. 11-25.

8. Helen Merritt, *Guiding Free Expression in Children's Art* (New York: Holt, Rinehart and Winston, 1964) , p. 15.

9. McFee, *op. cit.,* p. 172.

10. *Ibid.* p. 159.

11. McFee, *op. cit.,* pp. 168-174; Wilson, *op. cit.;* and Norma Fass, "Art in the Difficult School/Problems," *Art Education,* A Journal of the NAEA, *op. cit.* pp. 9-14.

12. Frank Riessman, "Teaching Culturally Disadvantaged Children Today," *Hexagon* (Vol. 1, No. 2 Logan Printing Company, 1964) , Printed speech from lecture given at a Human Relations Symposium at Crane Technical High School, Chicago, November, 1963. pp. 123-136.

Suggested Readings

Ausubel, David P., "A Teaching Strategy for Culturally Deprived Pupils: Cognitive and Motivational Considerations." *The School Review.* Vol. 71, No. 4. Winter, 1963.

Conant, Howard, *Art Education.* Washington, D. C.: Center for Applied Research in Education, 1964.

Conant, Howard, and Arne, Randall, *Art in Education.* Peoria, Illinois: Chas. A. Bennett, 1959.

Conrad, George, *The Process of Art Education in the Elementary School.* New Jersey: Prentice-Hall, Inc., 1964.

D'Amico, Victor, *Experiments in Creative Art Teaching.* New York: Museum of Modern Art, 1960.

D'Amico, Victor, Frances Wilson, and Moreen Maser, *Art For The Family.* Museum of Modern Art, Distributed by Simon and Schuster, New York, 1954.

De Francesco, Italo L. *Art Education: Its Means and Ends.* New York: Harper and Brothers, 1958.

Fass, Norma, "Art in the Difficult School/Problems," *Art Education:* A Journal of the NAEA. Vol. XVI, No. 6. June, 1963.

Fearing, Kelly, Clyde Martin, and Evelyn Beard. *Our Expanding Vision.* Art Series, Grades 1 through 8: Teacher's Manual, Austin: W. S. Benson & Company, 1960.

Gaitskell, Charles D., and Margaret R. Gaitskell, *Children and Their Art.* New York: Harcourt, Brace, 1958.

Jefferson, Blanche. *Teaching Art to Children.* Boston: Allyn and Bacon, 1959.

Jefferson, Blanche, and Barbara McGeary. *My World of Art.* Graded workbooks and Teacher's Manuals grades 1 through 6. Boston: Allyn & Bacon, Inc., 1963.

Lanier, Vincent, *Teaching Secondary Art.* Scranton: International Textbook Co., 1964.

Linderman, Earl W., and Donald W. Herberholz, *Developing Artistic and Perceptual Awareness.* Dubuque, Iowa: Wm. C. Brown Company, 1964.

Lowenfeld, Viktor, Lambert, Brittain, *Creative and Mental Growth.* Fourth Edition. New York: The Macmillan Company, 1964.

McFee, June K. "Art Education for the Culturally Deprived Child," *Art Education,* Sixty-fourth Yearbook of the National Society for the Study of Education. Part II. Bloomington, Illinois: Public School Publishing Company, 1964.

McFee, June King, *Preparation for Art.* San Francisco: Wadsworth Publishing Company, 1961.

Merritt, Helen, *Guiding Free Expression in Children's Art.* New York: Holt, Rinehart and Winston, 1964.

Ocvirk, Otto G., Bone, Robert, Stinson, Robert, and Wigg, Philip, *Art Fundamentals* Dubuque, Iowa: Wm. C. Brown Company Publishers, 1960.

Riessman, Frank, "Teaching Culturally Disadvantaged Children Today," *Hexagon.* Vol. 1, No. 2. Logan Printing Company: 1964. Printed speech from lecture given at a Human Relations Symposium at Crane Technical High School, Chicago, November, 1963.

Wilson, Delius E. "Art in the Difficult School/A Study." *Art Education.* A Journal of the NAEA. Vol. XVI, No. 6. June, 1963.

Chapter XII

EVALUATION AND THE DISADVANTAGED PUPIL

William Itkin*

OBJECTIVES

W HAT ARE WE TRYING to accomplish in education? Some of our objectives are mainly academic. They involve cognitive learnings —the acquisition of information and understandings. These include the tools for attaining cognitive learning—skills in the use of tools of communication: speaking, writing, gesture, language, mathematical symbols, and the language of the electronic computer. They include a comprehension of concepts—democracy, justice, principle, comprehension of quantitative relationships, and comprehension of cause and effect relationships in the physical and social world.

Some of our objectives are immediate, some long-term. Examples are preparation for economic competence, for accepting vocational responsibilities, development of esthetic interests, and enjoyment of wholesome leisure.

Some educational objectives may involve both cognitive learnings and psychomotor skills, for example; surgery, typewriting, stenography, playing musical instruments, piloting airplanes. Some may be concerned primarily with affective, attitudinal, and behavioral outcomes; the ability to get along with others in the family, at work, and play; appreciation of our democratic heritage; acceptance of our responsibilities as citizens; commitment to values. The three types of learning objectives—cognitive, psychomotor, and affective—are often interrelated. It is difficult and sometimes impossible to separate the three.

Educational objectives are usually expressed in general terms, but in order to be implemented they must be spelled out in terms of specific goals and specific activities. It is not enough to set a

---

*Professor of Psychology, Chicago Teachers College North.

general goal for ourselves to teach Johnny to read. We need to give him a background of experience from which to understand the meaning of the words we expect him to read; we need to teach him to listen; we need to give him confidence in his ability to learn; and we need to make learning enjoyable. Spelling out general objectives into more and more specific and immediate terms helps to suggest the specific activities we must provide in order to carry out our long term goals.

General educational objectives represent the values of a society, and local objectives reflect the values of a community, but the implementation of educational goals depends upon the local administrator and the classroom teacher. Both administrator and teacher must keep their educational goals clearly in mind if they are to carry them out. The administration must have a program that makes it possible for objectives to be carried out. Time, facilities, and appropriate personnel must be provided for within the educational program. Noble words alone will not do the job. The classroom teacher must aim for specific attainments if he expects to accomplish any specific goals or to contribute to the achievement of any long term goals. Planning is essential.

For both administrator and teacher diagnostic information is essential to planning. The principal needs to know how his school stands with respect to achieving the objectives set for the community as a whole, and the teacher needs to know how his classroom stands. Does a school in a disadvantaged neighborhood need the same emphasis upon general objectives as a school in an advantaged community? What are the particular needs that require emphasizing? What are the lacks? What are the handicaps? What are the factors which block the attainment of essential goals? Are all of the children in a classroom similarly handicapped? Do they all need the same things? Should they all be required to work at the same assignments? Are there some who need more of the same, but others who need less, and still others who need quite different learning activities?

How can principal and teacher know whether their plans are relevant to the needs, and whether their educational program is doing the job that needs to be done? Is the program of the school exactly the same as it would be if the school were not in an economically and culturally disadvantaged community? Do the teacher's units, lesson plans, instructional materials, and specific assignments take into consideration knowledge of the culture and the specific educational needs of his pupils?

Evaluation of Instruction

What is evaluation? How good is a school or a school system? How effective has a teacher been? Has a course succeeded in getting across what it planned to accomplish? How well have educational objectives been accomplished? All of these are questions pertaining to evaluation. These are the types of questions which need to be answered if progress in education is to be made.

How can a school system be evaluated? This is an exceedingly complex problem, but one on which there has been much loose discussion. Without presuming to present a solution to this problem within two or three short paragraphs, let us suggest a few guiding principles.

1. First, does the school system have a philosophy, a statement of objectives?

2. What are its goals?

3. Are the goals realistically related to community conditions?

4. Does the school have appropriate facilities for carrying out its goals? Buildings? Equipment? Personnel? Time? Training? Supervision? Instructional Materials?

5. Does the school attempt to do its job alone, or is there coordination with other agencies in the community?

Does the school appropriate use of community resources? Of community personnel?

6. How good is the school's rapport with parents? Does the school understand and appreciate the cultural backgrounds of its families? Is it apparent that the educational program presented takes cognizance of the cultural backgrounds of the children?

7. Does the school do anything appropriate to determine whether its objectives have been carried out? What objective data are there to show that the school has attempted to assess its effectiveness in terms of its professed objectives?

Evaluating Teacher Effectiveness

Assessing teacher effectiveness is almost as complex a problem as evaluating a school system. A teacher's effectiveness cannot be measured simply by computing the average increase of his pupils' scores in reading and arithmetic over a semester or year interval. Testimonials are nice, and they are especially complimentary when solicited, but they are of questionable value as evidence. The principles suggested earlier for evaluating a school or a school system may be applied to the problem of evaluating a teacher, but the teacher is probably in the best position to apply these criteria to himself.

1. Does the teacher have a philosophy? Does he know what his long term goals are?

2. What are his goals?

3. Are his goals realistically related to the needs of his community? Are they realisticaly related to the needs of his pupils?

4. Are the teacher's instructional plans well suited for carrying out his goals? Are his teaching plans adapted to the cultural backgrounds and achievement levels of his pupils? Are his teaching plans differentiated according to the needs of individual pupils?

In formulating his daily lesson plans, can the teacher say: "Exactly what am I trying to accomplish with this assignment today? Is this the best activity or assignment I can think of for accomplishing this objective? Do all of the children need this activity, or will a different assignment for some pupils better accomplish my aims for them? Are the instructional materials I plan to use appropriate for accomplishing my objectives for my class? Do my units need modification? Can I find more appropriate materials? What teaching aids do I need to help me get my meaning across? If I don't have them, what can I do to get them?"

5. Does the teacher try to do the job completely by himself, or does he make use of available auxilliary school personnel and of community resources? Is the teacher secure enough to ask his principal and his colleagues for advice? Does the teacher know when he needs the help of the school psychologist, counselor,

remedial reading specialist, nurse, speech therapist, librarian, physical education teacher? Does the teacher make use of pupil personnel files? Does the teacher know the community's formal and informal social service resources: community clergy; settlement houses, recreation centers, scout leaders; juvenile police officers; family service agencies; public assistance agency social workers; and children's home personnel?

6. How well does the teacher coordinate his efforts with parents? Does he make an effort to meet his children's parents? Does he provide time in his schedule for conferences with parents? Does he understand the cultural backgrounds of his children's parents? Does he respect their backgrounds? Does he have faith in their intentions?

7. Does the teacher test himself as well as his pupils to determine whether he has in fact carried out his objectives? Does he constantly revise his plans in efforts to do his job more effectively?

8. How does the teacher feel about his pupils? Does he really like them? Does he respect them? Does he have faith in them and hope for them?

There are subtle indicators which cast reflections upon the effectiveness of an educational program. The metaphor *climate* has been adopted to conceptualize these indications. It is actually possible to experience affective tones of warmth or coldness in a classroom atmosphere, sparkling brightness or dreariness, impending turbulence, and explosive storminess.

Pupil participation and obstructionism may be judged from objective observations, as Ryans has suggested.[1] Apathy and alertness may similarly be inferred.

Evidence of pupil participation, however, is not of itself evidence that instructional goals have been achieved. We need measuring instruments to tell us whether gains have been made in terms of our teaching objectives. How can we determine how much improvement our group has made in communication skills? How much better are they in reading, spelling, and arithmetic at the end of the year than they were at the beginning? We may think this question is easy to answer through the use of commercially available achievement tests, but what do we use to determine whether our children are becoming better citizens, or that they are developing in such a way as to become competent in their jobs and happy in their family relationships? How do we know how well the unique needs of individual pupils have been met? How do we find out what these needs are, and after we have found out what they are, how can we measure how much progress has been made? What do we evaluate with?

The Tools of Evaluation

Evaluation is far from simple. It is not enough to know whether our pupils have progressed, and how much they have progressed. We need to know how much they have progressed in relation to their *ability to progress,* in relation to their potentiality. Therefore, we need measures of potentiality, of aptitude or ability, as well as of achievement. The problem is even more complex than this. We not only need to know how our pupils' progress has been affected by their learning ability, we also need to know what conditions other than ability affect learning, so that pupil progress may be evaluated in terms of these factors.

Two studies, one with mentally handicapped children, the other with academically talented, show how conditions other than measured IQ affect the learning of school children. In a study of correlates of achievement of educable mentally handicapped (EMH) children from predominantly culturally disadvantaged backgrounds, Mullen and Itkin found Stanford-Binet IQ's to be only one of a number of factors associated with achievement or nonachievement of mentally handicapped children.[2] Stanford-Binet Mental Age scores were significantly related to reading and arithmetic achievement, as reflected in Pearson coefficients of correlation of .65 between MA and reading and of .73 between reading and arithmetic. Correlations of .81 were also obtained between MA and scores on a test of general information and general comprehension. Mullen and Itkin demonstrated, however, that a substantial number of educable mentally handicapped children remain virtual nonachievers despite apparently sufficient learning ability as indicated by their mental age scores. On the other hand, they found that a similar proportion of their educable mentally handicapped subjects achieved relatively well for their level of tested ability.

Their study identified a number of variables in the backgrounds of the achieving EMH children which differentiated them as a group from the nonachievers of the same Stanford-Binet mental age scores: one, a higher degree of family integration; two, higher socioeconomic status; three, more favorable family attitudes toward education; four, fewer physical and neuorolgical handicaps; and five, better personality and behavioral adjustment. The most striking differences between the achieving and nonachieving EMH children came, however, from several converging lines of evidence that the mental ability of a greater proportion of the achievers had been underestimated by the individual intelligence tests. A substantial number of the achievers were apparently pseudo-retarded rather than actually retarded. A study of correlates of adjustment of well adjusted and poorly adjusted EMH children was also carried out by Mullen and Itkin. The backgrounds of the well adjusted EMH children were found to be generally similar to those of the achievers and the backgrounds of the poorly adjusted to the nonachievers.

In work with academically talented adolescents, Elizabeth Drews found socioeconomic factors and personality variables associated with scholastic achievement and creativity of high school and young college students.[3] With the qualification that her types were neither *pure* nor *stable* Drews classified gifted students into four categories: the high achieving studious, the social leaders, the creative intellectuals, and the rebels. Two of her categories, the creative intellectuals and the rebels, were nonconformist and non-grade-oriented. The creative intellectuals came from the entire socioeconomic range, while the rebels were predominantly from families of low socioeconomic status. The high achieving studious students were characterized by conformity, productivity but not necessarily creativity, ability to put work ahead of pleasures, a feeling for logic and a sense of organization, and a preference for structured rather than unstructured assignments. The gifted adolescents who were social leaders generally achieved adequately and even very well, but they placed social and economic motivations first. In contrast, the creative intellectuals did not tend to be social leaders and did not want to be; they rarely dated; their interests tended to be unique; they neither cared about monetary nor grade rewards; and they did not like explicit assignments.

A consideration of the findings of the Mullen-Itkin and Drews studies makes it clear that the academic progress of children and adolescents cannot be accounted for by tested IQ or teacher effectiveness alone. A child's academic achievement and, in fact, educability is affected by his own motivation and his family's interest in education, by sex, socioeconomic status, family stability, health and physical factors, attitudes and values, and general adjustment. The degree to which his tested IQ reflects his educability will depend very much on the extent to which his IQ test score is an adequate measure of his academic potentiality, i.e., upon the validity of the IQ test score. These findings indicate, therefore, that neither schools nor teachers may be compared in terms of tested achievements alone. Before making such comparisons, it is necessary to know whether the schools and teachers being judged were comparable in terms of the factors which affect learning. To compare progress of groups which are not comparable in terms of correlates of achievement or adjustment without providing either proper experimental or statistical controls is naive. The kind of evaluation research which provides such controls involves rather complex experimental design and statistical analysis. The use of electronic computers, however, now makes this kind of research feasible.

Measurement Methods

What kind of measurement methods do we have? Measures differ in precision and in apparent precision. Some tests yield measures on a continum or on a continuous scale. The Revised Stanford-Binet Intelligence Scale, for example, yields Mental Age scores which progress continuously in single steps from 2-0 to 22-10. Achievement batteries may offer continuous grade scores from 1.0 to 12.9. A teacher-made test may be scored in terms of number of correct responses. Relative standing in a group may be given in terms of standard scores, stanines, percentile ranks, or simply rank order. Performance may be classified into a number of categories on the basis of subjective judgment, when, for example, essay questions are categorized as Outstanding, Excellent, Highly Adequate, Adequate, Marginal, Unsatisfactory, and Completely Inadequate. Sometimes it is not possible to make confident discriminations between more than two categories, for example, Pass-Fail, Average or Above Average vs. Below Average; Shows signs of creativity vs. Gives no evidence of creativity.

How precise do our measurement methods have to be in order to be useful? This depends upon our purpose in measuring. If our task is to make decisions about individuals, our measures should be as precise as they can meaningfully be made. If our task is to compare performance between groups, the more precise our measurement instruments are, the better chance we have of demonstrating differences which exist. Even dichotomous classifications, i.e., Pass-Fail, can be useful in making meaningful comparisons between groups. With gross measures our chances of finding small but real differences are reduced, but it may nevertheless be possible to demonstrate the existence of large ones.

The classroom teacher of the disadvantaged pupil may have no evaluative tool more useful to him in accomplishing his educational objectives than the simple dichotomous classification. That knowledge of results facilitates learning has been demonstrated in numerous research studies.[4] Some teachers have a philosophical position about traumatizing children with the sight of red ink. Then let them use bright royal blue! The quality of an essay question may be difficult to grade with precision and consistency. The teacher owes it to his students to let them know whether they are making themselves understood, however. Otherwise, it is pointless to speak of *communication*. If the teacher is able to make only a two-way evaluation of a sentence—clear or not clear, correct or incorrect, this is a judgment his pupils may very greatly need. The same applies to errors in spelling. Otherwise, they may reach college and even graduate school greatly handicapped by their deficiencies in communication skills.

Knowledge of results applies to the nonacademic areas as well as the academic areas of learning. Children need to know what the limits are, what goes and what does not go. Simply telling them: "We don't do this; this is acceptable behavior, and this is not," helps them to learn what the standards are. To give a few additional examples: "We do not spar on the playground;" "We do not throw garbage out of the window;" "We do not mark up school property." These are application of the dichotomous method of evaluation which should not be underestimated.

Measurement Problems

We may not assume that a test is equally good for all purposes and for all populations. We need evidence of the screening efficiency of a test for specific screening purposes. It may be that some group tests are more efficient in predicting mental retardation in some cultural groups than others, some more efficient in identifying the potentially academically talented. Some may be extremely inefficient for their intended purposes. For all of the money spent on group testing, a relatively infinitessimal investment in rather simple research could have answered these questions.

How useful are IQ tests for predicting the academic potentiality of culturally disadvantaged pupils? Table I presents longitudinal data on a single eighth grade classroom in a culturally disadvantaged area. This table shows relationships between IQ, economic status, grades, and reading achievement. The IQ's in Column 4 are derived from whatever IQ tests were available, in chronological order of administration. The reading scores are based on tests given in 6A. These data are presented for illustrative purposes only. The evaluation of any one intelligence test on the basis of these data is unfair, since this table is based upon different tests, given at unequal intervals. To the extent that judgments about the ability of individuals are sometimes quite uncritically made on just such data, there is a degree of realism in considering these data.

For almost one half of the group, IQ findings are remarkably stable, with deviations of less than ten points from highest to lowest scores. For approximately one-third, however, there are deviations in IQ of fifteen points or more, and for one fifth of the group, IQ deviations of twenty points or more were reported. Clearly, for some pupils the IQ in the generic sense in which the term is sometimes used is quite an unreliable measure of whatever it is that it attempts to measure. In the absence of other relevant data, it would be impossible to know which, if any, of the reported IQ's is most likely to be the true one for those pupils. The IQ's for the pupils classified as achievers seemed particularly inconsistent.

Does this mean that the IQ is a completely worthless bit of information for culturally disadvantaged pupils? Further examination of Table I yields some interesting observations. Six pupils

TABLE I
ONE EIGHTH GRADE CLASS IN A CULTURALLY DISADVANTAGED AREA

Student	Economic Status	Grade Average, Elementary School Years***	Available IQ's in Order	Reading Scores in 6A
*1	R	G—	71,101,101,88	4.2
2	Both W	F	87,91,78	3.6
3	W	F	84,79	4.4
**4	R	F	86,83,76,78	3.6
5	W	G—	94,92	3.3
6	W	F+	88,79	4.2
7	R	F	90,81	3.9
8	Unknown	G—	91,94,97	3.3
9	Unknown	G—	89,89	4.4
**10	W	F—	84,83,87	4.4
**11	R	F+	73	3.6
12	R	F+	63,63	2.8
**13	W	F—	95.91,93,83	3.4
14	W	G—	107,72,107,91	4.4
15	W	F	101,103,99	5.4
16	R	F+	83,100,98,96	3.8
17	R	F	92,96,82	3.5
18	R	F—	87,90,79,74	3.1
19	W	F—	96,97,78	3.9
20	W	F+	88,89,85	3.9
21	R	F	103,84,85	4.3
22	W	F—	80,90	5.7
23	Unknown	F	51,81,72	3.6
24	R	F	80,83,84	4.5
25	Unknown	F	80,77	4.3
**26	R	F—	97,93,67	3.1
**27	W	G	91,88,78	3.7
*28	W	F+	100,106,81,87	4.5
*29	W	G+	113,117,107,90	8.0
*30	W	G+	101,106,117	8.3
*31	W	G+	106,112	7.0

* Classified as achievers on basis of grade criterion and teacher judgment
** Classified as nonachievers on grade criterion and teacher judgment
*** G = Good, F = Fair
R Parents on Public Assistance
W Parent or Parents Working

were classified as achievers, twenty as average for the group. Of the six achievers, four had earned two or more IQ's of 100 or above. Of the twenty average achievers, only two had scores of 100 or above on two or more tests. None of the five poor achievers received even one IQ score of 100, and only two of the five had any scores in the nineties. The data on a single classroom is a most inadequate sample on the basis of which to evaluate a test. These data are offered here for illustrative purposes only because sweeping indictments of tests have been made in the literature, seemingly without a look at any data. The teacher is asked to compare these data with similar data from his own class.

What, then, can we say about the validity of intelligence test scores for culturally disadvantaged pupils? Intelligence tests are not all alike. A score from one test is not necessarily comparable to a score on another. We do not know which tests give us the best estimate of the academic potentiality of particular minority groups. The basic capacity or *true* measure of potential intellectual ability of any individual can only be estimated. It has to be inferred from his performance in various life and test situations, and his performance in these situations is influenced by his experience, his cultural background, his personality, and his health history. The potential learning ability of culturally disadvantaged children cannot be compared with the potential learning ability of nondisadvantaged children on the basis of scores on the same tests. Any one test score must be interpreted most tentatively. A psychologist should exercise clinical judgment in interpreting the validity of a single test score. Teachers' observations, achievement test data, observation in nonacademic situations, and inferences from personality tests should be considered in making an assessment of the learning ability of a culturally disadvantaged child. Two tests will give a basis for a more valid assessment than one. Revaluation from time to time is essential.

Single test findings should be regarded as probable minimal estimates rather than true estimates. Nevertheless, although intelligence test scores are not true measures of the basic capacity of culturally deprived children, consistent tests results are likely to predict academic performance with what must be regarded as a substantial degree of accuracy. Although the teacher should not quit trying for improved pupil academic achievement in the face of low test scores, he will not be able to help his students by accepting all of the blame for their lack of academic success.

Tests have been unjustly blamed for lack of validity which resulted not from weaknesses of the test, but from incompetence on the part of the test user or test interpreter. Test publishers provide manuals which supply norms for interpreting test scores. The manuals also give instructions for administering and scoring the test and contain evidence of reliability and validity. The norms are meaningful only when the conditions of administration specified in the manual are conscientiously followed. Similarly, the validity and reliability data are applicable only under conditions of standard administration.

The test user does not have the option of changing instructions given examinees, changing the timing of the test, providing help, changing the wording of test items, or in any other way modifying instructions provided in the manual. If he does so, he changes the test. He may not, then, use the norms given in the manual for interpreting test scores. He may not expect the reliability and validity data given in the manual to have the same meaning under the conditions of changed test administration. He may not blame the test for inadequacies that might be attributable to his own incompetent test administration. The test user may argue that in its present method of administration results from the test are unfair to his subjects. He may claim that his changes render the test more fair to his examinees. He may be correct, but the burden of proof is his, and the responsibility for proof is his. He is not free to enjoy his claims without supporting them with evidence of reliability and validity. He has changed the test by modifying items and administration procedure. He now has the same responsibility as the original test publisher to support his claims with evidence of the validity of his modifications. Otherwise, he has not improved upon the original product, but has been guilty of professional irresponsibility.

Another basic error in test administration is failure to obtain rapport or subject cooperation. It is the responsibility of the examiner to elicit the subject's best efforts. For his test results to be maximally valid within the limitations of the test, the examiner must be able to make his subjects comfortable and willing to do their best. If the examiner is unable to get the attention of his subjects or cannot make himself clearly heard, if he makes his examinees anxious, or antagonizes them, he should not be testing.

A third error in testing has to do with the use of a level or battery of a test which is inappropriate for particular subjects. Disregard of ceilings and basal scores reported in tables of norms is one aspect of this error. A test which may be valid for most subjects at a grade level may be either too difficult for subjects whose achievements are much below grade level or too easy for others. A student, for example, who somehow reaches high school with second grade reading ability may score at the fourth grade level of the achievement battery given in high school if the norms for that battery do not go below grade four. A third grade student whose reading ability is comparable to that of an average eighth grader may score at the sixth grade level if a ceiling score for an errorless performance on the battery given in third grade is at grade six. For these particular students, the battery given is invalid, regardless of the validity of the test for the general population.

Yet another error in interpretation of test results stems from a failure to take into consideration the error of measurement of a test. Many persons in a position to make administrative decisions about individuals on the basis of tests results treat test scores as if they were *true* and errorless measures. They treat a score as if it were an absolute rather than an approximate measure. To them, 7.4 means 7.4, and not 7.2 nor 7.7. If a cut-point of 7.5 on a reading test has been established as a criterion for going to high school, a student scoring 7.3 would be retained in elementary school. If a cut-point of 10.5 on a mathematics test were required for eligibility for an honors mathematics class, students falling a point short of this criterion would be denied enrollment in the honors class. Students receiving an IQ of 128 would be considered brighter than those receiving IQ's of 123, and so forth.

All test scores have an error of measurement. Standard errors of measurement are reported in test manuals. In interpreting these errors of measurement, one must consider that every test score represents a point within an interval of probability. If a test score has a standard error of five points, this should be interpreted as meaning that for that test, the chances of the obtained score being within five points of a hypothetical *true* score for any particular examinee is two to one, and the probability of the obtained score being within ten points, or two times the standard error, of a hypothetical true score are twenty to one. An implication of this point is that standard errors of measurement should be considered in making decisions affecting individuals. A Test score close to cut-points should not be used *as the single criterion.*

Teacher-made Tests

A teacher cannot reach for a test publisher's catalog to supply all of his evaluation needs. The teacher may have reason for believing that a standardized test is not appropriate for his particular group of children. For example, the teacher may feel that he wants to test for quite a different type of reading ability than is tested by a standardized test, or for a different kind of mathematical comprehension, or language ability. A published test may have generally adequate content validity, but its items may not adequately sample some of the objectives that are important in a particular school or a particular classroom. The social studies unit may be on India, for example, but this unit may stress quite different objectives in inner city than in suburbia. Further, for the one testing of some objectives, no appropriate commercially prepared measurement instruments may be available.

A teacher should use testing as an instructional tool to give students feedback or knowledge of results. Standardized tests *must not be used for this purpose,* because the security of standardized test items must be safeguarded. The teacher should use his own tests for this purpose. He must, therefore, know how to construct his own tests to meet his immediate measurement problems.

The possession of a teacher's certificate does not guarantee competence in test making. A good test is not achieved simply by writing a few essay questions or drafting a number of true-false, matching, or multiple-choice questions. Writing a good test requires considerable analytical ability and creativity. A teacher must identify the objectives he wants to measure, then draft test items to fit the objectives. The teacher has the same responsibility for determining whether his test is reliable and valid as any other test author. Reliability and validity may not be assumed, but they often are. Students who complain of a test being unfair may not be using the correct technical terminology, but they may be talking about validity, and they may be correct!

Essay Tests

Essay tests are laborious to score. They are difficult to grade because of the subjective judgments which have to be made in grading. Studies of consistency of the scoring of essay tests have given essays a poor grade for reliability. Regardless of these scoring problems for the teacher, college and graduate school instructors will generally agree that a substantial number of students reach even the graduate level unable to express themselves clearly and correctly in writing. Whether or not teachers are able to do a precise job of grading their written work, it is important that pupils be given ample experience in writing and consistent feedback to guide them in improving their writing skills.

Essay tests, properly constructed, have the following virtues:

1. They can be used to test for ability to generalize, and to organize facts and ideas.
2. They can be used to demonstrate reasoning ability, judgment, and comprehension of cause and effect relationships.
3. They can be used to test for comprehension of concepts.
4. They can be used to elicit the expression of feelings and attitudes.
5. They can be used to test for the application of principles to new situations.

As in the construction of any evaluation device, a major guiding principle is to identify the specific objectives to be measured. The objectives to be measured should determine the wording of the essay question. Writing good essay questions requires thought and creativity, but it is an art which can be improved with study and practice.

Scoring standards for an essay test should be decided in advance. The teacher should list the criteria of an adequate answer for each question. Scoring consistency may be improved by reading the answers for each question separately for an entire set of papers. Identity of writers should be anonymous during grading. The evaluation given previous questions should not be referred to in scoring subsequent questions by the same students. Evaluations for clarity of expression, spelling, and penmanship should be made independently of evaluations of content.

Short-answer Tests

Objective tests take longer to draft than essay tests. They take less time to score, and the seeming objectivity of a raw scores gives the teacher a feeling of complacency he does not experience in grading essay tests. This feeling of security is not always justified. It may be earned by testing the test by means of fairly simple methods of item analysis.

It is frequently assumed that on an objective test one test item is the equivalent of another test item, and that therefore similar total scores have the same meaning. Is this assumption justified? An examination of the literature indicates that this is not the case. Since, however, the argument advocating item analysis is the same whether the pupils tested are disadvantaged or not, it need not be developed here. Readers are invited to examine general works on evaluation for assistance in preparing an item analysis of their tests. The writing of an item for short answer tests is treated adequately in the same sources. In regard to these techniques, the insights into how to construct a test which evaluates the progress made in achieving the teacher's objectives can be utilized in any situation. Teachers are reminded that the tests must deal with the objectives and the learning activities which preceded the giving of the test.

One final caution is in order in regard to the use of a normal distribution curve as a basis for allocating marks to a group of disadvantaged pupils. Grading on a curve can be justified only if one is sure that he has a representative group in terms of learning ability and motivation. If his group is more academically talented than the average and better motivated or less so, grading on a curve is not warranted. One should be aware that setting cutpoints for different grades on an objective test involves a subjective judgment. Taking cognizance of this element of subjectivity in grading of objective tests takes some of the security away from the reliance on objective tests, but it may lead to more valid grading.

REFERENCES

1. David G. Ryans, "Some Relationships between Pupil Behavior and Certain Teacher Characteristics," *Journal of Educational Psychology*, 52; (April, 1961), p. 82.
2. Frances A. Mullen and W. Itkin, *Achievement and Adjustment of Educable Mentally Handicapped Children in Special Classes and Regular Grades,* Chicago: Board of Education, Chicago, Illinois, 1961.
3. Elizabeth Drews, "The Four Faces of Able Adolescents," in Joseph L. French, Editor, *Educating the Gifted: A Book of Readings* (New York: Holt, Rinehart & Winston, Inc., Revised Editing, 1964), pp. 105-113.
4. John A. McGeoch, *The Psychology of Human Learning: An Introduction* (New York: Longmans, Green & Co., 1946), p. 575.

Suggested Readings

Adams, Georgia S., *Measurement and Evaluation in Education, Psychology and Guidance,* New York: Holt, Rinehart and Winston, 1964.

Barnette, W. Leslie, Jr., *Readings in Psychological Tests and Measurements,* Homewood, Ill.: The Dorsey Press, Inc., 1964.

Gerberich, J. Raymond; Harry A. Greene; and A. N. Jorgensen; *Measurement and Evaluation in the Modern School.* New York: David McKay Company, Inc., 1962.

Guilford, J. P., *Psychometric Methods.* Second Edition, New York: McGraw-Hill Book Company, Inc., 1954.

Lyman, Howard B., *Test Scores and What They Mean.* Englewood Cliffs, N. J.: Prentice-Hall, Inc., 1963.

Thorndike, Robert L. and Elizabeth Hagen, *Measurement and Evaluation in Psychology and Education,* Second Edition, New York: John Wiley & Sons, Inc., 1961.

PART III

THE SCHOOL, THE COMMUNITY, AND THE DISADVANTAGED PUPIL

THE CHAPTERS IN Part III deal with the broad phases of the educational problem of the culturally disadvantaged. These are, in order, the teachers, the schools, and the community. The first of these chapters offers a graphic account of teachers for the inner city. Specific implications are drawn for the selection and preparation of teachers. Joyce directs his discussion to teacher characteristics, teaching skills and teaching styles, working conditions and the unique programs required for teacher education. In addition to highly qualified teachers, the necessity for cooperative action is stressed. Team teaching, especially, is recommended for the attack on the complex problems of the culturally disadvantaged. An important point is made of the need to provide future teachers with laboratory experience in inner-city schools which are designated by the community and the colleges as experimental centers for educating the culturally disadvantaged.

Next, Mendelson in his chapter describes the crucial role of the principal in the development of an effective educational program for the culturally disadvantaged. The focus is on the desirable behavior of the principal rather than on particular administrative traits. Both school and community situational factors are considered in defining the expected behavior patterns of the principal. The concrete proposals reflect the author's experiences in the inner-city schools.

What is evident in this discussion is that the principal can ill-afford to be content with traditional organizational and instructional approaches. Pupils, teachers, and the community increasingly depend on the dynamic leadership of the school principal. The attainment of an ever-improving education for culturally disadvantaged children, according to Mendelson, can be realized only if the principal is willing to move ahead with new ideas and experimental programs.

The major breakthrough in the education of the culturally disadvantaged may well depend on the success of community action programs. As Hobgood points out in the final chapter, the problems of the culturally disadvantaged pupils are always closely related to the problems of the communities in which they live. In the past, sporadic attempts have been made to link the school and community to augment the educational resources for improving the schooling of the culturally disadvantaged. Currently, federal subsidies for community and school programs to aid the culturally disadvantaged will insure a more effective relationship between the school and community.

Hobgood analyzes several aspects of this important school-community relationship. He presents the problems of community interaction and the task of reaching isolated groups. Different ways of establishing meaningful contacts with the culturally disadvantaged are described, including the use of "cultural interpreters" and auxiliary teachers where language is a barrier. A special note is made of existing community programs, such as school volunteers, tutors, and the highly successful Banneker project in St. Louis, Missouri.

Chapter XIII

TEACHERS FOR THE CULTURALLY DISADVANTAGED

Bruce R. Joyce*

Let us begin our discussion of the teacher for the culturally disadvantaged with a declaration of deep ignorance. We do not know—no one knows—even the best teachers of the culturally disadvantaged do not know just how we can describe the people who will be effective in the schools of the inner city. For the past ten years I have talked regularly with devoted, enthusiastic teachers who are identified by their colleagues as the pick of their cities. These people cannot tell us the secret of their success, are puzzled by the problem of recruitment for slum teaching, and many of them report that they are not at all sure how best to help student teachers who are sent to them.

Let us also agree to discuss the problem of identifying and preparing teachers for the slums with no more than a cursory review of the literature on the subject. On the whole, the literature is sparse and exploratory. One should read the chapters by Haubrich and Kornberg in the Passow volume.[1] Another must is Riessman's discussion.[2] All three provide some thoughtful advice about selecting and preparing teachers. On the whole, however, it seems to me that this is a time for hypothesis-setting and set-breaking. We should scour carefully the evidence that exists, attempt to build ideas that make the evidence more sensible, and then strike out with hypotheses on which we can act experimentally.

Hence, let us speak hypothetically in this chapter, and discuss a two-part question: who should teach the culturally disadvantaged and what should be his preparation for teaching?

---

*Director of Elementary Teacher Education, the University of Chicago.

What Describes This Teacher?

First, we can say that *he is not doctrinaire.*

The teacher for the inner city must know that he does not know. He must not think to himself: "The trouble with these kids is their language development. All they need is a little experience with words." If he approaches his job with any such simplistic formula, he will be sadly disappointed. These children have language problems, all right, but that is not their only problem. A little, or a lot, of experience with words is not going to do the trick all by itself.

The teacher for the inner city must not think to himself: "These children have low motivation because their parents do not teach them the value of education." One may hear this. He may even read it in the popular press or in the poorer professional literature. *It is not that simple.* Some of the most education-oriented parents are in slums. Some of the most highly motivated children are in slum schools.

The teacher for the inner city must not think to himself: "The reason they don't learn to read is because the readers deal with things outside their experience. The readers show ivy-covered cottages and dogs and cats and jolly grandmothers in the country. That stuff doesn't make sense to the slum child." While I personally have little brief with the content of many reading books, the logic in the quotation just made is about as valid as the argument that children will not like nursery stories about kings and dragons because they have not encountered them in their daily life.

What I am trying to say, of course, is that the teacher of the culturally disadvantaged has to enter teaching with a deep sense of our ignorance about inner-city children and how to treat them. He has to beware of shibboleths and treat with circumspection the doctrines of even the most successful teacher or the most careful psychologist. *This is no time for dogma.* Any beginning teacher in the slums who thinks he has the answers and who tries to teach in accord with the prescribed answers will come to grief very shortly.

He has a wide range of skills and teaching styles. Just as the teacher for the inner city has to beware of simple dogmas, so he has to beware of letting himself develop a single teaching style which he uses to meet all situations. He needs, instead, to cultivate a wide range of teaching styles which he employs as they seem to be appropriate.[3] For example, if he thinks that all lessons should be taught with pupil-teacher planning of objectives and procedures, and if he attempts to engage in cooperative planning with children who are not prepared to engage in democratic problem-solving behavior, chaos is likely to be the result. The teacher who wishes to plan cooperatively with the children needs to teach them how to participate in planning activity. Equally, the teacher who believes that: "The thing to do is to get tough at first, show them who's boss" will probably find that in the process of "getting tough" he has developed a teaching style that makes cooperative activity for mutual ends a virtual impossibility.

Many new teachers and many education professors think that disciplining children is not a desirable part of the teacher's repertoire. Some new teachers report that they feel guilty when they punish children or impose their will on a reluctant child. Yet the teacher has to learn how to punish and how to impose his will if he is to lead with success the children from the inner city. Some of these children will follow him eagerly. Others will have to be coerced whether we like it, or whether it is a final solution to their problems. The good teacher widens his repertoire and employs it intelligently.

Some teachers quite naturally teach tightly-sequenced lessons which lead the children step-by-step. Others prefer to teach through discussion. They present a problem or an idea and work it over with the children. The teacher of the culturally deprived needs to learn both of these styles (and many others). He has to be able to develop clear, tight lessons which build knowledge and skill and he has to learn to discuss common problems with groups of children. The teacher whose range of styles includes only one of these will only be able to do some of the things that he needs to be able to do. Thelen has reported that even relatively gifted children vary widely in the kinds of guidance they need to engage in inquiry.[4] The inner-city teacher will find equal dispersion of characteristics among the children he teaches. The teacher of the inner city has to be able to be firm when firmness is indicated; commanding when strong leadership is needed; gentle and comforting when someone is in need; determined and orderly in some lessons; loose and expressive in others. One may ask whether any one teacher can radiate all these styles with equal ease. We may forthrightly respond that of course he cannot. But he has to be able to produce them with reasonable efficiency. The teacher who can only discipline, who cannot work cooperatively with children, is a pedagogical cripple. Equally, the teacher who can only beseech cooperation but cannot impose or command is crippled with respect to many situations. Our teacher has to learn wide ranges of behaviors.

He has to learn to discriminate children on new terms. In education and psychology we have grown accustomed to thinking of children as academically able or not. In education and sociology we have learned to think of children as upper, middle, or lower class. It is on dimensions like academic ability and social class that most of us make distinctions among the children we teach.

All of us, and especially the teachers of the culturally disadvantaged, need to take care that the dimensions which we use to categorize our students are the most productive ones possible. For example, take the distinction between well-behaved and unruly pupils. Our first look at most unruly children might tell us that they are rebelling against control from outsiders. The psychologist David Hunt has been studying personality differences among culturally disadvantaged junior high school students in Syracuse, N. Y. On a basis of conceptual development, he has found differences in interpersonal behavior as follows:

One type is quite unruly. Their behavioral inconsistencies and unpredictability, their difficulties with authority-figures, apparently stem from early childhood environments so inconsistent that they have not internalized an adequate system of norms. Hence, they have great difficulty identifying rules and obeying them. Their interpersonal behavior is inconsistent and contentious. They respond only slowly to attempts to establish classroom procedures.

Hunt has been able to identify another type which at first seems like the unsocialized type that we have just described. This second group once was in a state of reasonably complete socialization. However, these children are in active rebellion against the standards which they once internalized.[5]

The difference in corrective procedure for these two types is enormous. The first type is, in a sense, presocialized. They need a consistent, firm, adult-dominated environment that will enable them to internalize norms and the ability to act in accord with agreed-upon standards. The second type needs to re-establish ties to other persons, to look realistically at standards and authorities, and to begin once more to relate to their society. They are a much more intelligent group, moreover, much more interesting to teach academic subjects, and quite willing to participate in discussion and debate, as long as they are able to express their hostility toward authority.

Unless the teacher learns to discriminate between these two types of unruly children, he will be unable to diagnose and treat their problems.

This is only one illustration of the new ways of describing children that the teacher of the culturally disadvantaged has to master. Ausubel has pointed out that many lower-class Negro girls suffer ego damage as a result of their inferior and discriminated-against position.[6] A child who has been damaged and fails to test reality adequately may appear simply to be rebelling against authority. The teacher has to learn the signs of ego-damage.

Until one has experience and training, emotional disturbance and mental retardation have many similar characteristics. A child, ritualistically changing and unchanging the diapers on a doll, humming to herself and talking to the play child, looks much the same whether she is taking solace in the action or whether she is playing a simple, happy game. A child who has difficulty talking because he knows few words and speaks in fragments of sentences may easily be confused with a child who is withdrawn and hostile.

Discriminating among children—identifying the real facts of the situation—is essential for accurate diagnosis and educational prescription. Typically, teachers are trained to the psychology of the middle-class child. They are sensitive to differences in gross intellectual capacity and to gross social class differences. The types of incapacity and the types of social differences that characterize the middle city are not those of the suburb or the middle-class school. The teacher has to learn a new psychology which will enable him to discriminate the characteristics of the lower class, culturally disadvantaged child. He has to learn *not* to lump all these children together as one type, obscuring the vast differences between them and the implications of the differences.

He has to learn to find out and use the frames of reference his pupils use to interpret the world. Every individual approaches life with characteristic points of view or frames of reference which affect the way he organizes and interprets his experiences. For example, some people view interpersonal relations as unilateral and mechanical. Such people tend to view leaders as authoritarian bosses. When a leader makes a suggestion, they tend to interpret it as an order.

Other persons view interpersonal relations as fluid and changing. They tend to see leadership as a process of interaction, a balancing of negotiation and influence. When a leader makes a suggestion, they tend to interpret it as the initiation of a decision-making process. Their *frame of reference vis-a-vis* interpersonal relations, leads to a different interpretation of essentially the same data as was available to the persons who view human relations unilaterally.

It is important for teachers to learn to recognize and interpret the frames of reference which their students use to approach important aspects of reality such as interpersonal relations, education, officialdom, work, and family. What do they expect of others? What is supporting and what is threatening to them? What do they see as their role with respect to teachers and vice versa? The teacher has to learn to seek the answers to these questions and to redirect his teaching accordingly. For example, a teacher may find that some of his pupils regard social workers as phonies and hypocrites. His strategies for teaching about social agencies needs to be different from those he might use with children who expect social workers to be sincere, impersonal, and effective.

The teacher of the culturally disadvantaged must also be a student to his trade. He has to be an experimenter. He has to contribute actively to knowledge about how to teach the culturally disadvantaged and what should be taught to him. On the face of it, it seems quite enough to ask the teacher to live and struggle all day each day with the culturally disadvantaged. How can we ask him to do more? Well, we can because we must. The teaching of the culturally deprived is an area in which we have very little wisdom that has accumulated out of the experience of the teachers who have worked through the years with the children of the inner city. They have written down very little of the insights and experiences that they have had. Further, the city colleges and teachers of the cities have done very little together to make available the wisdom of these teachers in systematic fashion to the young persons who would like to teach in the inner city. As a result, we start today to prepare new teachers for the slums with little practical knowledge we did not have forty years ago.

To remedy this situation, the teachers of the culturally disadvantaged have to be the major source of knowledge. They have to be experimenters, trying out ideas and methods and observing their effects. They have to be the ones who perform the experiments, who try and err, who communicate to new teachers and to psychologists and sociologists the things they have seen and the methods that have worked and the ones that have not worked. It is the teacher who has to allow observers to watch him, not only on good days but on bad. He has to try to communicate the secrets of his control of these children and to communicate unreservedly all he can about the children he has not learned to teach. The teacher of the slums has to be an assiduous student of his trade, constantly studying his performance and collecting knowledge that will improve it.

Let us look briefly at some of the directions in which he will have to experiment. Consider, for example, some of the implications of Bloom's hypotheses about the interaction between environment and mental development in the human child. Bloom has hypothesized that 50 per cent of mental growth occurs in the first four years of life and 30 per cent in the next four. He has further hypothesized that the effect of environment on mental growth is greatest during periods of most rapid change. (The first and second four-year periods of life are the periods of rapid intellectual change for most organisms.) "What we have hypothesized is that extreme environments can have far greater effects in the early years of development than they can in later years. That is, deprivation in the first four years of life can have far greater consequences than deprivation in the ten years from age eight through age seventeen."[7] If we are to take advantage of the years when school environments have the most opportunity to affect the mental growth of the child, then we will have to experiment with education from the age of two or even younger. No one knows just how extremely young children should or can be handled in large numbers. Suggestions can be made, hypotheses formed, and curriculums planned (and they should be), but the instructional decisions, the day-by-day handling of children will have to be worked out on the job by the teachers who first staff these earliest of early grades.

Think for a moment of another implication of Bloom's hypotheses. One of his corollaries is that the slower the period of change of the organism, the more extreme the environment has to be to have an impact on the child. This means that the years from about eight on require relatively more powerful environmental influences to affect mental growth. Also, the more deprived the child has been, the less responsive he is to any environment. Therefore, those who teach the child increase the influence of the school environment.

"Opportunities to solve problems, encouragement to think clearly about a variety of issues, and encouragement to attack problems in and out of school probably also differ in abundant and deprived environments. An environment which restricts these opportunities and which even discourages the individual from attempting to attack and solve problems on his own is likely to retard intelligence development, whereas an environment which encourages problem solving and clear thinking is likely to facilitate the development of intelligence."[8]

Yet, it is just the culturally disadvantaged for whom it is difficult to create problem-solving settings in school, because he is often so hard to handle or so docile. Experimentation will have to be undertaken into ways of increasing the potency of education for older culturally deprived children, by developing more powerful educational environments. New arrangements of teachers and children have to be sought in order to increase the potency of education. The teachers has to be the leader in this experimentation. If the potency of education is to be increased through the application of reference-group theory, for example, it is the teacher who will have to try to make the classroom group a reference group for the child. If new ways of leading the child through problem-solving activities are employed, the teacher will have to be the one to try them out.

Because large groups of inner-city children are frequently difficult to control, there is a temptation for the teacher of the culturally deprived to become a successful control artist whose attention is so taken by control problems that he restricts his teaching to carefully sequenced lessons. The teacher may learn to get along with the children, but he does not learn to get along with them and at the same time teach them. Perpetually, when he experiments with teaching methods, he risks losing control of the children. If he tries to use more concrete aids in teaching mathematics, he risks disruptive activity until the children have learned to use the aids properly. If the teacher tries to individualize his reading instruction, he risks chaos as the children learn to be independent. If he experiments with cooperative planning, he risks argument and division. (A compounding factor is that there is nothing that will bring the administration of the school district down on him faster than inability to control the children.) Therefore, the teacher's willingness to experiment is accompanied by another characteristic.

He is willing to fail, to risk failure because he recognizes that his own learning to teach requires him to step into the areas where we all are uncertain. Very, very few teachers experience quick success in teaching the culturally disadvantaged. Nearly every teacher I have ever talked to who has worked in the inner city reports that he went through an agonizing period in which he felt either that he couldn't control the children or that he couldn't find a way to reach them or both. We can say that up to the present time it is virtually a certainty that no one will learn to teach these children effectively who cannot tolerate a substantial period of failure before he becomes able. There can be no "I tried that once and it didn't work" attitude on the part of the teachers of the inner city. Nearly everything they try the first (and perhaps the tenth) time will not work. An abundance of error is involved in learning to teach these children. He who would teach in the inner city has to assume that he will not be a success right off.

Every student teacher that I have placed in a slum school has reported sadly to me, "I had to yell to get them quiet. What am I going to do?" Somehow, we have had to convince these beginners that they will only gradually learn to control difficult children unobtrusively, that it took their cooperating teachers a long while, too. Sometimes we are not able to convince them of this. The ones who want to be good "right away" tend to drop out and seek the surer success of the middle class schools.

The teacher of the culturally disadvantaged is a member of a team. He engages in experimentation into ways that teachers can work together, playing different roles in the lives of children, managing groups of children cooperatively, observing one another's teaching, helping one another out. A situation I watched a few weeks ago illustrated simultaneously the minimum and maximum of such cooperation. The school is organized into self-contained classrooms with minimal formal interchange of teaching responsibilities, although the administration is cooperative and the teachers work together on resource units and other mutual projects. One morning the regular teacher of a very difficult class was absent, leaving a substitute and a student teacher in charge. The class became extremely unruly. I went in and lent assistance, but the class was too difficult for three strangers unless all were present. Miraculously, neighboring teachers began to appear, each taking off one of the more difficult and hard-to-reach children until the class had become manageable. Only a few words were exchanged, but the situation of cooperation was well-understood. In this incident, the self-contained classroom represented the minimum of teamwork. The unspoken rush to the rescue represented the maximum in sensitivity and mutual support.

Now, in any effective attack on the problems of inner-city education, we are going to have to employ teachers in teams. The individual teacher, working by himself in the relative isolation of the self-contained classroom in the elementary school, or teaching any subject by himself in a departmentalized high school, is a relatively small-bore weapon compared to a team of mutually reinforcing adults. Especially is this true when the major educational problems involve the socialization, or the resocialization of the children. A single teacher is not as effective a socializing agent as is a group or a small society of interacting adults. Hence, whether we are attempting to work with the very young children and provide a warm society which will help them find stability, or whether we are attempting to organize the secondary school into an effective society which will help the adolescent find values and learn to direct his life productively, we need to work in groups. The adult interaction in groups provides examples, provides a sense of solidity and purpose, that individuals working alone cannot do. The depressed-area school that will be effective will be a school whose faculty is a well-coordinated team whose members reinforce and assist each other, and subteams which demonstrate to the children the kinds of cooperative behavior which they have to learn if they are to participate effectively in our society.

Consequently, the teacher of the culturally disadvantaged needs to learn to participate in the building of a school society whose social climate is designed to be an effective educative agent in its own right. This teacher has to learn how to teach as a member of a team whose function is the development of an integrated child society. One of the often mentioned advantages of team-teaching is that it enables each member of the team to play the roles with children that he fulfills best. Some of these children need softness and motherliness, some need command and sureness, some need to be brought out of their docility, and some need to reestablish ties with other humans. By working together, a team can supply many of these needs effectively and consistently.

The teacher of the disadvantaged knows his subject. With all the social and emotional problems of the inner city, one could forget that no one needs to have greater control of the things he teaches than those who teach the very slow, the disturbed, and the socially needful. The individual curriculum areas have been dealt with in separate chapters, so we will not here dwell on subject matter except generally.

First of all, each teacher of the inner city needs to have a comprehensive knowledge of the teaching of reading and other facets of language development. All the teachers on the teams of the inner city have to coordinate an intensive effort to improve language usage. Every subject, every minute, has to be squeezed for language value. All teachers at all levels need to have a knowledge of the experience approaches to reading, for, even in the secondary school, experience records will have to be made to provide materials which the students can read, as well as material that has personal meaning for them.

Second, each teacher needs to control some academic area thoroughly and precisely. In the first place, this control over subject is needed for diagnosis. The mathematics teacher needs to be able to pick out precisely the student's critical problems. The language teacher needs to identify the most serious and pivotal grammatical lacks as well as minor problems.

Control is needed, also, so the teacher can identify the most critical focus for instruction. Given a learning problem in arithmetic, where does instruction lead? What principle will, if taught, make the greatest difference? Given a language problem, what suggestion for writing, what principle of grammar, will improve language usage most?

Control of the subject provides, also, a greater variety of approaches. The teacher who knows mathematics knows a half-dozen ways to teach the long division logarithm. The teacher who knows English well can identify several ways to approach the use of commas and periods. Knowledge of English literature provides the teacher with knowledge of more stories and novels of greater variety—he is more likely to find the intelligible and meaningful. He is less tied to standard materials.

Control over subject is needed, also, if the teacher is to help prepare the materials needed for the culturally disadvantaged.

The standard commercial materials which are marketed as texts are, on the whole, badly suited for the inner-city schools. Reading levels, special vocabulary, and the approaches of these materials make them unsuitable for the inner city. Hence, the teacher must construct original materials. Hopefully, teachers will soon be participating in materials-development projects which will systematically provide teaching materials for the inner city. When that day comes, it will be the teacher whose knowledge of subject is vast who will make the large-size contributions.

The Prototype Teacher

The teacher for the culturally disadvantaged, then, is an experimentalist. He does not shy away from our general societal ignorance about the inner-city children. Rather, he participates in the research and development programs which seek to attack the problems of the inner city. He is a skeptic when it comes to pat solutions or easy and simple styles of teaching. He is flexible in teaching style, not limited to a few patterns of teaching behavior, but capable of teaching in many ways. He is socially skillful, both in working with colleagues and in creating social climates that will have impact on children. He realizes that creating a society in school is an important aspect of educational method, and he cooperates with his fellow-teacher to produce a vigorous educational community. He is not a second-grade teacher, nor a mathematics teacher, but a team member who is as skillful at blending in with colleagues of different strengths as he is at handling children. He is persistent, for much of his work ends in apparent failure, and it takes him a long time to learn how to teach in his difficult situation. He is a shrewd observer of children, and distinguishes them from each other by many criteria. He is not limited to criteria of conventional academic ability or social class. He is a good student of his trade and of the subject he teaches. He learns to control the areas of knowledge which he shares with children.

Because no one can have all these needed characteristics, the teacher of the inner city is part of a team.

What Conditions Does the Teacher Need?

It should be plain from the foregoing that we cannot discuss the teacher without reference to the conditions under which he works. One of the critical conditions of teaching is the materials with which one has to work. The libraries of the inner-city schools need to be carefully and plenteously stocked with books on every topic and of every type. The high school libraries need reference books the children can handle—this means those provided for elementary and junior high children in many places. Special materials need to be created for the culturally disadvantaged child. Science equipment and audio-visual aids need to be built in abundance. The city cannot satisfy its obligation by suggesting topics in curriculum guides and then leaving to the individual teacher the job of creating the learning materials which he needs to get the job done. If a curriculum guide suggests that the city of London be a focus of instruction in the fourth or fifth grades, then the teacher needs to be supplied with a store of carefully made and tested materials that are suitable for the children he teaches. The teacher should not have to beg for films and film-strips from travel agencies simply to have *something* to use with his children. He may communicate with travel agencies and he may use their products, but he should not have to depend on his begging bowl for his teaching materials. Imaginative teachers should be gathered together and given the raw materials and resources to write and otherwise manufacture the teaching materials that the city needs. Individual creative teachers do and always will create many of their own materials, but this should not be because the storeroom and library are impoverished.

Another condition of teaching has to do with one's relations with colleagues. In the inner city, teachers need to not be alone, and should not work alone. They need the companionship of colleagues and, to be effective, they need assignment to teams of teachers who have complementary strengths. The administration needs to see that these teams carry on a dialogue about teaching, that they experiment together and work out patterns of education that capitalize on their varying strengths. To some extent, the

teacher will welcome this. To some extent existing teachers—
even many very good ones—will not welcome the necessity for
cooperative action. The old privatism of the classroom provides
a kind of security, because one can err without discovery, he can
worry without revealing weakness, he can discipline without
shame. I am convinced, however, that the day for this privatism
is past. The inner city will not yield to the efforts of uncoordi-
nated individuals. In a sense, the very isolation in which we have
worked has permitted it to grow so bad. The question is not
whether we will have team teaching or not, but who could be so
foolhardy as to try to assault the problems of cultural deprivation
all by himself?

Another condition for teaching has to do with the deployment
of ancillary personnel. The team of teachers needs access to
psychologists, social workers, instructional materials specialists,
and medical advice. It is curious that the public school systems
have lagged so badly in the provision of ancillary personnel. Even
prisons are not so laggard as schools in this respect. People to diagnose psychological ills and prescribe remedies, people to care for
family and other social ills, people to make instructional materials,
and people to help with the location and eradication of health
problems, should be abundant in schools. Intelligent laymen can
help with many tasks in school and classroom, and could help to
increase the adult-child ratio. Possibly every teacher in the inner
city should have a teacher's aide assigned to help him in every
way possible, with clerical work, with management of children
and with instructional materials. Since we have such trouble recruiting talented teachers for the inner city, perhaps the trained
professional should not be seen as a classroom teacher, but as a
leader or coordinator of a team of subordinate personnel. A few
of the highly-qualified teachers that we have been describing in
this chapter might well count for more, backed up by ancillary
personnel and subordinate team members, than a great many half-
qualified personnel.

The schools of the inner city, groping for effective patterns of
education, should become very different from each other. Some
should operate extensive out-of school recreational, cultural, and

social programs. Some should be staffed with teams of subject specialists, working with psychologists, sociologists, guidance counselors and social workers. Some should include intensive nursery education. Others should be centers of experimentation in creative arts.

Universities and colleges should jointly operate experimental schools in which the ideas of scholars and teachers are hammered into usable form and tried out. The teachers who volunteer for the experimental inner-city schools should be prized and rewarded for their skill and courage.

How do we prepare the teachers for the inner city? As our purpose here is not to produce an essay on teacher education in general, we will concentrate on the education that should be unique for the person who is preparing for teaching in the culturally-depressed areas of the city.

In the first place, the laboratory experience of the future teacher should take place at least partially in the schools of the inner-city, in schools which are designated by the city and the college as experimental centers for educating the culturally disadvantaged. There is no point in starting the young teacher out in a school which is not frankly experimental or one in which college and school personnel do not intimately share an experimental life. I do not mean to imply that college and university faculty members have very much sure knowledge to offer the slum school. They do not. There are those who feel that if the so-called great private universities will only attack the problem of the city, then it will somehow melt before the brain-power of their faculties. This is nonsense. However, the reason that university people have so little to offer at present is that the mainstream of American life and the mainstream of American academic life in particular have bypassed, or been bypassed by, the development of the society of the inner city. This condition will improve as soon as university personnel and teachers join hands in experimentation. Academia does not offer much until it has a base of experience and a dialogue about that experience. Cumulative inquiry into the society of the inner society has only just begun—is so fragmentary that we are not really sure that it *has* begun. So the conditions under which the analytic scholar makes his contribution have barely begun to develop.

On the other side of this coin, the inner-city schools are, generally, difficult places to find good situations for student teachers. In the sections of the city where there is the highest transiency rate, it is hardest to run a coherent school, most difficult to recruit good teachers. Once there are too many unqualified teachers in combination with the instability of the community, the school subtly changes from an educational institution into a holding company. The teacher becomes a control artist, and the school is lost for teacher education purposes.

It is no secret that it is difficult to recruit teachers for *any* school in the inner city. Hence, many teacher education programs have tended to place their students with good teachers rather than schools. As a result, students are often placed, one and two in a school, with the best teachers that can be found. I think that this is a serious error of procedure, although it is brought about by the well intentioned effort to place students with the best qualified individual teachers.

The basic unit in laboratory experience should not be the placement of the individual student with the individual co-operating teacher. It should be the group of students (the *team*, again) placed in a school where the total school program is viewed as the educative agent. School district and college should work together to staff that school and develop an experimental program to produce knowledge about the education of the culturally disadvantaged and at the same time provide a laboratory for the education of the student teacher. These experimental-training schools should not be the casual results of mere long-term cooperation between district and college. These schools should be deliberate creations whose financing is shared by college and district and into which special resources can be poured as necessary.

Let us consider how these laboratories should be run in order to help the future teacher develop the qualities we need.

First, if the teacher is not to be doctrinaire, the school must not be doctrinaire. It should not pretend to the new teacher that we know what we are doing with the education of the culturally disadvantaged. It should convey to the new teacher the message that he will have to join the ranks of those who declare their ignorance, who are skeptical of dogma, who are beyond the glib and pat solution.

Second, it needs to be experimental, in the literal sense of experimental. The teachers need to identify their assumptions, test them out, and frankly share their results. The teachers should discourage the impression that they are "master teachers." They should expose their fears and ignorance to their student teacher-helpers, and join hands with them in the attempt to seek a better education.

Third, the school should involve teams of teachers and student teachers in a constant dialogue about teaching. It should be a place of continual open discussion and analysis of the trade. Tape recordings, videotapes and films should be made of lessons taught by all concerned, and these should then be analyzed in seminars involving student teachers and cooperating teachers. Particularly, the special methods for the disadvantaged should be analyzed and means of controlling the children should be discussed and analyzed.

Fourth, in these schools, the educational team should include proper ancillary personnel. The future teacher should experience being part of an instructional team in which he has to play many roles, and he should see ancillary personnel working with the teacher to affect family and community as these relate to the work of the school.

Fifth, educational psychology, sociology, and methods courses should be taught right in the schools and utilize demonstrations and illustrative material gathered by the professors and teachers. These courses should relate closely to the shaping of the experimental program of the schools. Hence, arithmetic methods courses, English methods courses, and other courses should rationalize for the new teacher the program of the school and should be taught by cooperating teams of psychologists, teachers, and education professors.

Special attention should be given to training the new teacher to identify and interpret the frames of reference of children.

Weinstein and Hunt at Syracuse University and Joyce at the University of Chicago and at Manhattanville College, are developing procedures for helping teachers identify the frames of reference of children.

Sixth, the new teacher should be aided consciously to develop a wide range of teaching skills and styles. He should learn to use inductive and deductive methods, to plan cooperatively with children and to command attention when he has to. He should listen to his lessons on tape and analyze them with teachers and professors. He should see himself on videotape and analyze his nonverbal behavior. He should construct lessons on the basis of special knowledge about the children he teaches and have these lessons criticized by the team of his peers. He should learn to play various instructional roles on teams of teachers, sometimes assisting other teachers, other times being the key man on the team.

Seventh, the school should be operated in such a fashion that the new teacher is supported realistically through the failure that attends the first attempts of almost everyone to teach in the inner city. Everyone should expect that he will have control problems and he should not be pressured because he has them. He needs a long period of careful tutelage to bring him through the first long insecurity of not knowing whether he will be able to teach.

There are some other desirable characteristics of programs to prepare teachers for the inner city which do not have to be built into the laboratory situation.

A component of teacher education programs needs to be devoted to helping the new teacher cope with himself and his own feelings. Teaching in the inner city produces particular pressures on the new teacher. He needs to understand why this kind of work appeals to him. He needs to learn how he feels about lower-class children, and about himself as a leader of people.

The academic education of the inner city, as we have already pointed out, has to be as vigorous as that of the teacher of any group. The methods courses should teach how to use the power of his disciplines for the benefit of the disadvantaged child. They will not be able to do this if he does not first control the subjects of his specialty.

The teacher education program should develop high group esprit with respect to teaching the inner city child. The physics student will doubt at times whether slum teaching will be as satisfying, from an academic standpoint, as teaching the upper middle class in the suburbs. If he feels that he is part of the front phalanx of education, part of the group of teachers who will man the experimental schools of the inner city, part of the team of scholars, teachers and psychologists who are going to lick the problems of the slums, he will put his scientific knowledge to work for the culturally disadvantaged child.

The huge city school systems convey an impression of monolithic impersonality that literally devastates their recruiting efforts. High-quality cooperative teacher education programs in which city and college join with humility and high spirits can reverse this trend. The inner city teacher education, the inner city school, can be the place of the warmest and most human challenge.

REFERENCES

1. Vernon F. Haubrich, "Teachers for Big-City Schools," pp. 243-261, and Leonard Kornberg, "Meaningful Teachers for Alienated Children," pp. 262-278, in *Education in Depressed Areas* by A. Harry Passow (Ed.) (New York: Bureau of Publications, Teachers College, Columbia University, 1963).
2. Frank Riessman, *The Culturally Deprived Child* (New York: Harper, 1962).
3. Bruce R. Joyce and Richard E. Hodges, "Instructional Flexibility Training," University of Chicago, 1965 (unpublished manuscript).
4. Herbert A. Thelen, *Education and the Human Quest* (New York: Harper, 1962).
5. David E. Hunt, "A Conceptual Systems Change Model and Its Application to Education," Syracuse University, 1964.
6. David P. Ausubel and Pearl Ausubel, "Ego Development Among Segregated Negro Children," pp. 109-141, in *Education in Depressed Areas,* by A. Harry Passow (Ed.) (New York: Bureau of Publications, Teachers College, Columbia University, 1963).
7. Benjamin S. Bloom, *Stability and Change in Human Characteristics* (New York: Wiley, 1964).
8. *Ibid.,* p. 72.
9. *Ibid.,* p. 77.

Chapter XIV

THE ROLE OF THE PRINCIPAL
Lloyd J. Mendelson*

Perception of the Job

IN DEVELOPING POSITIVE school programs in disadvantaged communities, the principal plays a crucial role. His perception of the major tasks confronting the school, the way he works with staff, community leaders, and other groups determine to a large extent the effectiveness of the program. The crucial role of the principalship stems from the nature of the position as one invested with educational leadership in the school and community, and the chief source of authority in the school building. How the principal utilizes his leadership position sets the pattern for what can or cannot be accomplished through the formalized educational process.

The emphasis in this chapter, therefore, is on what the principal does and how he does it (or what he can do and how he can do it). This approach reflects the recent trend in the study of educational administration to focus on the behavior of administrators rather than on what traits can be postulated for being a *good* administrator.[1] In our case, the administrator is the elementary school principal, and the setting is the inner-city school.

As a starting point, the principal must have a fairly well-defined concept of the nature of his job. He normally operates within the framework of a large bureaucracy characteristic of big city school organization. His responsibilities are spelled out by board of education policy and administrative rules. Other tasks may be assigned by the principal's immediate superiors in the organizational heriarchy. Additional demands may be placed on him by staff, parents, and community groups. An awareness of the situational factors that impinge on the performance of his tasks are tantamount to the principal developing a realistic point of view

---

*Principal, John Farren Elementary School, Chicago.

with regard to the directions in which his efforts should be concentrated.[2]

Within the milieu of school policies and community demands, nevertheless, the principal has latitude in developing programs applicable to his school's needs. In the inner-city school, four major task areas may be projected with which the principal ought to be concerned. The first of these is developing priority goals for the school. For example, to what extent should certain curriculum areas, such as language arts, be stressed within a balanced program? What should be the school's approach to curriculum building? Should priority goals be determined by the principal and his staff, or should interested groups outside the school be brought into this kind of decision making?

The second area of concern is the role of the principal in providing educational leadership for the entire school staff. This task involves organizing the routine aspects of school administration to the point where faculty involvement is minimized and major effort is devoted to assessing the educational needs of children. Opportunity for faculty participation in developing instructional techniques is maximized.

A third factor pertains to the principal's understanding and respecting the values of families served by the school. Acceptance of many patterns of family organization and varying aspirational levels for children must be seen in the context of attitudes toward the school and possible barriers that exist between the home and school. In this connection, the fourth factor of developing relationships within the community becomes germane. That the school has the child for a portion of the day, and that what goes on among youth in the community has considerable bearing on educational attainment are reasons enough for the principal to be concerned with community involvement as part of his job.

Are the Demands Different in the Inner-city Schools?

The role of the principal can be viewed as similar regardless of the community setting in which the school is located. He is responsible primarily for seeing that the instructional goals of the school are attained. He relates to the faculty, pupils, and parents. He has specific responsibilities for budgeting, organizing the school, implementing the curriculum, ordering textbooks, and providing guidance services. He may delegate some of these duties to subordinates, but in the last analysis, the principal is the person responsible for whatever happens in the school.

It can be projected, therefore, that the competencies needed to be an effective principal would be the same whether the principal functions in a favored or so-called disadvantaged community.

Principals, like other administrators, exhibit leadership styles. A current research study has identified eight administrative styles of elementary school principals.[3] The study revealed relationships between patterns of administrative performance and personality variables associated with principals. In general, principals who were most highly regarded by their superiors were those who were better prepared professionally, who stressed preparation for decision-making, who seemed to grasp more completely the complex nature of educational problems, and who exhibited a higher degree of work output.[4]

Although the functions performed by principals in any situation may be quite similar, and appropriate leadership styles may be discerned, it would appear that situational factors affecting the inner city schools influence the nature of the principal's role in terms of major problems faced as to markedly differentiate it from that in more favored school-communities. In the latter communities, for example, parents in general are actively interested in the school program. They are concerned about instructional matters, come to school more readily, and support an organized, articulate, Parent Teachers Association. In the impoverished areas, parents are less knowledgeable about school affairs (although they may be quite concerned about their children's education) , are more reluctant to visit the school, and reflect much less experience in parent organizations. Clearly, the principal's task of communicating meaningfully with parents in the inner-city school is quite different from that in middle class communities.

Essential differences affecting the principal's job in disadvantaged areas arise from the sociology of the city characterized by great population shifts and changing social communities. A larger proportion of children with educational handicaps are enrolled in school. A general comparison between children who come to school from disadvantaged homes with those who come from middle class homes accentuates the problems of inner-city children whose quality of experiential background is meager, whose speech patterns are immature, and whose physical health needs are more prevalent.[5]

The principal in the inner city must have some knowledge and depth of understanding with regard to what is transpiring in the city. In his pre-service preparation or in-service education, he must acquire a background in minority group problems and an understanding of the implication of social class differences. He must be able to assist his staff in accepting changes that take place in the school-community. He must utilize staff initiative judiciously and encourage staff growth in understanding the cultural values of families served. Above all, the principal has to develop the total effort of the school towards achieving realistic instructional goals among a sizeable group of professionals who in turn have varying personality needs.

The Principal Determines the Organizational Climate

A visitor entering the school building can almost *sense* the atmosphere that exists within the school. The way he is greeted by the secretary in the office, the general relationships he observes as people converse, the manner in which teachers talk to children —all reflect the tone of the school. The tone has little to do with the physical structure of the building *per se*. Rather, it is rooted primarily in the pattern of interrelationships that prevail among school personnel.

It was this pattern of interrelationships, the social interaction between the principal and teachers, that Halpin and Croft assessed in their study of organizational climates within schools.[6] Prototypes of six organizational climates are described ranging on a continuum from *closed* to *open*. A partial description of a school characterized by an "open climate" follows.

> The open climate depicts a situation in which the members enjoy extremely high *esprit*. The teachers work well together

without bickering and griping. They are not burdened by mountains of busy work or by routine reports; the principal's policies facilitate the teachers accomplishment of their tasks . . . .

The behavior of the principal represents an appropriate integration between his own personality and the role he is required to play as principal. In this respect his behavior can be viewed as "genuine" . . . . He possesses the personal flexibility to be "genuine" whether he be required to control and direct the activities of others or be required to show compassion in satisfying the social needs of individual teachers. He has integrity in that he is 'all of a piece' and therefore can function well in either situation. He is not *aloof*, nor are the rules and procedures which he sets up inflexible and impersonal. Nonetheless, rules and regulations are adhered to, and through them, he provides subtle direction and control for teachers.[7]

It is our contention that the open climate is the desirable organization that should characterize the school in a culturally disadvantaged community. It provides for an operational flexibility that enables personnel within the school to work towards the achievement of the difficult instructional goals with a high degree of interaction at the professional level. In effect, the principal provides the basis for warm, friendly relations among school personnel within the framework of professionally oriented objectives. Leadership acts or solutions to problem situations will emanate, therefore, from faculty members as well as the administrative staff.

The organizational climate extends beyond principal-faculty relations. Within the school, the principal deals with other groupings: his secretarial staff, the maintenance crew, and the lunchroom staff (if the school has such facilities). It is a responsibility of the principal to establish the climate by which these groups feel a real part of the school enterprise and achieve satisfaction from a realization that their contributions are appreciated. The principal can call attention of the faculty to good work done by the para-professional staff. He can involve the personnel formally in necessary committees where common interests are concerned, such as a school safety committee or an anti-vandalism committee. In short, the principal creates situations or responds to situations whereby positive interaction can occur among various personnel groupings on the school staff.

The secretarial staff is especially important to the principal in this respect. The secretaries are the front line of human relations in the school. It is they who normally have initial contact with parents, visitors, children, and teachers *vis-a-vis* the school office. The principal must work with his clerks or secretaries in developing appropriate behavioral approaches with all who enter the office. In any setting, people take priority over reports. Friendly recognition on the part of the secretarial staff is especially important in communities where parents tend to be reluctant to call on the school or where they perceive coming to school solely a matter of their children being in trouble.

In summary, then, the tone or climate of the school is largely determined by the attitude of the principal. The principal who is sufficiently secure in his position so that he can provide a flexible, informal structure will develop a high degree of interaction among all staff members on a professional basis. This approach would seem to provide a more favorable setting for achieving instructional aims as well as meeting faculty needs than a rigid, highly formalized, closed structure. The open climate would tend to involve school staff, children, and parents in a more genuine commitment to the school. In no sense does the principal abrogate his responsibility or weaken his authority. Rather, he sets the pace by his own example, and shares decision making where instructional aims and implementation are at stake.

The Principal Develops Staff Competencies

School programs are really no more effective than the competencies of the teachers. Acquiring, developing, and maintaining a stable faculty is a task of paramount importance to the principal. Certain difficulties beyond the control of the principal are present in this regard due mainly to the rapid growth of the inner-city school population and the problem of teacher demand exceeding supply. It is a considerable challenge for teachers to make the commitment to work in lower socioeconomic areas where value positions may be in conflict, where there is a lack of educational orientation in the home, and where traditional methods of instruction have to be modified. As school systems move in the direction of making inner-city teaching more attractive through various incentives, this situation will be assuaged.

There are many things the principal can do to develop faculty stability and increase teaching effectiveness. Basic to any approach is a realization on the part of the principal that teachers are professionally oriented and will meet the special challenges of teaching in the inner city if given the opportunity to develop their own potentialities and if they can derive satisfaction and recognition for teaching performance. The principal's efforts in this phase relate partially to the type of school climate discussed in the previous section. The other factor pertains to the techniques the principal can utilize in working directly with his faculty.

First of all, the principal must help the staff understand the background and needs of children from disadvantaged environments. The immediate goal, whether in a changing community or in a long-established deprived area is to develop a basic respect for children on the part of staff and a sincere belief in the ability of these children to learn. In this regard, patronization or condescension are pitfalls to be avoided as much as negative feelings. There must be genuine acceptance of the children *qua* children and a recognition of their particular educational needs.

The principal can initiate in-service programs within the school designed to improve understanding of inner-city children. Such programs may assume a format of small group discussions with faculty members presenting reports based on their special interests. Experts in facets of urban sociology may be invited to speak with the staff and function as resource persons. The principal may encourage staff members to take course work at local colleges and universities which are designed to develop understanding of urban problems and the education of disadvantaged children. In Chicago, through the cooperation of Chicago Teachers College and Chicago Junior College, credit courses are offered in the local school districts on an after-school extension basis. Travel time for teachers is reduced through this decentralized process.

Encouragement of professional growth, of course, should not be limited to courses on the culturally disadvantaged child. The principal should stimulate faculty members to take advanced college work to improve subject matter competency, to learn about new teaching methods, to develop better insights into the learning process. It is helpful if the principal knows each teacher's strengths and weaknesses so that he can discuss and suggest appropriate programs for the teacher.

In the large cities, numerous professional associations provide many opportunities for professional activity. Teacher participation in such organizations should be supported by the principal. Furthermore, the principal himself must set the example by evidencing concern for his own professional growth and by participation in appropriate activities.

Developing a well balanced, productive staff requires that the principal understand the role needs of staff members. He has to provide situations or conditions that enable staff members to feel adequate in their teaching performance, to feel thoroughly involved in school problems, and to feel they are making some contribution towards the solution of these problems. The principal can create opportunities for faculty to work together and assume leadership positions in problem solving situations.

Part and parcel of this awareness on the part of the principal is the development of two-way communication. The fact that the principal is approachable, that his door is known to be open, provides an informal basis for faculty contact to discuss problems and to make suggestions. At a more formalized level, the committee structure is a vehicle for communication. Usually a faculty committee will consist of four to six members working on a specific problem; e.g., the improvement of social studies instruction, with the principal serving as consultant. General faculty meetings and written bulletins by the principal are necessary components in interpreting school administrative policies to the staff, but such techniques normally reflect one-way communication.

The principal also realizes that his staff has varying degrees of competency, experience, interest, and talent. It is easier to give recognition to the able and more talented teachers through committee chairmanships or through representing the school at professional gatherings. For the many new or relatively inexperienced teachers in his school, the principal must provide strong in-service programs. In this connection, he must be aware of and utilize the many services provided by central office staff personnel, various curriculum consultants and subject matter supervisors. The astute principal does not assume the burden of in-service education alone. He establishes the conditions for encouraging teacher self-improvement and he utilizes the considerable resources of the large school system.

There is one final point to be made about staffing in the inner-city schools. To the extent that the principal has control over assignments (and this varies according to personnel practices in each school system), he should be alert to the potentialities of recruiting competent male teachers. In many families, the strong adult male image is lacking. The positive contact that youth, especially boys, can have with empathic male teachers in the elementary school could prove quite significant in their lives. The school principal may very well be in a position to increase the proportion of male staff members, thus meeting a real need for the children.

The Principal Provides Leadership for Instructional Improvement

Organizing the School for Effective Instruction

By virtue of the size of inner-city schools, the principal normally has considerable flexibility in developing organizational patterns for effective instruction. Grouping arrangements of pupils can be determined to best meet learning needs. Culturally disadvantaged children have great need for individualized attention to meet learning demands. Yet unless the school district has substantial additional funds available to provide for greatly reduced pupil-teacher ratios, it is difficult to provide optimum small group situations for children.

This situation would seem to augur well for some aspects of *homogeneous* grouping in inner city schools, although research does not seem to indicate the superiority of either homogeneous or heterogeneous grouping. Nor is there such a phenomena as completely homogeneous grouping. Nevertheless, reducing the range of ability or achievement levels within a given classroom does enable the teacher to organize instruction in order to better meet the learning needs of the class.

Grouping patterns may be advisable among classes in certain subject areas for part of the school day. In the intermediate grades, for example, grouping for reading or the broader language arts for a double period daily can permit teachers to work with children who have similar reading and language deficiencies, or conversely, have special abilities in these areas. What the principal must be alert to is that any grouping pattern, especially one designed to enable children to learn more effectively in the skill areas, is accompanied by careful evaluation designed to determine whether in fact children are learning better through the special program.

Two organizational patterns that seem most promising for inner-city schools are the nongraded program and cooperative or team teaching approaches. The nongraded primary program (although the entire school may be organized on a nongraded basis) has a great advantage in flexibility of pupil movement in so far as traditional grading has been replaced by a plan of continual upward progress.[8] With attention focused on levels of development rather than on annual promotion, learning blocks are more specific and shorter in time span. Achievement gains are more readily discernible. Children progress at their own pace according to their abilities in particular subject areas.

The nongraded approach helps the culturally disadvantaged child by eliminating the stigma of failure. At the end of the first year in the traditional graded program, many children not ready for second grade work would be retained in first grade; and the failure process, another step in the child's later alienation from school, would begin. In the nongraded program, the child progresses as he is able to achieve, and the longer readiness program that many children need (hence, the current revival of interest in pre-kindergarten education) does not handicap them in meeting success in school.

Much passes under the guise of team teaching; and assuredly

the kinds of facilities available in a school have much to do with the kind of teaming that can function, let alone the attitudes and abilities of staff. Yet, with relatively large numbers of teachers and children, it would behoove the principal to interest teachers in cooperative practices, and in turn to be open to suggestions for trying out experimental programs. The team approach permits teachers to specialize in areas of interest and abilities and to work cooperatively. Special large-group and small-group arrangements characteristic of cooperative teaching result in enthusiastic response on the part of pupils, thus stimulating learning potential. There seems to be growing evidence that cooperative teaching practices are adaptable to a variety of situations and result in creative teacher performance in developing instructional techniques with disadvantaged children.[9]

The principal is in a position to try out a variety of organizational and grouping patterns to serve instructional ends. New practices in organization must have faculty understanding and support. Much can be said for moving slowly in changing organizational patterns long established in a school. Educational practitioners can err in too rapid or too comprehensive a change all at once, as much as to err in doing nothing. It would seem advisable for a principal to launch changes in organization practices cautiously and to evaluate progress carefully, rather than to make precipitous changes.

Adapting the Curriculum to the Special Needs of Children

The principal plays a key role in directing staff attention to the motivational aspects of teaching culturally disadvantaged children. Nothing is as significant as far as the school is concerned as providing meaningful learning experiences for pupils. This involves the selection of content material within the ability of pupils to comprehend and the projection of teaching methods that stimulate pupils to want to learn as well as to learn. Because the subject of curriculum itself is so vast, the discussion will be limited to a few ideas with which the principal should be concerned. He must be prepared to give direction in these areas of curriculum as well as to elicit self-direction among the staff.

The content of the curriculum must be realistic and it must be an outgrowth of the pupils' experiences. If handled correctly, children will learn new content and extend their horizons. But the point of departure must be what the children know at the level where they are, Furthermore, highly charged motivational techniques must characterize the instructional program. The attractive classroom with its colorful bulletin boards, meaningful displays, and variety of interest centers is crucial to the effective learning situation.

The principal must see that the teacher has varied learning materials in the classroom or has access to them. This includes the availability of audio-visual equipment and materials. Especially important is the utilization of many kinds of reading materials. The standard developmental reading series is not sufficient to insure reading stimulation or growth.

At the primary level, the principal should encourage the use of teacher-pupil-made experience stories, outgrowths of class activities in various areas of study. If possible, two or three reading series should be available to every primary classroom. More phonics and word attack aids may also be necessary in primary classrooms. At the intermediate level, the principal has to acquire additional reading materials of high interest but controlled vocabulary level. Work-type texts, charts, magazines, and newspapers should also be drawn upon. For many pupils, the school will be their only or prime source of contact with these kinds of reading sources. The well-stocked school library with adequate references books and developmental material on minority group life, particularly Negro history, is a necessary adjunct to the instructional program.

Although there may be budget limitations in acquiring all of the kinds of equipment, aids, and materials considered optimum for the school, the principal has to be attuned to the special needs of inner-city children, and acquire his materials accordingly. For example, assuming the principal has decided to allocate a certain sum for science in any given year, he wisely may order a variety of resources that lend themselves to activity or demonstration approaches on science topics, rather than investing the money solely in one given science series so that every child has the same text. By acquiring a variety of resource material which may include small numbers of several texts, the principal provides some conditions for the faculty to adapt teaching methods that will involve pupils in *doing* science projects rather than just reading about science out of a single textbook.

The integrated unit approach to instruction, while not particularly new, seems especially suitable for providing meaningful instruction to disadvantaged children. Chicago's Special Elementary Summer Schools have had considerable success in motivating learning through the unit method.[10] By selecting a topic based upon pupil interests, one that is broad enough to draw learning experiences logically from several subject areas, teachers have been able to stimulate pupil learning and to differentiate instruction to meet individual needs. Pupil's experiences are extended as they explore the world about them through experimentation, committee undertakings, project demonstrations, and field trips throughout the community. By building these varied activities around a unit theme in which the objectives are clear to the learners, a high interest level is maintained, and growth is evidenced for all pupils.

A unit may be subject matter based with other areas correlated, or it may be derived from an immediate problem of some significance to the pupils. At any rate, the teacher and pupils conjointly develop the objectives and determine the learning activities. Pupils see the culmination of a few weeks effort in terms of solving some problems in which they have become immersed, problems which have meaning for their daily living.

It is up to the principal to encourage his faculty to adopt unit approaches in curriculum development. Such approaches not only provide for varied motivation to learning, essential for inner-city children, but also project the school beyond its confines to utilize the vast resources for education that are available in the broader community.

The Principal Focuses on Pupil Growth

In culturally disadvantaged communities, the school in many cases becomes a major element in providing emotional security for children. Here again, the principal by example and orientation determines the school's attitude toward children. He must set in motion the kind of school program in which pupils can receive satisfactions in a variety of ways, in which pupils feel a real stake in the school.

Guiding pupils to put forth the consistent effort that learning requires is a signal task facing inner-city schools. Providing a program in which children have many opportunities to develop interests and talents, where cognizance is taken of realistic expectations, and where the value of positive awards is understood, would seem to offer the best chance for optimum pupil learning. The school then becomes truly significant in the lives of the children.

How a principal and staff work toward these goals will differ among schools, depending on the particular circumstances. Some essential ingredients would include: (1) consideration of individual learning needs as much as is feasible; (2) providing for a host of extra-class activities based on pupil interests, and (3) utilization of school and community resources beyond the normal school day.

The learning needs of disadvantaged children basically center around the reading and language areas. The principal can provide special reading classes and remedial sessions on a small group or individualized basis contingent on his school organization and availability of staff. The adjustment counselor or some other staff person especially skilled in reading techniques may be programed for small group remedial sessions. Whether in the regular classroom or in special coaching groups, pupils must be able to see improvement and achieve appropriate awards. Such awards may be the smile or kindly comment of the teacher, a satisfactory grade on a paper, or a positive check on a class record.

Providing opportunities for status building activities is achieved through the school-wide program. The perceptive administrator recognizes the value of encouraging special interest clubs, a school newspaper, patrol, monitor and playleader groups, student council activities, and assembly programs. Such varied activities enable pupils to gain recognition and assume leadership roles. Moreover, such activities if properly directed develop a strong school identification among both pupils and staff.

The principal can determine the after-hours utilization of the school building within limitations. It is becoming widely accepted that compensatory education programs are a necessity for children and youth in culturally disadvantaged areas. The trend is toward greater utilization of school facilities after regular hours as funds become available. The principal can provide leadership in assessing the particular activities most needed by pupils in his school. Together with staff and community assistance, he can develop enrichment, recreational, study, and remedial programs. An elementary school may be used after school for social center activities, for remedial reading and arithmetic classes, and for library and study purposes. Through the faculty and guidance staff, pupils may be directed into these supplementary activities.

The school is by no means the only resource for needed enrichment. The principal should know the community centers, settlement houses, park district and other community agencies that conduct programs for young people. Through inter-agency cooperation, he should be able to guide pupils into worthwhile after school activities.

The cities also have vast resources for cultural enrichment. Schools can make arrangements for pupils to attend plays, concerts, and special events at no cost or at nominal fee. The principal has the opportunity to encourage parent and community involvement since many of these events may take place on weekends. Joint school-parent sponsorship may help build parental responsibility and confidence in taking children to interesting places. The responsibility of the principal and staff extends beyond promoting cultural ventures. If a school supports a planned program in cultural enrichment, the principal must ensure that such programs reflect a developmental approach for pupils in which there is adequate preparation and follow-up.

Handling Disciplinary Problems

Pupil behavior problems in schools serving culturally disadvantaged children seem more severe because of the conflict in value systems between the expectancies of the middle class school and the realities of community life. The findings of the NEA

Juvenile Delinquency Project document the clash in value systems in which delinquency, interpreted as norm-violating behavior brought to the attention of official agencies, reflects a complex interaction of personality with cultural and subcultural forces.[11] Fighting, which the school interprets as norm-violating behavior, may well be the accepted pattern for solving differences in the community, particularly among peer group subcultures. Similarly, a principal may hear from a parent that his child has been taught to "fight for his rights." Or parents may advise the principal to have teachers use corporal punishment on their children. "The only thing he understands is a good beating."

There are two immediate sources for disciplinary problems that confront the principal. One is school centered, some incident that takes place among pupils or between pupil and teacher in the classroom or on other school premises. The other is a community or gang conflict that originates outside the school and is carried over into the school. While solutions to such problems will vary according to the specifics in each case, certain principles seem clear.

1. Most youth want and need an orderly arrangement in their lives which the school program offers.
2. A good, varied instructional program in the school will engage the energies of most pupils in constructive learning situations.
3. There must be a clear-cut, fair, and consistent procedure for handling all behavioral problems that occur. This procedure must be understood by staff, pupils, and parents.
4. Symptomatic indications of behavioral difficulties will be recognized by the classroom teacher who should attempt to solve these problems utilizing administrative and counselling staff if needed. The teacher's position is strengthened if he maintains control over the class by handling lesser behavior problems directly with pupils and parents.
5. For more serious problems, written descriptions of behavioral incidents should be maintained by the classroom teacher, so that when a given pupil is referred to the office

and follow-through with parents and other school resources, such as psychological services, is indicated, there is objective data with which to assess the nature of the problem.

Basic responsibility for discipline in the school rests with the principal although he may delegate authority in this area to others on the staff, particularly the assistant principal. From an overall standpoint, discipline and guidance functions in the elementary school are closely related and require working with parents and community agencies as well as directly with children. Thus, the principal, or delegated staff person, may have to take the initiative in helping parents develop alternative ways of disciplining children than by beating them, an over-simplified reaction to the complex business of child rearing, and a practice that becomes ineffectual in the long run.

Gang problems that carry over into the school must be understood by staff leadership as manifestations of the real world that goes on outside the school. The principal and staff should get to know the gang leaders, assess their learning problems, and develop positive programs for them. Constructive status-building activities within the school have to be designed for these youth. Special service jobs in the school may have to be created. If possible, programing of peer group leaders who are boys with an able male teacher for whole or part of the day would help develop appropriate identification for some youth.

Another point needs to be explored here. Administering inner-city schools will bring the principal into more frequent contact with the police and other juvenile authorities. An increasing number of youth officers are trained in skilled ways of working with delinquent youth. For the best interests of pupils who get into serious difficulty, the principal will find it to his advantage to develop cooperative relationships with juvenile officers.

The Principal Encourages Parent Involvement

In the inner city, school-home-community cooperation is essential for the implementation of educational goals. The principal normally is the person who must take the initiative in launching programs that develop positive relationships between the school on one hand and between parents and community leaders on the other. Stimulating parents to take an active interest in their children's education is a particularly challenging task.

A study of school-home relations in inner city schools of five major cities undertaken by the U. S. Office of Education indicated that parents in general were reluctant to visit their school, did not become involved in the activities of school-related organizations, and tended to shy away from school personnel.[12] The following admonition is contained:

> School staff awareness of the profound effect of the cultural environment on pupil behavior, attitudes, and learning should lead to efforts to bridge the gap between school and home. If the school staff does not take the initiative in developing an action program to generate school-home interaction, it is not likely that such activity will be assumed by the parents.[13]

The school principal can initiate various practices which will enable parents to become genuinely involved in educational affairs. The active support of the school by parents and the development of know-how among parents in helping their children with learning-readiness tasks supplement efforts of the school. The following suggestions indicate kinds of practices the schools can effect.

1. Schedule regular parent-teacher conferences. Such conferences may be group based to interpret facets of the school program, or individual to discuss the progress and problems of individual children. The school must not simply invite parents to come for individual conferences, but must *insist* on their attendance.

2. Have parent institutes or parent education classes at school designed to give parents confidence in understanding children and making the home a place for study and learning readiness. Such topics might include how to provide places for quiet study in the home, how parents can help pre-school children with readiness activities, how to utilize the public library, and learning about

child growth problems and sibling rivalry. Outside authorities as well as school personnel may be called on to lead discussion on these topics. The use of group dynamics techniques will help parents become active participants.

3. Invite parents to participate in special school activities, such as assembly programs, science and book fairs, school exhibits, kindergarten teas, and open houses. Special invitations made by children to bring parents out to such affairs may be the touch needed for parental response.

4. Communicate with parents in a variety of ways and for a variety of purposes. Brief written communications in attractive leaflet form are more effective than lengthy letters. Such bulletins may contain suggestions for parents with regard to after-school activities or they may deal with specific school concerns, such as the importance of children being in school every day on time.

5. Involve parents in assisting teachers on field trips and in utilizing community recreational and cultural resources.

6. Assist parent-teacher organizations in building their memberships and in developing meaningful programs. The school must be flexible enough to schedule meetings at a variety of times, including the evening, in order to induce working parents to attend. The typical, middle-class PTA structure may or may not be the best vehicle for involving parents in school affairs in the disadvantaged areas. Much would depend on the nature of the program or activities presented by the organization. Parents will participate in school organizational work if the program is attractive to their needs and the formal structure is not threatening.

The basic goal of the school in this sense is the development of an emerging parental responsibility and leadership. Again, the establishment of a climate in which parents really are welcomed in the school to confer with teachers and to participate in school-related activities, is the underlying thread that must accompany the best of prepared programs. The principal must be oriented to reach out to these parents, to be available to them, and to get into the homes and community.

The Principal Works with Community Agencies

Lower socioeconomic neighborhoods are characterized by the presence of a variety of agencies: community centers, settlement houses, Y.M.C.A.'s, churches, welfare agencies, all of which are concerned partly or to a large extent with youth and youth problems. These agencies and their facilities will vary in kind and in quality from one community to another, and when considering the magnitude of the problem and population density of inner city communities, it is quite likely that there are not enough personnel or facilities in any given area to meet all the needs of young people. (Assistance from the federal government through the Economic Opportunity Act of 1964 portends considerable growth in community services.)

Nevertheless, many agencies do exist and conduct active programs for youngsters. They should be regarded by school principals as allies in the persistent struggle to develop worthy self-identification, sense of purpose, and acceptable behavior patterns among youth in impoverished areas. The implication, therefore, is that the principal should establish working professional relationships with the key personnel of such groups.

Liaison between the school and various community agencies stems from the common interest of all these institutions in making the community a better place in which to live. What happens to the child outside of school, how he spends his leisure time, the family pattern and peer group activity, all bear on the child's adjustment to school and his ability to make normal academic progress.

Cooperative working relations between the principal and community agents may take many forms. The principal may have an *ad hoc* community advisory council comprising important neighborhood people. There may be an inter-school council in which several principals serving a generally contiguous area meet regularly with civic and business leaders to discuss common needs and plan effective utilization of community resources. The school principal in turn may serve as an advisor or participant in community youth projects. Whatever the format, the principal must assume some leadership role to interpret the school program and aims, and to seriously involve himself in community affairs.

An interesting illustration of a kind of school-community cooperation is the Family Relations Committee of the John Farren Public School in Chicago. At the initiative of the school, which primarily serves children who reside in a large high-rise public housing development, agency personnel were invited to develop coordinated services and approaches in working with the families of children who were exhibiting special difficulties in school. Several social workers and supervisors from the local public welfare office and the settlement house, together with tenant relations aides of the housing authority, meet regularly with school personnel to staff cases. School personnel include those who have more direct contact with the parents; the assistant principal as chairman of the committee, the adjustment counselor, the teacher-nurse, and the attendance officer. The board of education social worker in the area attends some meetings as an advisor, while the principal serves as consultant. The classroom teacher is brought into discussions and recommendations as the need arises.

Over a two-year period, this committee has provided services for the children of some forty families. Normally, the children's problems can be traced directly to conditions in the home and community. By utilizing agency services that have contact with the home in varying ways, greater understanding of pupils' difficulties has been possible, and action taken to alleviate home conditions has been expedited. Several youth have been guided into appropriate after-school programs in the local settlement house and park district; community counselling has been procured for some; mental health referrals where necessary have been speeded up and therapeutic treatment launched, and needed health and physical care have been provided.

Improved communication patterns between the school and community agencies are clearly within the province of the principal. Establishing lines of contact, of course, is a two-way proposition, and community agencies must understand the basic function of the school. The school cannot do the job that parents and other institutions in the community must fulfill. Nonetheless, the principal must be cognizant of the value of knowing community resources and utilizing them for the benefit of children. Developing cooperative relations between school personnel and responsible community agents to a large extent depends on the interests of the principal. In disadvantaged communities especially, the stakes are too great for the principal to ignore such opportunities.

The Principal as Innovator

The elementary school in disadvantaged communities stands squarely in the midst of social and educational ferment. Proposals for improving the quality of education for inner-city children flow in a steady stream from many sources. Contrary to what sometimes appears in the popular literature, city school systems not only know a great deal about how to work in these communities, they have conducted several model programs. Under the coordination of the Great Cities School Improvement Program, numerous pilot projects have been launched in the largest public school systems of this country. These programs are designed to help disadvantaged youth in a variety of ways; to raise their school achievements, to identify and assist able youngsters, to raise the level of aspirations, to develop competencies for urban life, to increase parental responsibility, and to mobilize community support.[14] In addition, large cities on their own, as exemplified by Chicago's Special Elementary Summer Schools and New York's Higher Horizons project, have developed a variety of approaches to meet the challenge of educating the culturally disadvantaged.

With all that is going on in this field, the principal is thrust in a position of great responsibility. He must be caught up in the contagious fervor of the times, and be willing to forge ahead with new ideas and experimental programs. School leadership cannot afford to remain static, locked in by traditional organizational and instructional approaches. If the principal is to provide real leadership in these communities, he must be able to grasp the essence of social forces unleashed, must be a willing participant in changing educational practices, and provide a dynamic influence on the behavior of others—faculty, pupils, community.[15]

The effective principal not only understands the needs and expectations of individuals and groups with whom he works, he is also able to mobilize their talents and energies toward the attainment of an ever-improving education for culturally disadvantaged girls and boys. The balance between the role of the principal as innovator and his opposite role as conservator of the cultural heritage of the past is usually heavily weighted on the side of stabiliztaion, of maintaining the *status quo*. The choice of action is clear. The *status quo* cannot be preserved. The principal must break new trails. As he does this, he must evaluate as he innovates. Move, he must, but with a purpose, a plan, and a means to determine if the direction is true and the rate of progress satisfactory. "Keeping school as usual" is a decision: a decision to fail. This is a time for dynamic leadership by school principals everywhere.

REFERENCES

1. Two major studies which are illustrative of this point of view are Roald F. Campbell and Russell T. Gregg (eds.), *Administrative Behavior in Education* (New York: Harper and Brothers, 1957), p. 547 and Daniel E. Griffiths (ed.), *Behavioral Science and Educational Administration,* The Sixty-third Yearbook of the National Society for the Study of Education, Part II (Chicago: The University of Chicago Press, 1964), p. 360.
2. Roald F. Campbell, "Situational Factors in Educational Administration," *Administrative Behavior in Education,* pp. 228-234.
3. John K. Hemphill, "Personal Variables and Administrative Styles," *Behavioral Science and Educational Administration,* p. 197-8.
4. *Ibid.,* p. 191.
5. *Compensatory Education in the Chicago Public Schools,* Study Report Number Four, 1964 Series (Chicago: Chicago Public Schools, 1964), pp. 25-35.
6. Andrew W. Halpin and Don B. Croft, *The Organizational Climate of Schools* (Chicago: Midwest Administration Center, The University of Chicago, 1963), p. 7.
7. *Ibid.,* pp. 60-62.
8. John I. Goodlad and Robert H. Anderson, *The Nongraded Elementary School,* Revised Edition (New York: Harcourt, Brace, and World, Inc., 1963), pp. 248.
9. Charles H. Hayes, "Team Teaching in Culturally Deprived Areas," *The National Elementary Principal,* XLIV (Jan., 1965), pp. 60-65.
10. *The Story of the Special Summer Schools* (Chicago: Chicago Public Schools, 1963), 48 pp.
11. William C. Kvaraceus et al., *Delinquent Behavior: Principles and Practices* (Washington: National Education Association, 1959), pp. 11-21.

12. Gene C. Fusco, *School-Home Partnership in Depressed Urban Neighbor-hoods* Office of Education Publication #31008 (Washington: U. S. Government Printing Office, 1964), p. 59.

13. *Ibid.*

14. Frederick Shaw, "Educating Culturally Deprived Youth in Urban Centers," *Phi Delta Kappan,* Vol. XLV, No. 2 (Nov., 1963), p. 93. See also *Promising Practices from the Projects for the Culturally Deprived* (Chicago: The Research Council of the Great Cities Program for School Improvement, 1964), 80 pp.

15. Martin Haberman, "Leadership in Schools Serving the Educationally Disadvantaged," *The National Elementary Principal,* Vol. XLV, No. 2 (Nov., 1964), pp. 21-22.

Chapter XV

THE COMMUNITY AND THE DISADVANTAGED PUPIL

John J. Hobgood*

T HE PROBLEMS OF culturally disadvantaged pupils are always intimately related to the problems of the communities in which they live. (Because the culturally disadvantaged tend to be concentrated in communities which show a high incidence of unemployment, poor housing, and other social problems, many school systems have tried to develop programs tailored to the needs of culturally disadvantaged neighborhoods.)

In the development of specialized programs for the culturally disadvantaged, a gradual evolution has taken place that is reflected by a slow change in attitude towards the poor. A very short time ago, educators used to speak of the culturally deprived as if there were very little to build on in the culture of poverty. Because of a reaction against this attitude, the term "culturally deprived" is giving way to the more accurate term "culturally disadvantaged." A culturally deprived person is a person "deprived" of our middle class culture. He is "deprived" because of the implication that our culture is the only one of any importance, at least in our modern industrial society. The urban teacher who complains about "those people without a culture who move into the city," usually also wonders how to "Americanize" southern whites, southern Negroes, and others, foreign to the teacher's urban background.

The history teacher who says that; "I never really could appreciate the bad feelings that existed between the 'steadfast,' 'stubborn' American Colonists and the British during the Revolutionary War until southern whites first entered my classroom," is a little closer to understanding that there are no people that do not possess a valid culture. The problem is that in our modern

---

*Human Relations Officer, Chicago Commission on Human Relations.

urban society some cultures, especially our dominant middle class American culture, have such a distinct advantage that the values, behavior and the cultural differences that exist among the poor are recognized primarily as a hindrance to education and adjustment to urban life.

Lack of understanding for the culturally disadvantaged student's point of view contributes to a breakdown in communication that sometimes occurs between educators and the people they serve, because of differences in class or cultural orientation. The middle class professionals who administer and staff normal schools, schools in slum areas, social welfare agencies and local community organizations can subject many points of view based upon middle class ethnocentrism to insights acquired through learning to relate more effectively with the culturally disadvantaged. Some teachers spend their entire working lives with a lack of sensitivity to cultural differences that would be immediately disastrous for a street worker and would not allow him to even begin his job.

The question of being culturally disadvantaged and how this works both ways was illustrated rather eloquently for me during a social service workshop in Puerto Rico. Our group, which was made up largely of social workers and school teachers, had spent the morning on a conducted tour of the old city of San Juan. The tour ended on a narrow side street when our guide announced that he was leaving us to have lunch in the Old City, after which we should walk back to the plaza and take a Rio Piedras bus to the University of Puerto Rico where the group would assemble again in the afternoon.

The problems of finding a "suitable" restaurant and of taking a bus across metropolitan San Juan proved to be quite a test for many in the group. In fact, several took a taxi rather than risk using public transportation in a strange city. That afternoon, the first speaker spent a lot of time hearing the trials and tribulations of the group in their efforts to reach the University. He then stated that in San Juan, Puerto Rico it was the teachers and social workers who were culturally disadvantaged, and they had just experienced a taste of some of the problems a Puerto Rican has on the mainland.

Even those who on the mainland complain, "Why don't these

people speak English—the language the Bible was written in?" gain some insight into the problems of the culturally disadvantaged if they have the opportunity of submerging themselves in a strange culture. In a slum school, this opportunity is not nearly so apparent. Just as a soldier in an invading army can travel the length and breadth of a foreign land, always associating with the same sergeant, in the same company and always receiving his supplies through the PX, but cannot make meaningful contact with the people of an unfamiliar country without making a special effort, so the school needs to make a special effort to have meaningful contacts with the culturally disadvantaged.

The culturally disadvantaged that cluster in the neighborhoods surrounding the schools that serve them are in addition to their ethnic identity, part of the culture of poverty. The culture of poverty has been defined by Oscar Lewis in his book *The Children of Sanchez*[1] as follows:

> To those who think that the poor have no culture, the concept of a culture of poverty may seem like a contradiction in terms. It would also seem to give to poverty a certain dignity and status. This is not my intention. In anthropological usage the term culture implies, essentially, a design for living which is passed down from generation to generation. In applying this concept of culture to the understanding of poverty, I want to draw attention to the fact that poverty in modern nations is not only a state of economic deprivation, of disorganization, or of the absence of something. It is also something positive in the sense that it has a structure, a rationale, and defense mechanisms without which the poor could hardly carry on. In short, it is a way of life, remarkably stable and persistent, passed down from generation to generation along family lines. The culture of poverty has its own modalities and distinctive social and psychological consequences for its members. It is a dynamic factor which affects participation in the larger national culture and becomes a subculture of its own.
>
> . . . We are prone to view . . . slum conditions as transitional or temporary phases of drastic culture change. But this is not necessarily the case, for the culture of poverty is often a persisting condition even in stable social systems . . . Only the size, location, and composition of the slums have been in flux. I

suspect that similar processes have been going on in many other countries of the world.

It seems to me that the culture of poverty has some universal characteristics which transcend regional, rural-urban, and even national differences. In my earlier book, *Five Families* (Basic Books, 1959), I suggested that there were remarkable similarities in family structure, interpersonal relations, time orientations, value systems, spending patterns, and the sense of community in lower-class settlements in London, Glasgow, Paris, Harlem, and Mexico City. Although this is not the place for an extensive comparative analysis of the culture of poverty, I should like to elaborate upon some of these and other traits in order to present a provisional conceptual model of this culture based mainly upon my Mexican materials.

In Mexico, the culture of poverty includes at least the lower third of the rural and urban population. This population is characterized by a relatively higher death rate, a lower life expectancy, a higher proportion of individuals in the younger age groups, and, because of child labor and working women, a higher proportion of gainfully employed. Some of these indices are higher in the poor colonies or sections of Mexico City than in rural Mexico as a whole.

The culture of poverty in Mexico is a provincial and locally oriented culture. Its members are only partially integrated into national institutions and are marginal people even when they live in the heart of a great city. In Mexico City, for example, most of the poor have a very low level of education and literacy, do not belong to labor unions, are not members of a political party, do not participate in the medical care, maternity, and old-age benefits of the national welfare agency known as Seguro Social, and make very little use of the city's banks, hospitals, department stores, museums, art galleries and airports.

The economic traits which are most characteristic of the culture of poverty include the constant struggle for survival, unemployment and underemployment, low wages, a miscellany of unskilled occupations, child labor, the absence of savings, a chronic shortage of cash, the absence of food reserves in the home, the pattern of frequent buying of small quantities of food many times a day as the need arises, the pawning of personal goods, borrowing from local money lenders at usurious rates of interest, spontaneous informal credit devices (tandas) organized by neighbors, and the use of second-hand clothing and furniture.

Some of the social and psychological characteristics include living in crowded quarters, a lack of privacy, gregariousness, a high incidence of alcoholism, frequent resort to violence in the settlement of quarrels, frequent use of physical violence in the training of children, wife beating, early initiation into sex, free unions or consensual marriages, a relatively high incidence of the abandonment of mothers and children, a trend toward mother-centered families and a much greater knowledge of maternal relatives, the predominance of the nuclear family, a strong predisposition to authoritarianism, and a great emphasis upon family solidarity—an ideal only rarely achieved.

The definition of the culture of poverty given by Oscar Lewis is certainly applicable to the situation in the United States.

Jane Addams in her book, *Twenty Years at Hull House* mentions the extreme isolation of many of the people living near Hull House in 1910.[2] In her chapter on "Problems of Poverty," Jane Addams does not theorize, however, she does describe Mrs. Moran, a public assistance recipient, who "went to the root of the matter and roundly cursed poverty."[3]

In this chapter, Jane Addams also anticipates Michael Harrington by fifty-five years when she describes "the inadequacy of the charitable efforts of the city and an unfounded optimism that there was no real poverty among us."

Michael Harrington, whose book *The Other America*[5] influenced the war on poverty, also mentions conditions of extreme isolation in slum neighborhoods that closely parallel those described by Oscar Lewis.[6] Harrington describes the condition of the poor by using the terms "the subculture of misery" and the "culture of poverty" in a way that emphasizes many of the points brought out by Oscar Lewis.[7]

It is interesting to note that both Michael Harrington and Oscar Lewis obtained their insight into the culture of poverty by using the technique of participant observation and actually living with the poor and for a while sharing some of their trials and tribulations.

The value of this technique has been recognized by both the

Peace Corps and its domestic counterpart VISTA. (Volunteers in Service to America), as both organizations emphasize the importance of their volunteers living in the neighborhoods they are serving.

Most of the educators who work in culturally deprived neighborhoods may not be able to live in the communities where they work but they can begin to visit and establish a network of contacts with parents and others who can contribute a surprising amount to the education of the children in the school in spite of the fact that a great proportion of those living in the community may not be as far advanced educationally as their culturally disadvantaged children.

The isolation of these communities is phenomenal. All of the usual methods of contact through parent conferences, PTA's, settlement houses and local community organizations usually attract a small percentage of the residents who, while they may not all be middle class, usually belong to the middle class oriented group that exists in even the worst slum neighborhood in the country.

Problems of Community Interaction

In considering the problems of establishing effective contact with even the middle class oriented group in the community, complications often arise because the school itself is usually over-committed in its use of staff time and has its own problems of maintaining institutional stability.

If the internal and external situation produces a constantly changing stream of professionals and semi-professionals moving through the schools and through the community, all of them saying "now you people be stable" to the local inhabitants before moving on, there is little wonder that they achieve a minimal effect. Often, even the professionals in adjacent public and parochial schools do not know each other by name, nor do they know the staff in the social service agencies serving the community, nor the community leadership outside of the few who are active in the PTA. Public Health nurses and case workers working with families receiving public assistance are a built-in source of much information on conditions in the neighborhood. Even if case workers and Public Health nurses were encouraged to take their meals in the school whenever they were visiting in the neighborhood, useful knowledge could be exchanged on an informal basis.

More effective contact with the community can be established if teachers are encouraged to visit the homes of their students and if some teachers can become involved in the activities of local community organizations as volunteers. An increase in neighborhood contact can be achieved by expanding the role of the truant officer through hiring additional staff with enough preparation to assist with other family problems in addition to those directly related to the problem of truancy. An example of a family problem with which the school cannot even begin to cope at present would be the many families living in culturally disadvantaged neighborhoods that tend to change their place of residence almost as often as people in middle class neighborhoods change shoes. The phenomenon of schools with close to 100 per cent turnover in the student body for an academic year has a deadly effect on the efforts of even the best teachers and reflects just one of a network of economic and social problems that call for the development of a new specialist who would be a "cultural interpreter." The cultural interpreter would be a type of urban extension agent who would use his sensitivity to cultural differences in urban extension programs that would serve as a communication link channeling the results of research and community development activities into programs meaningful to both educators and the culturally disadvantaged.

The cultural interpreter relates to the middle class oriented group but he should be partially effective with ethnically oriented groups in the neighborhood. In getting help from the community for the culturally disadvantaged pupil, organized ethnic groups are a tremendous potential resource for the public school that takes the trouble to integrate its program with positive elements in the local ethnic cultures. The school that operates on the premise that their contact with ethnic groups should be purely one of assimilation (with the object of divesting the ethnic of his old culture) has to ignore as much as possible of the ethnic culture they are trying hard to eliminate. It should be remembered that among the old "national" parishes of the Roman Catholic Church many "ethnic" parochial schools were created which usually did an excellent job of assimilating the group into the mainstream of American life. These parochial schools were successful because they were integrated with the community through numerous channels both within and outside the church.

Public and parochial schools located in the inner city find that neighborhoods tend to be handed down from generation to generation like second-hand cars to the latest group of newcomers migrating from rural sections of the country and from abroad. A cultural interpreter would be useful in helping the schools shift gears a little for each new ethnic group on the problems that prevent adequate communication and tend to restrict social mobility. For a cultural interpreter to be effective with the older generation, it would be necessary to have many schools develop adult education programs in the evening and, where space is available, in the daytime so that the school would function very much like a settlement house. One aspect of the isolation of disadvantaged neighborhoods is that many people who will not travel out of their immediate neighborhood to take advantage of adult education opportunities respond quite well if this service is available at the local school. If these people are contacted by the same persons who will help them register for adult education courses at the school, the response is even greater.

In the New York City Public Schools, some use is made of teachers from Puerto Rico who serve as Puerto Rican coordinators and as substitute auxiliary teachers in an attempt to meet some of the needs that would be met by a cultural interpreter.[8]

The group that is hardest of all to work with in disadvantaged communities is the isolated group. The ethnically oriented group should be differentiated from the isolated group. This isolated group is often considered to be made up of southern Negroes, southern whites, and those second and third generation migrants from Europe and Latin America who are losing contact with their fellows. Actually a great many southern whites and southern Negroes really belong to the ethnically oriented group. You will rarely see a southern white organization that cares to identify itself as such by name, even if it is a store-front church. The same is true of churches and social groups made up of newcomers in the Negro community. However, many people clustering in the same neighborhood do come from the same county or town and many of them are closely related by marriage. Although they do not come together formally as a group for weekly meetings with a secretary to take the minutes, migrants from the same locality can be reached by those who take the time to go out into the community to find them. Sometimes whole apartment buildings are nearly filled with people who have migrated to the city from the same village. This situation affords as much opportunity for community organization as work with a national group, especially if the cultural interpreter working with them is assisted by subprofessional people who are members of the group.

Frank Riessman, in his recent article on "Cultural Styles of the Disadvantaged,"[9] mentions that more use is being made of nonteaching personnel as aides within the schools to help the teachers with duties such as attendance taking and field trips, as well as working in the playground and cafeteria.[10]

Riessman goes on to suggest "the use of low-income youngsters who are doing relatively well in high school to help elementary school children who are doing poorly . . ." as well as low-income college students to teach in high schools under close supervision: "They could go to college while doing apprentice teaching in the communities from where they had come. They might have some special ability because they would be familiar with the communities and with the types of problems that the children in these communities faced."[11]

The use of semi-professional community organizers drawn from local culturally disadvantaged neighborhoods to work under a school-based cultural interpreter, would also be an effective way for the school to reach out into the community.

With the launching of the war on poverty, there has been much recent emphasis on the active participation of the poor in the planning and carrying out of local programs. A key aspect of these programs will be the hiring of outstanding people from the culture of poverty to assist the professionals. With an economic base provided by such employment it is hoped that many people from culturally disadvantaged communities will continue their educations and join the ranks of the professionals working in their area.

The Task of Reaching the Isolated Group

Regardless of the amount of assistance available, the school serving rural or urban culturally disadvantaged communities has the most difficult task of all in reaching the isolated group. The isolated group can be defined as the group that cannot be reached through any means that would require active participation of the individual in some aspect of community life. Because they are part of no group, they will not attend PTA's, Block Club meetings or community conferences, they are not members of any club or special interest group, and usually they are not active members of any church. Because they do not belong to any of these associations, they cannot be contacted through a group even if every association in the community has been reached by the community organizer. Many people in culturally disadvantaged communities do not participate in community activities; however, this is not solely a characteristic of the disadvantaged. If you examine the most advanced community in a city or in the suburbs, you will still find that only a fraction of the people living there, participate in clubs and community activities. Culturally disadvantaged communities have no monopoly on apathy.

About the most isolated group in any community, with the possible exception of the A.D.C. mother tied down with small children, is the dweller in a high rent-high rise apartment. Clergymen as well as community organizers have done no better than the door-to-door salesmen in getting past the doorman.

Reaching the isolated group depends upon much door-to-door contact. In rural Puerto Rico, the community education program is built largely upon the fact that the community organizer (who, incidentally, is recruited from the district he is working in) spends over half of his day going from house to house visiting the isolated homesteads scattered over the Puerto Rican countryside. The Puerto Rican community organizer consumes endless cups of coffee every day during these conversations. Also, he has to have an excellent memory for names and faces. During the day he gets excellent feed-back on community problms by using this technique but if this visiting were not followed up by a sustained record of effective leadership on the part of the community organizer, you would not get the excellent attendance these meetings draw nor would you see the excellent record of progress that has been made by the community education program of Puerto Rico.

However, the most massive program of door-to-door contact can be no more than a colossal waste of time if this effort is not backed up by an effective community program. Those who do show up will be disappointed and community involvement will quickly slip back to the same few who are always active in the community.

On the other hand, if many people are contacted by the door-to-door method and the first ones to respond do find something worthwhile to be involved in, those who have been contacted will assist in door-to-door recruitment by at least contacting their friends.

If one looks at the problems of the schools working effectively with the middle-class-oriented group, the ethnically oriented group and the isolated group, it can be seen that even an expanded staff that is made up of specialists working with the culturally disadvantaged who are supported by paid subprofessionals from the community will not be a large enough group to meet all of the needs or to make a massive attack on the educational sector of the war on poverty. Also, what is to be done in those schools that cannot undertake an extensive expansion of their program in the near future?

Samuel Shepard, director of the Banneker Project in St. Louis, has received national publicity because of the success of his program in a large culturally disadvantaged section of St. Louis where low income Negroes are concentrated. Additional help in the Banneker Project is limited to "four teachers assigned to assist in administration, a few extra remedial reading classes in the summer, and an average classroom size that is slightly smaller than that for the entire city."[12]

Harold Baron, in writing about the Banneker Project, does not attribute the success of the Banneker Project so much to program content as to the leadership abilities and commitment of Samuel Shepard.

> Samuel Shepard does not place a barrier of a middle-class patronizing manner between himself and his working-class student . . . He directly challenges his middle-class teachers, mainly Negro, to change their manner.
>
> As he told me:
>
> Most of the teachers would drive to school and not even recognize the neighborhood. I had to challenge them by asking "how many people do you know in the school community?" They hardly knew anyone.
>
> The teachers are now required to visit the homes of their pupils.[13]

Visiting the homes of pupils can be a very educational experience for teachers. For example, in a 1964 study of 882 welfare recipients in Illinois, one of the comments most often made by interviewers who had M.A.'s in social work and an average of twenty years experience, was on the amazing ability of the A.D.C. mother to survive from day to day under tremendous psychological, social and economic pressures and tensions. Many of the interviewers could not see how *they* could possibly survive living under similar conditions.[14] Such an observation begins to open the way to understanding of what Oscar Lewis was trying to get at when he included in his definition of the culture of poverty that it was "something positive in the sense that it has a structure, a rationale, and defense mechanisms without which the poor could hardly carry on."[15]

These problems are important for a teacher to understand when trying to get students to see the importance of turning in their homework assignments and doing good work in school. Effective challenges can be made by the most understanding teacher:

> Shepard also challenged the students' parents. Forthrightly, he told them that the children had to be in school in order to learn:
>
> > If you child stays home to pay the bill collector, he won't be in school. If he has to baby sit, he won't be in school. You can't send him around the corner to get bread and milk at ten minutes to nine and expect him to be at school on time.

Shepard understands the life-style of his community. While he does not stand with an air of superiority in moral judgment of his constituents, he does not shrink in pity from forcefully posing the realities of modern urban life to them. The approach works. On the day I visited Shepard, he received notice that one of his schools, serving in a housing project, had the best attendance record of any school in the city for the previous month.[16]

Samuel Shepard has achieved success because he was able to move from the culture of poverty to his present status without making the mistake of becoming so middle class in his outlook that he lost contact with the culturally disadvantaged. Many lose much of their effectiveness as teachers by reacting so negatively to the shortcomings of their students that they prevent the student from using the teacher as a model. This is particularly unfortunate if the teacher is a male, especially if the teacher belongs to the same ethnic group as his students:

The sheer fact that [Shepard] is a male who in his poise and professional history conveys his physical prowess, presents an adult figure who is appealing to the children; they perceive more in physical than verbal dimensions. Also, he can partially fill the gaps of a childhood in a family that frequently lacks a powerful male adult figure. His style and emphasis go a long way to overcome the mutual hostility that exists between middle-class value orientations of the teacher and the values of the working-class culture of the children. Unlike too many other educators, he does not appear as an outsider who alienates his constituents by putting primary importance on their acknowledgment of his superior status.[17]

Use of School Volunteers

Samuel Shepard has demonstrated what can be done by an already heavily committed professional staff reaching out into the community. The great need for additional services in culturally disadvantaged communities has, however, focused the attention of many educators on the possibility of using nonpaid volunteers to work with the culturally disadvantaged, especially with reading problems and homework.

The rapid growth of volunteer tutoring movements in many

parts of the United States has thrust this question upon educators. Most of the growth of volunteer tutoring over the past four years has taken place largely without the initiative of the schools whose students are being served. Even those school systems that are active in recruiting volunteers in the playgrounds and lunch-rooms and for trips have not usually made use of volunteers to aid with the academic problems of the culturally disadvantaged.

Most of the exceptions to this practice occur in culturally advantaged neighborhoods where honor society students sometimes work with classmates who need academic help. Also, in middle-class neighborhoods a student's own parents are usually expected to give some help and guidance with homework assignments. Some middle-class schools even hold special courses for parents in the new math system so they will be able to help their children. These activities are in no way construed to be an intrusion of amateurs upon the educational task of the professional teacher but rather as much needed support in solving the academic problems of the students in middle-class schools.

In neighborhoods where parents have insufficient education to guide their children, tutoring centers are important and should be encouraged by the school. It is a rare occurrence for an illiterate child to come out of a home where the parents are well educated, unless there has been some terrible family tragedy. Conversely, if the parents have a third grade education or if they do not speak English, they are at a tremendous disadvantage when they want to assist in the education of their children. Help is also hard to find outside the family in disadvantaged neighborhoods without the assistance of at least some volunteers with adequate educational backgrounds. Where parents are not sufficiently interested in their children, or one or both parents are absent entirely, the personal interest of a volunteer tutor can do much good beyond purely academic achievement; this is as true of an A.D.C. family without a father in the home, as it is of orphans. In one Chicago orphanage where tutoring was started last year, it was learned that over half of the orphans were a year or more below grade. When tutoring was started among those who were behind in school, many youngsters with excellent academic records also requested a volunteer tutor. The need to relate to a person outside the institutional setting was strong, regardless of the educational problems involved.

The tutoring movement can be of tremendous significance because of the unifying effect it has among people of various races and cultural backgrounds within a city as well as among the people of the city and the suburbs. Yet, because these lines of communication are usually first established by volunteer groups who may not be known to the school, the school often hesitates in taking advantage of these services.

The basic problem that always arises when nonprofessionals become involved in any aspect of education has been clouded by the lack of a clear definition of what volunteer tutoring is. It is definitely *not* a substitute for professional education. The tutor is needed because he does what the child's parents would do if they had the skill and education to help. The educational skills found to be adequate for effective volunteer tutoring range all the way from those possessed by volunteer professional educators to the skills of volunteers with college or even good high school educations. The combination of an adequate educational background and the interest and time to devote at least one hour a week to volunteer tutoring over a period of at least three months are the essential resources of every volunteer tutor.

The leadership for volunteer tutoring programs is drawn from the faculty and students of colleges and high schools, organizations related to churches and synagogues, fraternal groups, business service organizations and interested adults from many walks of life.

The tutoring programs' success in terms of helpfulness to the whole metropolitan community is very marked, both for the volunteer and for the person he is trying to help. The one-to-one or one-to-two relationship between tutor and student brings the volunteer into contact with the resident of the inner city in a closer way than most programs make possible. Through volunteer tutoring, many individuals from the suburbs have gained an understanding of what it means to live in the inner city. Contact with the people of the inner city is an invaluable help in correcting much loose thinking concerning those "ignorant, lazy people" who "would rather receive public assistance than work." The volunteer can always contribute a great deal to any discussion of urban problems by saying, "come see for yourself."

After noting the valuable experience gained by volunteers, some schools of education and several universities and high schools interested in giving their students a significant service-oriented experience are using tutoring and related activities to familiarize their students with the inner city. Should the student of education later be assigned to teach in a culturally disadvantaged community he suffers less cultural shock from his initial experience in a slum school. As the tutoring relationship is an informal one, the teacher-to-be gains a broader view of the whole child than he will get later in the more authoritarian school setting. The tutoring projects which place the volunteer tutor in the child's homes are particularly valuable for future teachers. As a professional teacher, the one-to-one relationship of tutor and student will be one that will be no more than a fond memory. Many volunteers have gained so much satisfaction from tutoring that they have changed their vocational interest to teaching or social work. Tutoring programs have definitely become an effective recruiting tool for the teaching profession.

For the child who is being tutored, an extra benefit has been the enlargement of his environment. Children who had never been out of the ten-to-fifteen block radius of their homes have been taken to see a university, taken on trips to the country, and on visits to the public library. Another benefit has been the stimulation of interest in higher education on the part of high school students who are being tutored in their last two years of high school. One tutoring group in Chicago has a prep program at a girls' vocational school. In addition to furnishing information on existing scholarships, several volunteers have secured college scholarships for the students they are tutoring by making known the need for additional help at their own colleges. Another effect of tutoring in the city has been the establishment of study centers in the suburbs by suburbanites who have recognized that the culturally disadvantaged are by no means confined within the city limits. In a few localities, tutoring programs have spread to rural areas.

Another interesting development in Chicago is that about fifty foreign students studying in Chicago area colleges have become involved with several volunteer tutoring programs. This group, which includes some students from the so-called underdeveloped nations, constitutes a sort of reverse peace corps. These foreign students tutoring in the inner city have a very positive relationship with people from one underdeveloped section of the United States. Volunteers also benefit from association with others who are tutoring. I remember one group of suburban college students who decided to tutor in Chicago in order to help the "poor Negro." They were quite surprised to find Negro school teachers participating in the orientation program for new tutors, and to find that they were joining hands with several Negro volunteers from the neighborhood who were already tutoring at this location.

If one were to put a price tag on volunteers' time and add up the many small personal expenses included in terms of dollars and cents, the combined efforts of all the volunteer tutors in the United States would equal an enormous foundation grant or a sizable portion of the funds now earmarked for the war against poverty. More schools should attempt to cooperate with and direct this enormous resource, as volunteer tutoring represents a very effective way of establishing meaningful contact with the community and the disadvantaged pupil.

In the years ahead, we will need all of the help we can get!

REFERENCES

1. Oscar Lewis, *The Children of Sanchez* (New York. Random House, 1961), p. 24-27.
2. Jane Addams, *Twenty Years at Hull House* (New York: The New American Library, 1961), p. 89.
3. *Ibid.,* p. 121
4. *Ibid.*
5. Michael Harrington, *The Other America* (New York: Macmillan Company, 1962).
6. *Ibid.,* pp. 152-153.
7. *Ibid.,* pp. 12-15, 134-135.
8. Benjamin E. Strumpf, *Your American Pupil From Puerto Rico* (New York: Noble and Noble, 1956).
9. Frank Riessman, "Cultural Styles of the Disadvantaged," *Learning Together* (Chicago: Integrated Education Associates, 1964), p. 25-31.
10. *Ibid.,* p. 30.
11. *Ibid.,* p. 31.

12. Harold Baron, "Samuel Shepard and the Banneker Project," *Learning Together* (Chicago: Integrated Education, 1964), p. 46.
13. *Ibid.*, p. 46-47.
14. Personal communication, Emery Biro, Director of the Greenleigh Associates Literacy Study in Illinois.
15. Lewis, p. 24-27.
16. Baron, *Learning Together*, p. 47.
17. *Ibid.*

EPILOGUE:

PROSPECTS FOR THE DISADVANTAGED

Raymond M. Cook*

T EACHING THE disadvantaged child is not an entirely new problem. Pestalozzi was forced to improvise constantly with his "seventy wild beggar-children" in Switzerland in the winter of 1798-99. The Monitorial System devised by Lancaster and Bell about the same time was solely for the purpose of giving an education to the underprivileged and the poor.

Nevertheless, it has been in the past few years that great progress has been made in the education of disadvantaged children. Part of this has been due to recent developments in theory. The leaders of our public schools have at last become persuaded that the disadvantaged child is not a hopeless case. His intelligence quotient was not necessarily fixed at birth. If society tries hard enough and begins early enough, this child can usually make normal and satisfactory progress through the elementary school and beyond.

Another force for progress has been the civil rights "revolution." It was in 1954 that the U. S. Supreme Court ruled against *de jure* segregation in the public schools. Since then, the aspirations of the civil rights leaders with respect to the schools have changed. Where once they were content to have all legal barriers to integration stricken down, now they wish to do away with *de facto* segregation. But perhaps more importantly, many leaders have come to the conclusion that compensatory education is the proper solution. In their minds, separate but equal education has been rejected. "Integrated and equal" education is not enough. Compensatory education, which seeks to make up for present and accumulated deficits, is required.

The concept of compensatory education is not entirely a new

---

*Dean, Chicago Teachers College South.

one. For many years the cities, the states, and even the federal government have maintained schools and classes for those children who were handicapped physically, mentally—or more recently, socially. Society has not hesitated in the past few generations to provide special facilities for the education of the deaf and hard of hearing, the blind and partially seeing, the crippled and the cardiacs, the socially and emotionally maladjusted, and the mentally handicapped. Sometimes their efforts have been marred by sentimentality; often they have suffered from inadequate learning theory; typically they have been hampered by getting the handicapped child too late, years too late, to do an adequate job of educating him.

The American people have cheerfully poured out many millions of dollars to give special education to the "lame, the halt and the blind," plus the moron and imbecile, plus the juvenile delinquents. There have been instances when a highly skilled and highly paid teacher was furnished on a one-to-one basis for a multi-handicapped pupil. This generosity was not to insure that the handicapped pupil would be self sufficient and not become a public charge. It was due to a settled conviction on the part of the people that every child should have an opportunity to get as much education as he can absorb.

Why not then, compensatory education for the culturally disadvantaged child? It will be necessary to spend more on this program than we have on all the other forms of special education combined. A crash program that will break the cycle of the disadvantaged producing more disadvantaged, generation after generation, is required. We must beware of the dangers cited above. There must be no sentimentality; we must have an adequate learning theory; and we must get an early start.

The day will come when all children coming to school are fed and clothed properly. If the family cannot or will not manage this, then another agency must take over the task. The day will come when all children coming to school will have had medical and dental examination and the treatment indicated. Here again, if the family is insufficient for its obligation, another agency must step in .The day will come when public nursery schools for three and four year olds are as common as public kindergartens are for five year olds.

What is the role of the nursery school for the disadvantaged child? Too long we have thought of it as, at best, a day care agency for working mothers, at worst a baby sitting service for lazy mothers. The evidence is overwhelming that the home experiences of a typical disadvantaged child are not and cannot be of the kind that will properly prepare him for school at age five or six or seven. He starts in school with his own age group at a disadvantage, and he gets farther and farther behind as the years go on. The nursery school can awaken him to the richness of the world around him, give him a sense of self-hood, and make him eager to learn and go on learning.

There are other new programs besides the nursery school that have proven their worth and will become accepted parts of our all out attack on the problems of the disadvantaged child. Special summer schools, after school classes and clinics, and widening of cultural horizons are a few of them. School systems alive to the problem have poured supplementary funds into the schools where the need was great in the form of more text books, supplies and equipment, additional staff, and new school buildings.

The disadvantaged child very much needs to have a sense of accomplishment, and to feel the thrill of visible success. A type of school organization, especially in the early years, that provides for flexible grouping and "continuous progress" is much to be desired. Differentiated teachers' guides to learning are also essential. A vast amount of work needs to be done in preparing guides to teachers of the three and four-year-old pupils.

Where will the teachers come from for these new tasks? Many will be converted kindergarten or primary teachers, taking advantage of in service courses to be given by established teacher education colleges or by the school systems themselves. The colleges will shortly, when details of certification are worked out, prepare students directly for preschool teaching. In the meantime, much use must be made of partly trained teacher aides, and of volunteers. It is also essential that the parents of pre-school children become involved in the program. (Good nursery schools have always accomplished this.)

Pioneers in the struggle to solve the special problems of the disadvantaged child have been the great city school systems. Sixty to seventy years ago these same great city school systems were assimilating millions of culturally disadvantaged immigrant children of trans-Atlantic origin. From what the written record tells us, this was accomplished "in stride," with little trouble. Why, then, are the great cities so exercised about the task of educating Negro and Appalachian children from our own Southland, and Spanish speaking children from our own continent?

In the first place, the assimilation process was not so easy in the early 1900's as it may seem in retrospect. The failure of the school, and it often failed, was not so apparent as it is now. A school drop-out, even though he would not yet read, could get a job and hold it. In the second place, the Negro child (and persons of this race form the bulk of the disadvantaged children in the great cities) has been the victim of a degree of prejudice for three and a half centuries that never afflicted the immigrant child from across the Atlantic. The effect of this prejudice is a part of his cultural heritage, a part of his disadvantage.

Earlier, we spoke of a landmark decision of the U. S. Supreme Court that had a profound effect on the education of the disadvantaged child. This was the 1954 case which outlawed school segregation. Another more recent decision will also be important in solving what is perhaps the great cities' most pressing problem. The one-man-one-vote decision will give the great cities their fair voice in both houses of the various state legislatures and in the United States House of Representatives. The cities can then get the needed funds to carry on the vital programs for disadvantaged children. And they must do this; or they will become the true wastelands of the nation.

SELECTED BIBLIOGRAPHY

Bloom, Benjamin S., *Stability and Change in Human Characteristics,* New York: John Wiley and Sons, Inc., 1964.

Bloom, Benjamin S. (editor), *Taxonomy of Educational Objectives, Handbook I: Cognitive Domain,* New York: Longmans, Green and Company, 1956.

Bloom, Benjamin S. (editor), *Taxonomy of Educational Objectives, Handbook II: Affective Domain,* New York: David McKay Company, 1964.

Bloom, Benjamin S., Davis, Allison, and Hess, Robert, *Compensatory Education for Cultural Deprivation,* New York: Holt, Rinehart, and Winston, 1965.

Board of Education of the City of New York, *Puerto Rican Profiles,* New York: The Board, 1964.

Chandler, B. J., Stiles, Lindley, J., and Kitsuse, John I.: *Education in Urban Society,* New York: Dodd, Mead and Co., 1962.

Clark, K. B., *Prejudice and Your Child,* Second Edition, Boston: Beacon Press, 1963.

Conant, James Bryant, *Slums and Suburbs,* New York: McGraw Hill Book Co., 1961.

Davis, Allison, *Social Class Influences Upon Learning,* Cambridge: Harvard Press, 1948.

Deutsch, M., *Minority Group and Class Status as Related to Social and Personality Factors in Scholastic Achievement,* Society for Applied Anthropology, Monograph No. 2. Ithaca, New York: Cornell University, 1960.

Edwards, Newton, and Richey, Herman, *The School in the American Social Order,* Boston: Houghton-Mifflin, 1963.

Festinger, L. A., *A Theory of Cognitive Dissonance,* Evanston, Illinois: Row, Peterson, 1957.

Flavell, J. H., *The Developmental Psychology of Jean Piaget,* New York: Van Nostrand, 1963.

Frankenstein, C., "The School Without Parent," in A. M. Dushkin, and C. Frankenstein (Editors), *Studies in Education,* Vol. 13, Jerusalem: Hebrew University, Magnus Press, 1964.

Educational Policies Commission, *Education and the Disadvantaged American,* Washington, D. C.: NEA, 1962.

Goodman, Paul, *Compulsory Mis-Education,* New York: Horizon Press, 1964.

Harrington, M., *The Other America,* New York: Macmillan, 1962.

Harris, Albert J., *Effective Teaching of Reading,* New York: David McKay Company, 1962.

Harris, I. D.: *Emotional Blocks to Learning,* New York: Free Press, 1961.

Hollingshead, A. B., and Redlick, F. C.: *Social Class and Mental Illness: A Community Study,* New York: Wiley, 1958.

Havighurst, R. J., *The Public Schools of Chicago: A Survey for the Board of Education of Chicago,* Chicago: The Board of Education, City of Chicago, 1964.

Hunt, J. McV., *Intelligence and Experience,* New York: Ronald Press, 1961.

Kerber, August, and Bommarito, Barbara, *The Schools and the Urban Crisis,* New York: Holt, Rinehart, and Winston, 1965.

Lennon, R. T., *Testing and the Culturally Disadvantaged Child,* New York: Harcourt, Brace and World, Inc., Test Department, 1964.

Loban, Walter D., *The Language of Elementary School Children,* Champaign, Illinois: National Council of Teachers of English, 1963, pp. 82-89.

McClelland, D. C., *The Achieving Society,* Princeton, New Jersey: Van Nostrand, 1961.

McGeoch, Dorothy M., and others, *Learning to Teach in Urban Schools,* New York: Teachers College Press, Columbia University, 1965.

Miller, David R., and Swanson, Guy E., *Inner Conflict and Defense,* New York: Henry Holt, 1960.

Ministry of Education, *Half Our Future* (A Report for the Central Advisory Council for Education), London: Her Majesty's Stationery Office, 1963.

Passow, A. Harry, *Education in Depressed Areas,* New York: Teachers College Columbia University, 1963.

Pettigrew, T. F., *A Profile of the American Negro,* Princeton, New Jersey: Van Nostrand, 1964.

Riessman, Frank, *The Culturally Deprived Child,* New York: Harper and Row, 1962.

Sexton, Patricia C., *Education and Income: Inequalities of Opportunity in our Schools,* New York: Viking, 1961.

Silberman, Charles E., *Crisis in Black and White,* New York: Random House, 1964.

Teaching English to Puerto Rican Pupils in the Secondary School, Language Guide Series, The Puerto Rican Study, Board of Education of the City of New York, 1960.

U. S. Department of Health, Education and Welfare, *Program for the Educationally Disadvantaged,* Washington, D. C.: U. S. Government Printing Office, 1963.

U. S. Office of Education, *Improving English Skills of Culturally Different Youth in Large Cities,* Bulletin No. 5, Edited by Arno Jewett, Joseph Mersand, and D. V. Gunderson, 1964.

INDEX